PCs For Dummies, 11th Edition

W9-BMO-651

My PC!

Fill in the following essential information about your computer.

Make and model: _____

Serial number: _____

Network name (if any): _____

Microprocessor: _____

RAM (MB): _____

Hard drive capacity (GB): _____

Keys to press on startup to enter PC Setup program:

_____

Drive A is ❑ 3½-inch floppy ❑ Missing

Drive C is ❑ My PC's first hard drive

Other drives

Drive ___ is a hard drive.

Drive ___ is a hard drive.

Drive ___ is a CD-ROM drive. ___ Recordable

Drive ___ is a DVD drive. ___ Recordable

Drive ___ is a memory card drive, Type:

_____

Drive ___ is a memory card drive, Type:

_____

Drive ___ is a memory card drive, Type:

_____

Drive ___ is a memory card drive, Type:

_____

Drive ___ is _____.

Drive ___ is _____.

What Plugs into What?

Circle the proper connection for your PC goodies.

Keyboard	Keyboard port	USB
Mouse	Mouse port	USB
Printer	Printer port	USB
USB hub?	Yes	No

Other USB devices

NIC	Scanner	Modem
Sound gizmo	Digital camera	Webcam

External USB drives: _____

_____

_____

FireWire?   Yes   No

FireWire devices: _____

_____

_____

Important Phone Numbers

My dealer: _____

Sales rep (name/ext.): _____

Dealer tech support: _____

Operating system support: _____

ISP: _____

ISP tech support: _____

Computer guru: _____

For Dummies: Bestselling Book Series for Beginners

PCs For Dummies,® 11th Edition

Cheat Sheet

Helpful PC Hints

The Help key in Windows and in most other programs is F1.

Always save your stuff. Save when you first create something, save as you go along, save when you stand up to take a break, and save before you quit your programs.

Delete only the files or folders that you created yourself.

It's okay to delete a shortcut file; doing so doesn't delete the original.

When you mess up, immediately press Ctrl+Z, the Undo keyboard command. That should rectify whatever transgression you just committed.

Always unplug the computer console before you open it.

It's okay to connect USB devices to the computer while the computer or the device is on.

Get used to working with the mouse by playing some computer games, especially card games.

The best gift you can buy your PC is more memory.

Remember to unmount any removable media in Windows before you yank something out of your PC. Properly eject the media. For USB drives, properly remove them before disconnecting.

The key to understanding software is to know what a file is.

When e-mailing a graphical image, be sure to save or convert the image into the JPG or PNG file format.

Internet Info

Internet login name: _____

Internet password: (Write down elsewhere)

My e-mail address: _____

My e-mail password: (Write down elsewhere)

My ISP's domain name:_____

My e-mail address on Yahoo: _____

My Yahoo e-mail password: (Write down elsewhere)

Hotmail e-mail address: _____

Hotmail password: (Write down elsewhere)

Other e-mail address: _____

For Dummies: Bestselling Book Series for Beginners

PCs

FOR

DUMMIES®

11TH EDITION

PCs
FOR
DUMMIES®
11TH EDITION

by Dan Gookin

BICENTENNIAL
1807
WILEY
2007
BICENTENNIAL

Wiley Publishing, Inc.

PCs For Dummies,® 11th Edition

Published by
Wiley Publishing, Inc.
111 River Street
Hoboken, NJ 07030-5774

www.wiley.com

WILEY

About the Author

Dan Gookin has been writing about technology for over 20 years. He has contributed articles to numerous high-tech magazines and written over 110 books on personal computers, many of them accurate.

Dan combines his love of writing with his gizmo fascination to create books that are informative, entertaining, and not boring. Having sold more than 14 million titles translated into over 30 languages, Dan can attest that his method of crafting computer tomes seems to work.

Perhaps his most famous title is the original *DOS For Dummies,* published in 1991. It became the world's fastest-selling computer book, at one time moving more copies per week than the *New York Times* #1 bestseller (though, as a reference, it could not be listed on the *NYT* bestseller list). That book spawned the entire line of *For Dummies* books, which remains a publishing phenomenon to this day.

Dan's most popular titles include *Word 2007 For Dummies*, *Laptops For Dummies*, and *Troubleshooting Your PC For Dummies* (all published by Wiley). He also maintains the vast and helpful Web page www.wambooli.com.

Dan holds a degree in communications/visual arts from the University of California, San Diego. Presently, he lives in the Pacific Northwest, where he enjoys spending time with his sons in the gentle woods of Idaho.

Publisher's Acknowledgments

We're proud of this book; please send us your comments through our online registration form located at www.dummies.com/register/.

Some of the people who helped bring this book to market include the following:

Acquisitions, Editorial, and Media Development

Sr. Project Editor: Mark Enochs

Executive Editor: Gregory Croy

Copy Editor: Rebecca Whitney

Technical Editor: James F. Kelly

Editorial Manager: Leah Cameron

Media Development and Quality Assurance: Angela Denny, Kate Jenkins, Steven Kudirka, Kit Malone

Media Development Coordinator: Jenny Swisher

Media Project Supervisor: Laura Moss-Hollister

Editorial Assistant: Amanda Foxworth

Sr. Editorial Assistant: Cherie Case

Cartoons: Rich Tennant (www.the5thwave.com)

Composition Services

Project Coordinators: Heather Kolter, Lynsey Osborn

Layout and Graphics: Stacie Brooks, Carl Byers, Joyce Haughey, Stephanie D. Jumper, Christine Williams, Erin Zeltner

Proofreaders: Laura Albert, Linda Seifert

Indexer: Potomac Indexing, LLC

Anniversary Logo Design: Richard Pacifico

Publishing and Editorial for Technology Dummies

    Richard Swadley, Vice President and Executive Group Publisher

    Andy Cummings, Vice President and Publisher

    Mary Bednarek, Executive Acquisitions Director

    Mary C. Corder, Editorial Director

Publishing for Consumer Dummies

    Diane Graves Steele, Vice President and Publisher

    Joyce Pepple, Acquisitions Director

Composition Services

    Gerry Fahey, Vice President of Production Services

    Debbie Stailey, Director of Composition Services

Contents at a Glance

Introduction 1

Part I: Your Computer Will Not Explode 7

Chapter 1: A Painless Introduction to Computers 9
Chapter 2: The Nerd's-Eye View 17
Chapter 3: PC Setup 29
Chapter 4: The Most Powerful Button (On-Off) 43
Chapter 5: Windows Rules 59

Part II: Computer Guts 69

Chapter 6: Mysteries of the Console 71
Chapter 7: Jacks on the Box 85
Chapter 8: Temporary Storage (Memory) 93
Chapter 9: Permanent Storage (Disks and Media) 105
Chapter 10: Glorious Graphical Goodness 119
Chapter 11: Input Buddies: Keyboard and Mouse 133
Chapter 12: The Printer's the Thing 149
Chapter 13: Sounds Good 163
Chapter 14: Mighty Modems 175
Chapter 15: Positive PC Power Management 185

Part III: It's a Digital Life 191

Chapter 16: Picture This 193
Chapter 17: PC TV 207
Chapter 18: The Digital Ear 219

Part IV: Networking and Internet-Working 229

Chapter 19: N Is for Networking 231
Chapter 20: I've Been Working on the Network 243
Chapter 21: Cowboy Dan's Internet Roundup 253
Chapter 22: Flinging Files Freely 263
Chapter 23: Internet and PC Security 271

Part V: The Soft Side of Computing 283

Chapter 24: Files: The Key to Understanding Software 285
Chapter 25: Organizing Your Compu-Junk 297
Chapter 26: File Control.............................307
Chapter 27: Software, Programs, Applications 317
Chapter 28: Making Your Own Discs.............................327

Part VI: The Part of Tens 335

Chapter 29: Ten Common Beginner Mistakes.............................337
Chapter 30: Ten Things Worth Buying for Your PC.............................343
Chapter 31: Ten Tips from a PC Guru 349

Index 355

Table of Contents

Introduction *1*

What's New in This Edition? 1
Where to Start 2
Conventions Used in This Book 3
What You Don't Need to Read 4
Foolish Assumptions 4
Icons Used in This Book 5
Getting in Touch with the Author 5
Where to Go from Here...6

Part 1: Your Computer Will Not Explode *7*

Chapter 1: A Painless Introduction to Computers **9**

Simple Computer Concepts 10
  I/O 11
  Processing 11
  Storage..12
Hardware and Software 13
  The computer's operating system 13
  Other software 14
  The stuff you make (files)......................................15
The PC (As in PCs For Dummies)....................................15
"Uh, About That Exploding Thing" 16

Chapter 2: The Nerd's-Eye View **17**

PC Flavors 17
Your Basic PC Hardware...18
The Console Tour..20
  Major points of interest on the console, front...........20
  Visiting the console's seedy side...........................22
  Up close: The I/O panel 24
  Helpful hints, hieroglyphics, and hues 26

Chapter 3: PC Setup **29**

Unpack the Boxes..29
Set Up the Console First 30

A General Guide to Plugging Things into the Console 31
    Audio...31
    IEEE, 1394, FireWire..33
    Joystick or gamepad 34
    Keyboard and mouse 34
    Modem 34
    Monitor 35
    Network 35
    Printer 35
    S-Video 36
    Serial 36
    USB 36
    Wireless gizmos 37
The Final Connection: Power...37
    The mighty power strip...37
    The UPS power solution 40
    Using the UPS (a short play)...41

Chapter 4: The Most Powerful Button (On-Off) **43**
Turn On Your PC 44
    The Setup program..45
    Trouble in Startup Land!..46
Here Comes Windows!...46
    Who the heck are you? 46
    Log in, mystery guest..46
    Welcome to the desktop 48
Turning the Computer Off (Shutdown) 48
    Options for PC shutdown 48
    Log yourself off 50
    Lock the computer 50
    Switch users 51
    Sleep mode 51
    Hibernation 51
    Restart Windows 52
    Turn the darn thing off 52
Power Button, What's Your Function?...53
    Setting the console's power button function...................................53
    Setting the moon button's function 55
    Setting the Start menu's power button function 55
Should You Leave the Computer On All the Time?....................................56
    "I want to leave my computer off all the time"................................56
    "I want to leave my computer on all the time" 57

Chapter 5: Windows Rules 59

    The Smiling Face of Windows 59
        The desktop 60
        The taskbar 61
        The Start button 62
        The Start button menu 62
        The Notification Area 63
    The Control Panel 64
    Network Control 65
        The Network and Sharing Center 65
        The Network window 66
    Places for Your Stuff..66
    Windows Help...67

Part II: Computer Guts...**69**

Chapter 6: Mysteries of the Console 71

    A Look Inside the Console 71
        Discovering your PC's inner guts 72
        Opening the case (if you dare) 73
        Closing the case..74
    The Mother of All Boards..74
    The Microprocessor Is Not the Computer's Brain....................................75
        Name that microprocessor!..76
        Microprocessor muscle and speed 76
        Which microprocessor lives in your PC? 77
    Expansion Slots 78
        The PCI Express 79
        Older expansion slots 79
    The PC's Ticker..80
        "My clock is all screwy!" 80
        Set the clock...81
        Internet time to the rescue!...82
    About the PC's Battery 82
    The Chipset...83
    The Source of PC Power 83

Chapter 7: Jacks on the Box 85

    Is It a Port, a Jack, or Just a Hole?..85
    All Hail the USB Port 86
        Hanging around USB cables 87
        Connecting a USB device...87
        Where's the power cord?..87
        Removing a USB device 88
        Expanding the USB universe..88

The Port of Many Names, IEEE 89
Legacy Ports 90
    The mouse and keyboard 91
    The printer port 91
    The serial port 91

Chapter 8: Temporary Storage (Memory) 93

Why Memory? 93
Delicious Chocolate Memory Chips 95
Here a Byte, There a Byte, Everywhere a Byte-Byte 96
Some Memory Q&A 98
    "How much memory is in my PC right now?" 98
    "Do I have enough memory?" 99
    "Does my PC have enough memory?" 99
    "Will the computer ever run out of memory?" 99
    "What is virtual memory?" 100
    "What is video memory?" 100
    "What are kibi, mebi, and gibi?" 101
Adding More Memory to Your PC 101
An Homage to Gilbert and Sullivan 103

Chapter 9: Permanent Storage (Disks and Media) 105

Storage for the Long Haul 106
    Storage media roundup 106
    Ask Mr. Science: How does a disk drive work? 107
The Hard Disk Drive 108
The DVD Drive 109
    Disc capacity 110
    About the speed rating (the X number) 110
    Inserting a disc 111
    Ejecting a disc 111
The Floppy Disk Drive 112
Memory Cards 113
    Memory card roundup 113
    Inserting a memory card 114
    Ejecting a memory card 114
    When the memory card is canceled 115
External Storage 115
    Adding external storage 115
    Removing external storage 116
Permanent Storage ABCs 117

Chapter 10: Glorious Graphical Goodness 119

Proper Jargon Department 120
The PC's Graphics System 120
    Two types of monitors: LCD and CRT 121
    Adept graphics adapters 122

Love Your Monitor 124
    The physical description..124
    Adjust the monitor's display...124
Windows and Your Monitor 126
    Summoning the Personalization window 126
    Going for a new look 127
    Changing the background (wallpaper)..128
    Saving the screen..129
    Adjusting the display size (resolution) and colors.......................131

Chapter 11: Input Buddies: Keyboard and Mouse 133

Push the PC Keyboard's Buttons 133
    The basic PC keyboard 134
    Shifty keys 135
    The Lock sisters 137
    Specific keys from Any to the bizarre..138
    Special keys on special keyboards..139
Control the Keyboard in Windows...140
Proper Typing Attitude..141
You and Your PC Mouse Go Hand in Hand....................................142
    The basic computer mouse 142
    Optical versus mechanical..143
    Cordless mice...143
    Other mouse species 144
Basic Mouse Operations 144
Dink with the Mouse in Windows..146
    "I can't find the mouse pointer!" 146
    "Double-clicking doesn't work!" 147
    "I'm left-handed, and the buttons are backward!"........................148

Chapter 12: The Printer's the Thing 149

Behold the Printer...150
    Types of computer printer..150
    A look around your printer 151
    The mighty printer control panel..152
    Feed your printer, Part I: Ink..153
    Feed your printer, Part II: Paper 154
    Types of paper 155
Printer Set Up 156
Windows and Your Printer 156
    Manually adding a printer 158
    Setting the default printer 158
Basic Printer Operation 159
    "Where do I set my margins?"...160
    Print in reverse order...161
    Stop, printer! Stop! 161

Chapter 13: Sounds Good **163**

Audacious Audio 163
Noisy potential...164
Speakers hither and thither 164
Microphone options..167
Audio Control in Windows 167
Controlling the sound hardware...............................167
Configuring the speakers..168
Configuring the microphone 168
Adjusting the volume..169
Windows Makes Noise...170
Playing sounds in Windows 170
Assigning sounds to events 170
Recording your own sounds 172

Chapter 14: Mighty Modems **175**

What Does a Modem Do? 175
Types of Modem...176
The dialup modem 176
Broadband modems 177
Modem speed..178
Setting Up a Dialup Modem 179
Adding an external dialup modem 180
Configuring an internal dialup modem 180
Using the Dialup Modem 181
Setting up a connection 181
Making the connection 182
Hanging up the modem 183

Chapter 15: Positive PC Power Management **185**

What Is Power Management?..185
Power Management in Windows 186
Choosing a power-management plan........................187
Creating your own plan 188
Power-saving options for battery-powered PCs.....188

Part III: It's a Digital Life *191*

Chapter 16: Picture This **193**

Getting Images into the PC..193
The digital camera..194
The scanner 195

Working with Graphics Files 198
Graphics file formats...198
Changing graphics file types..200
Editing images...201
Viewing images in Windows...204

Chapter 17: PC TV **207**
How to Turn a PC into a TV 207
Connecting a TV tuner 208
Configuring Windows Media Center 209
Something's on Television! 209
Seeing what's on 210
Seeing what's on next 211
Recording on the fly 211
Scheduling a recording 212
Watching recorded TV 213
Burning a DVD from recorded TV 213
Purging recorded TV 214
Moving Pictures...215
It's live, and it's living on top of your monitor!.............................215
Video file types 216
Video editing 217

Chapter 18: The Digital Ear **219**
Your PC Is Now Your Stereo...219
Running Windows Media Player...220
Collecting tunes 221
Creating a playlist..222
Taking your music with you...223
Making your own music CDs...224
The PC Can Talk and Listen 225
Babbling Windows..226
Dictating to the PC 226

Part IV: Networking and Internet-Working **229**

Chapter 19: N Is for Networking **231**
The Big Networking Picture..231
Networking Hardware..232
Saint NIC 234
Network hoses 234
The hub..235

The Software Side of Networking 236
  Getting to Network Central 236
  Connecting to a network 237
  Setting your computer's network name 239
  Joining a workgroup..239
  Configuring the router 240

Chapter 20: I've Been Working on the Network 243

Windows Does the Network..244
  Browsing the network 245
  Turning on network discovery 246
  Viewing the network map 246
Network Sharing, Shared, and Unshared 246
  Configuring Windows to share stuff...............................247
  Sharing one of your folders...248
  Accessing a network folder 249
  Mapping a network folder as a disk drive letter...........250
  Unsharing a folder 251
  Disconnecting a mapped network drive..........................251
  Sharing a printer 251
  Using a network printer 252
  Unsharing a printer 252

Chapter 21: Cowboy Dan's Internet Roundup 253

What Is the Internet? 254
How to Access the Internet...254
  Choosing an ISP 254
  Configuring Windows for the Internet 256
  Connecting to the Internet 256
It's a World Wide Web We Weave 257
  Browsing tips 257
  Printing Web pages..258
  Searching tips 259
E-Mail Call!..259
Quiz Answers 261

Chapter 22: Flinging Files Freely 263

Snagging Stuff from a Web Page 263
  Saving an image from a Web page 264
  Saving text from a Web page to disk 264
Software from the Internet 265
  Downloading software from the Internet 265
  Installing from a Zip file 267
You've Got an E-Mail Attachment!...268
  Grabbing an attachment with Windows Mail.................268
  Sending an attachment in Windows Mail 269

Chapter 23: Internet and PC Security 271

Bad Guys and Superheroes 271
Internet Explorer Tools 273
  Blocking pop-ups 274
  Phighting phishing 274
The Windows Security Center 275
  Windows Firewall 276
  Updating Windows 277
  Defending Windows 279
  Dealing with annoying User Account Control warnings 280

Part V: The Soft Side of Computing *283*

Chapter 24: Files: The Key to Understanding Software 285

Do You Know What a File Is? 285
  Presenting the file 286
  What's in a file? 286
  Describing a file 287
  Files dwell in folders 288
Slap a Name on That File 288
  Choosing the best name 289
  Official file-naming rules 290
File Types and Icons 290
  The supersecret filename extension 291
  Filename extension details 291
  How to see or hide a filename extension 292
  Don't rename the extension 293
  Icons 293
Creating Files 294
  The Save command 294
  The Save As dialog box 295

Chapter 25: Organizing Your Compu-Junk 297

The Folder Story 297
Famous Folders throughout History 298
  The root folder 298
  Subfolders and parent folders 299
  The User Profile folder 299
  Famous yet forbidden folders 301
The Windows Explorer Program 302
Let There Be Folders 304
The Open Dialog Box 305

Chapter 26: File Control **307**

Working with Groups of Files...307
  Selecting all files in a folder 308
  Selecting a random smattering of files 308
  Selecting a swath of files in a row 309
  Lassoing a group of files 310
  Unselecting stuff...311
Files Hither, Thither, and Yon 311
  Moving or copying files to another folder.........................311
  Moving or copying files can be such a drag 312
  Duplicating a file..312
  Copying a file to removable media.....................................313
  Creating shortcuts..313
  Deleting files...314
  Undeleting files (Files of the Undead!)..............................314
  Renaming files 315
Finding Wayward Files 316

Chapter 27: Software, Programs, Applications **317**

Software Installation 318
Running a Program 320
  Finding a program on the Start button menu 320
  Accessing recent programs...321
  Putting your program in the pin-on area...........................321
  Creating a desktop shortcut icon.......................................322
  Putting an icon on the Quick Launch bar..........................323
Uninstalling Software...323
Updating and Upgrading Your Software...325

Chapter 28: Making Your Own Discs **327**

Your Personal Disc Factory 327
  Checking the hardware...328
  Obtaining the proper disc..328
  Disc-writing software 329
  Choosing the right format 329
Your Very Own Data Disc 330
  Inserting the disc..330
  Working with the disc in Windows.....................................332
  Ejecting a recordable disc 332
  Finishing a Mastered format disc 333
  Erasing an RW disc...333
  Labeling the disc 334
Disposing a Disc 334

Part VI: The Part of Tens 335

Chapter 29: Ten Common Beginner Mistakes 337
Not Properly Shutting Down Windows....................................337
Buying Too Much Software 338
Buying Incompatible Hardware 338
Not Buying Enough Supplies 338
Not Saving Your Work 339
Not Backing Up Files 339
Opening or Deleting Unknown Things....................................339
Trying to Save the World..340
Replying to Spam E-Mail..340
Opening a Program Attached to an E-Mail Message................341

Chapter 30: Ten Things Worth Buying for Your PC 343
Mouse Pad and Wrist Pad 343
Antiglare Screen 344
Keyboard Cover...344
More Memory 345
Larger, Faster Hard Drive 345
Ergonomic Keyboard 345
A UPS 346
Headset..346
Scanner or Digital Camera 346
Portable Digital Music Player 347

Chapter 31: Ten Tips from a PC Guru 349
Remember That You Control the Computer 349
Realize That Most Computer Nerds Love to Help Beginners.................350
Use Antivirus Software 350
Understand That Upgrading Software
    Isn't an Absolute Necessity..351
Don't Reinstall Windows 351
Perfectly Adjust Your Monitor...352
Unplug Your PC When You Upgrade Hardware 352
Subscribe to a Computer Magazine 352
Shun the Hype 353
Don't Take It So Seriously 353

Index...355

Introduction

. . . .

*H*o, boy! Fifteen years and about 60 pounds ago, I co-wrote the first edition of *PCs For Dummies* as a guide to helping folks understand their personal computers. So much has changed in those 15 years that it has required *11* editions of this book to keep up! Yet the basic concept here remains the same: "How does a computer turn a smart person like you into a dummy?"

You don't have to love a computer. Some folks do, most don't. The reason is simple: Computers are *not* easy to use. True, a computer is easier to use now than it was back when Grover Cleveland sent the world's first e-mail message, but some things remain cryptic. The Help files are mystifying. Technical support isn't even in English any more! So, you're left feeling numb and cold and wondering why no one bothers to sit down and explain things to you in plain human terms. Well, wonder no more!

This book explains the basics of your computer, the PC — how it works, what does what, and all that stuff you want to know or maybe didn't realize you wanted to know. Honestly, computers really aren't that difficult to use or understand. It's just that it has taken an author like me and a book like this one awhile to get the word out.

Between this book's yellow-and-black covers, you'll find friendly, helpful information about using your PC. This book uses friendly and human — and often irreverent — terms. Nothing is sacred here. Electronics can be praised by others. This book focuses on you and your needs. In this book, you'll discover everything you need to know about your computer without painful jargon or the prerequisite master's degree in engineering. And, you'll have fun.

What's New in This Edition?

This edition of *PCs For Dummies* has been polished and honed toward using modern PCs running the Windows Vista operating system. Yes, I recommend using Windows Vista, and I recommend that you get a PC capable of running it. Especially if you have a PC five years old or older, you're missing out on a lot of technology that truly makes using a computer better and easier. Upgrade now!

In going along with the theme of the 21st century, this book has a new part for the first time ever: "It's a Digital Life" covers using a PC as the new hub of your digital world. Activities such as recording live TV, interfacing your PC with a video camera, and the old standby of finding and playing digital music grace this book for the first time ever.

In addition to making the PC the focus of your digital life, this book covers the following new topics:

- Vital computer security issues are covered here, coupling well with Windows Vista and its new levels of PC security.

- Working with memory cards is now a key part of permanent storage on a PC, and that topic is covered here in depth.

- Now that Windows can create DVDs, that information is contained in these pages and includes steps on how to make your own movies.

- Information on home computer networking, including Internet connections and the ever-popular wireless networking options.

- Basic information on understanding what a computer is and how it works.

- Key information on the essence of a file. Truly, by understanding the file, you really get hold of the entire computer software concept.

- General up-to-date and current information on all aspects of PC technology, hardware, and software — stuff too numerous to mention here, so why not just start reading the book already?

As in years past, I present all the information in this book in a sane, soothing, and gentle tone that calms even the most panicked computerphobe.

Where to Start

This book is designed so that you can pick it up at any point and start reading — like a reference. It has 31 chapters. Each chapter covers a specific aspect of the computer — turning it on, using a printer, using software, or insulting the computer, for example. Each chapter is divided into self-contained nuggets of information — sections — all relating to the major theme of the chapter. Sample sections you may find include

- Turn the darn thing off
- The mighty power strip

✔ Stop, printer! Stop!

✔ Ejecting a memory card

✔ Disposing of a disc

✔ Downloading a file from the Internet

You don't have to memorize anything in this book. Nothing about a computer is memorable. Each section is designed so that you can read the information quickly, digest what you have read, and then put down the book and get on with using the computer. If anything technical crops up, you're alerted to its presence so that you can cleanly avoid it.

Conventions Used in This Book

This book is a reference. Start with the topic you want more information about; look for it in the table of contents or in the index. Turn to the area of interest and read the information you need. Then, with the information in your head, you can quickly close the book and freely perform whatever task you need — without reading anything else.

Whenever I describe a message or information on the screen, it looks like this:

```
This is a message on-screen.
```

If you have to type something, it looks like this:

Type me

You type the text **Type me** as shown. You're told when and whether to press the Enter key.

Windows menu commands are shown like this:

Choose File⇨Exit.

This arrow means to choose the File menu and then choose the Exit command.

Key combinations you may have to type are shown like this:

Ctrl+S

This line means to press and hold the Ctrl (control) key, type an *S,* and then release the Ctrl key. It works the same as pressing Shift+S on the keyboard produces an uppercase *S.* Same deal, different shift key.

What You Don't Need to Read

Lots of technical information is involved in using a computer. To better insulate you from this information, I have enclosed this type of material in sidebars clearly marked as technical information. You don't have to read that stuff. Often, it's just a complex explanation of information already discussed in the chapter. Reading that information only teaches you something substantial about your computer, which is not the goal here.

Foolish Assumptions

I make some admittedly foolish assumptions about you: You have a computer, and you use it somehow to do something. You use a PC (or are planning on it) and will use Windows Vista. This book doesn't cover any previous versions of Windows.

Various flavors of Windows Vista are available. This book attempts to cover them all. But as a so-called expert, let me recommend that you use either Windows Vista Home Premium for the home or Windows Vista Business for the office. (The Home Basic edition is just too little, and the Ultimate edition is overpriced.)

This book refers to all editions of Windows Vista as *Windows.*

This book refers to the menu that appears when you click or activate the Start button as the *Start button menu.* The All Programs menu on the Start panel is referred to as *All Programs,* though it may say *Programs.*

Icons Used in This Book

This icon alerts you to needless technical information — drivel I added because I just felt like explaining something totally unnecessary (a hard habit to break). Feel free to skip over anything tagged with this little picture.

This icon usually indicates helpful advice or an insight that makes using the computer interesting. For example, when you're pouring acid over your computer, be sure to wear a protective apron and gloves and goggles.

This icon indicates something to remember, like closing the refrigerator door when you leave the house in the morning or checking your zipper before you step before a large audience.

This icon indicates that you need to be careful with the information that's presented; usually, it's a reminder for you not to do something.

Getting in Touch with the Author

My e-mail address is listed here in case you want to send me a note:

    dgookin@wambooli.com

Yes, that's my address, and I respond to every e-mail message. Note that I reply to short, to-the-point messages quickly. Long messages may take more time for me to reply to. Plus, I cannot troubleshoot or fix your PC. Remember that you paid others for your technical support, and you should use them.

You can also visit my Web site, which is chock-full of helpful support pages, bonus information, games, and fun:

    http://www.wambooli.com/

Where to Go from Here

With this book in hand, you're now ready to go out and conquer your PC. Start by looking through the table of contents or the index. Find a topic and turn to the page indicated, and you're ready to go. Also, feel free to write in this book, fill in the blanks, dog-ear the pages, and do anything that would make a librarian blanch. Enjoy.

Part I
Your Computer Will Not Explode

The 5th Wave   By Rich Tennant

In this part . . .

Believe it or not, your computer won't explode. Inside its box, you'll find no hideous intelligence and no cool logic circuits calculating to destroy the human race or, at minimum, print an outrageous phone bill. Honestly, the computer is a rather dull device, tolerant of tedium yet eager to please. So, despite what you see in the media, a computer is nothing to fear.

This part of the book explores the basic concepts of the computer, specifically the PC, or personal computer. Here you'll find a welcome expanse of information designed to get you familiar with the PC, to understand some simple computer stuff, and to get up and running in no time. For though a computer lacks the heart to destroy you or the enthusiasm to spontaneously combust, it's still not quite as easy to use as its advertisements claim.

Chapter 1

A Painless Introduction to Computers

In This Chapter

▶ Understanding computer basics

▶ Admiring input and output

▶ Knowing about hardware and software

▶ Discovering the PC

▶ Realizing that your PC is actually quite dumb

*J*ust because you can buy a complete computer straight off the shelf, right down the aisle from the diapers, canned peas, and frozen burritos, doesn't imply that using a computer will be any easier to use today than it was 20 years ago. Don't believe the hype.

Yeah, I know: The advertisement said that you'd be up on the Internet in no time. The text on the side of the box promised that you could put your complete library of music and movies on the computer with less effort than it takes to make toast. And, naturally, everyone tells you how easy the programs are to use and how helpful and *user-friendly* the whole thing is. Yeah. And if you believe that, then you'll get out of bed tomorrow with tweeting birds and animated forest creatures helping you to get dressed.

You probably paid a pretty penny for your computer, so why not try to use the thing at more than a superficial level? It's not that difficult. All you need to do to have a friendly, productive, and long-term relationship with your computer is to *understand* it. No, this doesn't mean you need to do math. Nor do you need to have Einstein's IQ or Mr. Spock's pointy ears. Just a modicum of knowledge is all you need to overcome the computer's complexity and stop that cold intimidation that makes you feel like a dummy. That's what you'll find in this chapter.

Simple Computer Concepts

Most gizmos are rather simple: The coffee maker supplies you with delicious, hot, legal stimulant; the TV remote saves you the labor of walking a short distance to work the knobs on the television set; the lawn mower keeps the grass short and the gophers paranoid; and an ice tea spoon allows you to blissfully scratch inside a five-week-old arm cast. Despite any advanced features you may not use, the purpose of just about any device can be boiled down to the simplest description.

For the longest time, computers lacked a simple description. At one time, the computer was considered the ultimate solution for which there was no problem. That description, however, was based on too much focus. The computer isn't a single solution to anything but rather multiple solutions to many things. It's the world's most flexible device, versatile and almost indispensable.

Rather than clog your brain pipes with technical nonsense about the computer, it helps to understand how the thing works at the most basic, simple level. When you peel back all the mumbo jumbo, the computer is nothing more than a gadget that takes input and then modifies that input to create some form of output (see Figure 1-1). The enormous potential of that simple activity is what makes the computer capable of so many things.

Figure 1-1: What a computer does at its simplest level.

The act of taking input, modifying it, and then producing output involves three basic computer concepts:

- I/O
- Processing
- Storage

The following sections expand on these ideas, distilling for you what you could have learned in a computer science class, had you bothered to take one.

I/O

No one would accuse a computer of being a reliable moocher, but it's obsessed over the two letters *I* and *O*. It's *IO* as in "I owe," not as in Io, the third-largest moon of Jupiter.

IO stands for Input and Output. It's commonly written as I/O, which are the two things a computer does best. In fact, I/O is pretty much the *only* thing a computer does. Consider the popular nursery song:

Old MacDonald had a Dell,
E-E-E I/O

You get this whole I/O concept down and you've tackled the essence of what a computer is and what it can do.

- ✔ The devices connected to your computer are divided into input and output camps. There are input devices, there are output devices.

- ✔ The computer receives information from *input* devices. The keyboard and mouse are two input devices, as are a scanner and a digital camera. They all send information to the computer.

- ✔ The computer sends information from output devices. *Output* is simply anything the computer produces. The stuff displayed on the monitor is output, sound is output, and the pages the computer prints are output. The monitor, speakers, and printer are all output devices.

- ✔ Some devices can do both input and output. For example, a disk drive can supply input to the computer as well as store output. A modem both sends and receives information.

- ✔ Don't let terms like *disk drive* and *modem* bother you! If you're curious, you can look them up in the index. Otherwise, keep reading and nod occasionally, like you really get it. If anything, that will impress someone else who's watching.

Processing

What the computer does between input and output is *processing*. The computer processes input and produces output.

Without processing, the computer's output would be the same as its input — kind of like plumbing: Water goes into the pipe, and water comes out of the pipe. The water is the same before, during, and after the journey. With a computer, you have the added element of *processing,* which means doing something to the input so that you get something else as output. To continue the plumbing example, turning dirty water into clean water would be a type of processing.

✔ Processing is handled by a gizmo inside the computer called (logically enough) a *processor.*

✔ By itself, the processor doesn't know what to do with input. No, the processor relies on *instructions* to tell it what to do. Those instructions are referred to as *software.* The topic of software is covered later in this chapter.

✔ It's amazing when you think of it: Computer input is all digital. Yet with the proper processing, the output can be anything from a poem to a graphical image to a symphony. That's all thanks to the power of processing.

Storage

The final part of the basic computer equation is storage. The storage is necessary because the processor needs a place to perform its magic — a scratchpad for mad doodles, if you will.

On a modern computer, storage comes in two forms: temporary and long-term.

Temporary storage is supplied as memory, or RAM. *Memory* is where the processor does its work, where programs run, and where information is stored while it's being worked on. *RAM* is the microprocessor's playground, its workshop, its den.

Long-term storage in a modern computer is provided by storage media. Storage media includes disk drives, flash drives, media cards, and CDs and DVDs. Long-term storage allows information to be saved and recalled for later use — like putting clothes in a closet or all your junk in a storage unit. Media storage is the place where things go when the microprocessor isn't directly working on them — but from where stuff can be retrieved later, if need be.

✔ All computers need storage.

✔ RAM is an acronym for *random access memory.* It's often just called *memory.*

✔ The most popular form of long-term storage is the disk drive, primarily the computer's hard drive (or drives).

✔ Another term for disk drives is *disk memory,* although I don't prefer that term because it's easy to confuse it with RAM.

✔ Don't get all hung up on these terms. Computer jargon, such as *RAM* and *disk drive,* is explained later in this book.

✔ The computers on the Apollo moon missions had lots of storage for their day. This was so that the astronauts wouldn't have to manually type the programs the computer needed to run. Even so, a lot more typing and programming were going on in the capsule than you would imagine.

Hardware and Software

A computer system is a blend of two different things: hardware and software. Like other famous pairs — Astaire and Rogers, sweet and sour, bug and windshield — hardware and software must go well together to create the full computer system.

Hardware is the physical part of a computer — anything you can touch and anything you can see. The computer console, the monitor, the keyboard, the mouse — that physical stuff is hardware.

Software is the brains of the computer. It tells the hardware what to do.

In a way, it helps to think of hardware and software as a symphony orchestra. For hardware, you have the musicians and their instruments. The software is the music. As with a computer, the music (software) tells the musicians and their instruments (hardware) what to do.

Without software, hardware just sits around and looks pretty. It can't do anything because it has no instructions and nothing telling it what to do next. And, like a symphony orchestra without music, that can be an expensive waste of time (especially at union scale).

No, you must have software to make the computer go and complete the computer system. In fact, it's software that determines your computer's personality.

- ✔ If you can throw it out a window, it's hardware.
- ✔ If you can throw it out a window and it comes back, it's a cat.
- ✔ Computer software is nothing more than instructions that tell the hardware what to do, how to act, or when to lose your data.

- ✔ Contrary to what most people think, between hardware and software, it's the software that's more important. Just as a director tells actors what to do in a play, software directs the hardware, telling it what to do, where to go, and how best to convey the emotional context of the scene. Software's importance is especially valuable to note when first buying a computer because most people dwell on the new computer's hardware rather than on the software controlling that hardware.
- ✔ Without the proper software, your computer's hardware has nothing to do. That's when the computer magically transforms into a swell-looking paperweight.

The computer's operating system

The most important piece of software inside a computer is its *operating system*. It has several duties:

✔ Control the computer's hardware.

✔ Manage all the computer software.

✔ Organize the files and stuff you create on the computer.

✔ Interface with you, the human.

Doing all these things is a major task. Be thankful that computer designers have seen to it that only one program does all these things! The operating system is no slacker.

On PCs, the most common operating system is Windows. Other operating systems are available, all of which do the things just listed and can handily control the PC's hardware, but Windows dominates the marketplace. This book assumes that Windows is your PC's operating system.

How the operating system does its various jobs is covered elsewhere in this book.

✔ The big bully among all the software programs is the operating system. It's the most important piece of software, the computer's number-one program — the head honcho, the big cheese, Mr. In Charge, Fearless Leader, *le roi.*

✔ The computer hardware surrenders control of itself to the operating system mere moments after you turn on the computer. See Chapter 4 for information on turning the computer on and off.

✔ The operating system typically comes with the computer when you buy it. You never need to add a second operating system, although operating systems get updated and improved from time to time.

✔ When you buy software, you buy it for an operating system, not for your brand of computer. So, rather than buy software for your Dell, Compaq, or Crazy Larry's PC, you look in the Windows section of the software store.

Other software

The operating system isn't the only software you use on your computer. If you're a typical computer user, you'll most likely obtain dozens, if not hundreds, of other programs, or computer software, to help customize your computer and get it to do those things you want it to do.

Computer software is known by several different names. In addition to software, you find

Applications: This category of software is used for productivity or to create things. Applications are the software that does the work.

Programs: Anything that's a "computer program" is also software, but this category includes software that may or may not be used for productivity or to produce output, such as a computer game or a video editing program.

Utilities or tools: These programs are designed to help you manage the computer or diagnose or fix problems. For example, you may use a tool to optimize the performance of your computer's disk drives.

Drivers: A special type of program that allows specific hardware to work. For example, a *video driver* program is required for the operating system to use your PC's specific graphics hardware. This type of software comes with the hardware it supports.

Part V of this book goes into more detail on computer software.

The stuff you make (files)

When you use your computer to create things, those things are stored in units of information called *files*. A computer file can be a document you write with your word processor, a graphical image from a digital camera or an image you create with a digital paintbrush, a piece of music, a video, or just about anything. Whatever it is, the computer stores that information as a file.

The operating system manages files for you. It helps your programs *save* information from temporary storage (memory) to long-term storage (the hard drive). Further, when you need to work on the file later, you can *open* the file from disk; by opening the file, the operating system transfers the file's information into memory, where you can view, modify, print, or continue to work on the file.

Understanding files is *vital* to using a computer. Be sure to check out Chapter 24 for more detailed information on the useful topic of computer files.

The PC (As in PCs For Dummies)

The kind of computer you have, or will soon have, is a PC, which is why this book is titled *PCs For Dummies.* There are many varieties of computers, from large supercomputers to small handheld gizmos. The largest category by far, however, is the PC.

PC stands for *personal* computer. The design of the PC is based on its most ancient ancestor, the IBM PC, introduced in 1981. Back then, PCs were referred to as *microcomputers.* And although many, many microcomputers were available, the IBM PC proved the most popular and successful.

Now the term *PC* is used to refer to any computer that can run the Windows operating system. There are subtle differences between the PC's hardware from one manufacturer to the next, but, universally, if the computer runs Windows, it's a PC. (Note that this doesn't include cars, sewing machines, or heart–lung machines that also may run Windows.)

✔ The only thing not officially considered a PC is Apple's Macintosh computer. Although the Mac is a *personal* computer, Mac users get fussy about calling it a PC.

✔ Today's Macintosh can run Windows. In that mode of operation, this book and its contents apply. But to best understand the Mac, I recommend getting the book *Macs For Dummies,* 9th Edition (Wiley Publishing, Inc.), written by the average-looking guy Edward Baig.

✔ If you have a laptop PC, I highly recommend getting the book *Laptops For Dummies* (Wiley Publishing, Inc.), a well-written tome by the good-looking guy Dan Gookin.

"Uh, About That Exploding Thing"

Anyone who has ever seen an old episode of TV's *Star Trek* or any Irwin Allen television show from the 1960s knows that computers are capable of exploding, and doing so in a quite dramatic fashion. When given the most subtle yet illogical directions, the televised computer fidgets and heats up and eventually explodes in a shower of sparks and chunky debris.

In real life, computers die a much more silent death. The typical dead PC simply refuses to turn on when the switch is thrown. Oh, sure, sometimes the power supply may go "poof!" But that is so nondramatic compared to the exploding war computers of Eminiar VII in *Star Trek* Episode 23 or the perilously wimpy way the Landru computer deep-sixes itself in Episode 21.

Computers aren't evil. They harbor no sinister intelligence. In fact, when you get to know them, they're rather dumb.

Chapter 2

The Nerd's-Eye View

In This Chapter

▶ Recognizing different types of PCs

▶ Looking at the basic PC hardware

▶ Perusing things on the console

▶ Locating PC connectors, holes, and jacks

▶ Using helpful symbols and colors

Computers have come a long way since the days of the "beige box." Today's models feature designs that make them look sleek or even aerodynamic — despite the fact that "computer speed" isn't measured by how fast you can throw the thing. Some newer models have ominous internal lighting, an evil glowing red or a cool blue, hinting at some internal, hideous intelligence. Oh, the computer box can be a fun thing! But to many folks, it's still a mystery.

Behold computer hardware! Of the two basic parts of a computer, hardware and software, the hardware, sadly, gets the most attention — despite the software's being more important. This chapter provides you with the bird's-eye — or, rather, *nerd's-eye* — overview of what a PC is and where you can find interesting and useful things on that device.

PC Flavors

There is no such thing as a typical PC, just as there is no such thing as a typical car. Although both PCs and cars have common parts, their arrangement and design are different from manufacturer to manufacturer, not to mention the differences between sedans, coupes, pickup trucks, vans, SUVs, and so on.

The following list is a quick overview of the various types of PCs available. These are the official names for the various forms a PC can take:

Mini-tower: The most popular PC configuration, where the computer sits upright on a desktop or tucked away out of sight, below the desk.

Desktop: Once the most popular PC configuration, with a large, wide, slab-like console lying flat on the desktop with the monitor squatting on top.

Desktop (small footprint): A smaller version of the desktop, typically used in low-priced home systems. The *footprint* is the amount of desk space the computer uses.

Tower system: Essentially a full-size desktop standing on its side, which makes this PC tall, like a tower. Towers have lotsa room inside for expansion, which makes them the darlings of power-mad users. A tower typically sits on the floor, often propping up one end of the table.

Notebook/laptop: A specialty type of computer that folds into a handy, light-weight package, ideal for slowing down the security checkpoints in airports. Laptop PCs work just like their desktop brethren; any exceptions are noted throughout this book.

Choosing the proper PC configuration depends on your needs. Power users love the expandability of the tower or full-size desktop. Folks on the go love laptops. Small-footprint desktops can fit on any desk. (Just remember that the amount of clutter you have always expands to fill the available desk space.)

Your Basic PC Hardware

Figure 2-1 shows a typical computer system. The big, important pieces have been labeled for your enjoyment. It's important that you know which piece is which and what the proper terms are.

Console: The main computer box is the console, although it may also be called the system unit (geeky) or the CPU (incorrect). It's a box that contains your computer's soul, its electronic guts. On the outside, the console sports various buttons, lights, and holes into which you plug the rest of the computer system.

Monitor: The monitor is the device where the computer displays information, its output. A common mistake made by new computer users is to assume that the monitor is the computer. Nope. The console is the computer. The monitor merely displays information.

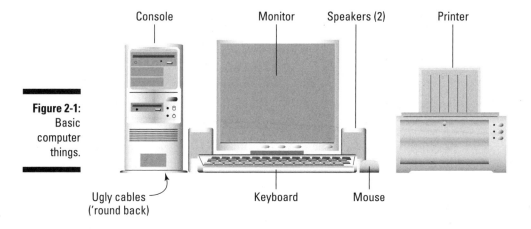

Figure 2-1:
Basic
computer
things.

Console   Monitor   Speakers (2)   Printer

Ugly cables
('round back)

Keyboard   Mouse

Keyboard: It's the thing you type on; it's the primary way you communicate with the computer, with input.

Mouse: No rodent or pest, the computer mouse is a helpful device that lets you work with graphical objects that the computer displays on the monitor.

Speakers: PCs bleep and squawk through a set of stereo speakers, which can be external jobbies you set up (refer to Figure 2-1), speakers built into the console or the monitor, or perhaps even headphones. Pay more money and you can even get a subwoofer to sit under your desk. Now, *that* will rattle your neighborhood's windows.

Printer: It's where you get the computer's printed output, also called hard copy.

You may find, in addition to these basic items, other things clustered around your computer, such as a scanner, a digital camera, a gamepad (or joystick), an external disk drive, a high-speed modem, and many, many other toys — er, vital computer components.

One thing definitely not shown earlier, in Figure 2-1 — and something you will never see in a computer manual and especially not in advertisements — is the ganglion of cables that lives behind each and every computer. What a mess! These cables are required in order to plug things into the wall and into each other. No shampoo or conditioner on Earth can clean up those tangles.

✔ Ensure that you know where the console, keyboard, mouse, speakers, monitor, and printer are in your own system. If the printer isn't present, it's probably a network printer sitting in some other room.

> ✔ Chapters in Part II of this book go into more detail on the individual computer components just introduced and illustrated in Figure 2-1.
>
> ✔ CPU stands for *central processing unit*. It's another term for the computer's microprocessor (see Chapter 6). Even so, some folks foolishly refer to the console as the CPU. Boy, are they wrong!

The Console Tour

That console, that main box that really is your computer system, doesn't stand alone. Into the console you plug every other gizmo that you use as part of the computer system. To accommodate those gizmos, the console has many, many holes into which those things plug. Not only that, the console has doors and slots so that you can access important things inside the console directly. Topping everything off like nuts on a sundae, the console has interesting buttons to press and switches to throw. The following sections mull it all over.

> ✔ Try to find on your own PC the items mentioned in the sections that follow. Get to know their locations as well as their official computer names.
>
> ✔ Not every console is the same. Use this section as a general guide.

Major points of interest on the console, front

The front of the console is for you, dear computer user. That's where you interact with the computer system directly, by adding or removing disks, observing lights, punching buttons, and perhaps even plugging one or two special items into the PC's tummy.

Use Figure 2-2 as your reference as you go hunting for the following items:

DVD drive: Like a music or video player, your computer digests CDs and DVDs through a slot or tray on the front of the console. The DVD drive consumes both CDs and DVDs, though your PC may have only a CD drive. Read more about this topic in Chapter 9.

Future expansion: Some spots on the console's nose may look like they're DVD or disk drives, but they're not! They're simply blanks that cover holes — holes you can use for adding things to your computer someday.

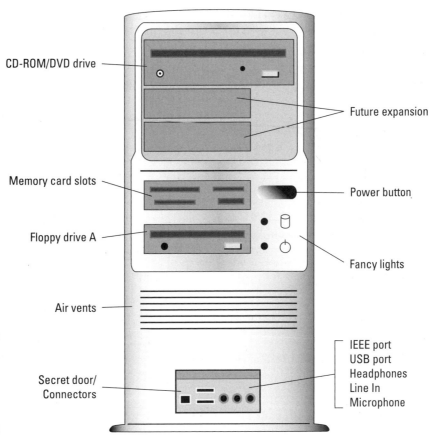

CD-ROM/DVD drive

Future expansion

Memory card slots

Power button

Floppy drive A

Fancy lights

Air vents

Figure 2-2:
Things to
note on the
front of the
console.

Secret door/
Connectors

IEEE port
USB port
Headphones
Line In
Microphone

Memory card slots: Found on many PCs are various slots for inserting digital memory cards, such as those used in digital cameras or other portable electronic gizmos.

Floppy drive: This slot eats floppy disks. Some software comes on floppy disks, and you can use floppy disks to move information from one PC to another. Not every PC sold today comes with a floppy drive.

Air vents: Okay, this one isn't impressive, but most consoles sport some type of air vent on the front. Don't block the air vents with books or sticky notes! The thing's gotta breathe.

The secret panel. Some PCs, especially home models, have a secret panel or door that pops open. Behind it, you can find connectors for joysticks, microphones, headphones, digital video, or other handy items you may need to plug and unplug from time to time. Having the secret panel is handier than having to reach around behind the computer and fumble for plugs and holes.

Buttons and lights: Most of a computer's buttons are on the keyboard. A few of the more important ones are on the console, and these buttons on fancier PCs are accompanied by many impressive, tiny lights. These buttons and lights include the following:

- ✔ **Power button:** It's no longer a plain on–off button — it's the *power button,* and it can do more than just turn the computer off or on. See Chapter 4 for the details.

- ✔ **Reset button:** Rare but still found on some computers is a button that forces the computer into a restart during times of woe. Consider it a plus if your PC has such a button.

- ✔ **Sleep button:** This rare button is designed specifically to put the computer into a coma (see Chapter 4). On some PCs, this button and the power button are the same.

- ✔ **Disk drive lights:** These lights flash when the hard drive, floppy drive, or DVD drive is working. On a hard drive, the light is your reassurance that it's alive and happy and doing its job. On all other types of drives (with removable disks), the light indicates that the computer is using the drive.

Other fun and unusual things may live on the front of your console, most of which are particular to a certain computer brand.

- ✔ The front of the console may also boast a brand label or manufacturer's tattoo.

- ✔ Some newer computers have stickers that show the secret Windows installation number or proclaim such nonsense as "I was built to run Windows Optimus Prime" or "A Pentium Wazoo lurks inside this box."

- ✔ For more specific information on the connectors lurking behind a secret panel, see the section "The I/O panel," later in this chapter.

- ✔ Don't block the air vents on the front of the console. If you do, the computer may literally suffocate. (It gets too hot.)

- ✔ A hard drive light can be red or green or yellow, and it flickers when the hard drive is in use. Don't let it freak you out! It's not an alarm; the hard drive is just doing its job.

Visiting the console's seedy side

The console's backside is its busy side. That's where you find various connectors for the many other devices in your computer system: a place to plug in the monitor, keyboard, mouse, speakers, and just about anything else that came in the box with the PC.

Use Figure 2-3 as a guide for finding the following important items on the back of your PC's console. Note that some things may look different and some may be missing, and some newfangled things may not be listed here.

Power: This thing is where the PC plugs into a cord that plugs into the wall.

Fan: Air gets sucked in here, blows around inside the console to keep things cool, and then puffs out the vents.

Voltage switch: Use this item to switch power frequencies to match the specifications for your country, region, or planet.

Expansion slots: These slots are available for adding new components on *expansion cards* to the console and expanding your PC's hardware. Any connectors on the expansion cards appear in this area, such as the digital video connectors on a high-end graphics expansion card.

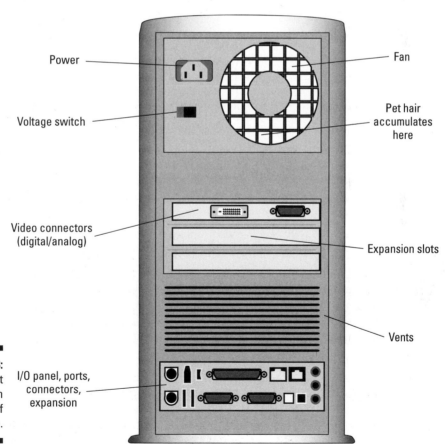

Figure 2-3:
Important doodads on the back of the console.

Vents: The breathing thing again.

I/O panel: Aside from the power cord, and anything attached to an expansion card, the rest of your PC's expansion options and plug-in-type things are located in a central area that I call the I/O panel. Details of what you can find there are covered in the next section.

Up close: The I/O panel

To either help keep all the connectors in one spot or just create the most intensely cable-crammed location on the console, your PC most likely has an I/O panel, normally found on the console's rear. This is where you add various expansion options to the PC as well as plug in the standard devices shown way over in Figure 2-1.

Use Figure 2-4 as your guide for what's what. The items you find on your PC's I/O panel may be labeled with text, or they may include the symbols listed later, in Table 2-1.

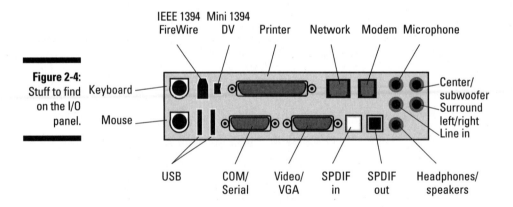

Figure 2-4: Stuff to find on the I/O panel.

Keyboard: The keyboard plugs into this little hole.

Mouse: It's generally the same size and shape as the keyboard connector, although this hole has a mouse icon nearby to let you know that the mouse plugs in there.

USB: Plug snazzy devices into these Certs-size Universal Serial Bus (USB) slots. See Chapter 7 for more information about USB.

COM/Serial: PCs have at least one of these connectors.

Video/VGA: Your PC's monitor can plug into this hole. The video connector is about the same size as the COM/serial connector, but it has 15 holes rather than 9. A second, digital monitor connector may be available for plugging in LCD monitors. Also, these connectors may be located on an expansion card rather than on the I/O panel (refer to Figure 2-3).

SPDIF In, SPDIF Out: These connectors are used for digital audio. Special fiber optic cable is required: Audio coming into the computer plugs into the In hole; the sound the computer generates goes out the Out hole.

Headphones/speakers: Into this hole you plug in your PC's external speakers or headphones, or it's where you hook up the PC to a sound system. (Also check the "secret panel" on the front of the console for a headphone connector.)

Line In: This jack is where you plug a traditional audio-producing device (stereo, phonograph, VCR, and so on) into the PC for capturing sound.

Surround left/right: Also for surround sound, this is the jack into which you plug the rear left and right speakers.

Center/subwoofer: For a surround sound audio system, you plug the center speaker or subwoofer, or both, into this jack.

Microphone: The computer's microphone plugs into this jack.

Modem: This is where you connect your PC's dialup modem to the phone jack in the wall. If two phone or modem holes are on the I/O panel, the second one is for a telephone extension. Note that this is *not* where you connect a broadband (DSL or cable) modem.

Network: This is where you plug in a local area network (LAN) connector or where you attach a broadband modem to the PC.

Printer: Older printers can plug into this connector.

Mini 1394: This special version of the IEEE 1394 connector is designed specifically for digital video and for connecting digital cameras.

IEEE 1394 (FireWire): This is another type of versatile connector, similar to USB. See Chapter 7.

The good news? You connect all this stuff only once. Then your PC's butt faces the wall for the rest of its life, and you never have to look at it again (well, unless you add something in the future or you just enjoy looking at PC butts).

- ✔ Your PC may also sport an S-Video output, which allows you to connect an S-Video monitor, video recorder, or television set to your computer.

- ✔ Older PCs may sport a specific joystick port, which is referenced in Table 2-1. On modern PCs, the joystick plugs into the USB port.

- ✔ The keyboard and mouse connectors *are* different! Be certain that you plug the proper device into the proper hole, or else the keyboard and mouse don't work!

- ✔ See Chapter 7 for more information on these holes and what plugs into them.

- ✔ See Chapter 14 for more on modems.

Helpful hints, hieroglyphics, and hues

Even though most PC connectors are different, manufacturers have a set of common colors and symbols used to label the various holes, connectors, and ports on the console's rump. These are listed in Table 2-1 to help you find things, in case the need arises.

Table 2-1	Shapes, Connections, Symbols, and Colors		
Name	*Connector*	*Symbol*	*Color*
Center/subwoofer			Brown
COM/Serial			Cyan
Digital video			White
Network			None
IEEE 1394			None

Name	Connector	Symbol	Color
IEEE 1394 mini			None
Infrared			None
Joystick			Mustard
Keyboard			Purple
Line In (audio)			Gray
Microphone			Pink
Modem			None
Monitor			Blue
Mouse			Green
Power			Yellow
Printer			Violet
SPDIF In		IN	Pink or white

(continued)

Table 2-1 *(continued)*

Name	Connector	Symbol	Color
SPDIF Out		OUT	Black
Speakers/headphones			Lime
S-Video			Yellow
Surround left/right			Black
USB			None

Chapter 3

PC Setup

In This Chapter

▶ Assembling your computer system

▶ Understanding computer cables

▶ Plugging things into the console

▶ Using a power strip

▶ Managing with a UPS

The PC has long been a member of the Pantheon of Incredibly Difficult Devices to Assemble. It has joined the ranks of the backyard grill, stereo equipment, pressboard Scandinavian furniture, bicycles, hammocks, and kid's playsets as one of the most dreaded assembly projects known to man. In fact, I would say that the computer is perhaps chief god of the pantheon.

I'm not going to lie to you: Setting up a PC isn't simple. On the other hand, it's truly not that difficult. Most of the things you need to connect are color-coded, and they fit together only one way. Yes, it's almost as easy as inserting the proverbial Tab A into the primordial Slot B — but I still had to write this entire chapter to help you through the process.

✔ This chapter covers basic computer setup. Turning the computer on is covered in Chapter 4.

✔ See Chapter 7 for additional information on what do to next, specifically after adding USB, IEEE, or other expansion options to your computer.

Unpack the Boxes

Computers can come in one, two, or multiple sets of boxes. If you're lucky, one of the boxes says Open Me First. Open that one first. Otherwise, attempt to locate the box containing the console. Open that one first.

Be sure to look through everything. Sometimes, manufacturers stick important items inside boxes inside boxes, or tucked away between pieces of packing material. Look over everything.

As you open boxes, check to ensure that you have all the pieces necessary for your computer system. (Refer to Chapter 2 for a review of the pieces.) If you're missing anything, call someone!

- ✔ Your computer runs faster when you take it out of the box.

- ✔ Keep the packing slip, warranty, sales receipt, and other important pieces of paper together.

- ✔ Don't fill out the warranty card until after the computer is set up and running fine. (If you have to return the computer, the store likes it best if you have *not* filled in the warranty card.)

- ✔ Keep the boxes and all the packing material. You need them if you have to return the computer. Also, the boxes are the best way to ship the computer if you ever have to move. Some movers don't insure a computer unless it's packed in its original box.

- ✔ Your computer may have come with a road map or flow chart type of diagram that tells you how to set everything up. If so, follow those instructions first and use the instructions here as suggestions.

Set Up the Console First

The *console* is the main computer box, the locus of all the PC's activities, so you should set it up first. Put it on the desktop or in the location where you you've always dreamed it would be. If you plan on putting the console beneath your desk, put it there now.

Don't back the console up against the wall just yet. You need to start plugging things into the console's back. Not until everything is connected to the console do you want to push it up against the wall. (Even then, leave some room so that you don't crimp the cables.)

- ✔ The console needs to breathe. Don't set up the computer in a confined space or inside a cabinet where there's no air circulation.

- ✔ Avoid setting the console by a window where the sun will heat it up. Computers don't like to operate in extreme heat — or cold, for that matter.

- ✔ Don't put the console in a cabinet unless the cabinet is well ventilated.

- ✔ Computers by a window also make a tempting target for a smash-and-grab thief.

It's a PC, not an oven or a refrigerator

Your PC wants to operate in just about the same temperatures as you, the human, enjoy. Most computers list their happiest operating temperatures on the case somewhere. Generally speaking, temperatures between 40° and 80° Fahrenheit (4° to 27° Celsius) are best for a computer. When it gets too hot, the computer starts to act funny and may spontaneously restart itself. When temperatures get too cold, the computer may not even start!

Also avoid humidity, which can really gum up a computer. Readers in tropical climes have reported mold growing inside their PCs — the humidity was that bad! If you're going to compute where it's humid, do so in an air-conditioned room!

A General Guide to Plugging Things into the Console

All major parts of your computer system plug directly into the console, which means that after you have the console set up, the next step in assembling your computer is to unpack other pieces parts and hook them into the console.

Don't plug anything into the wall just yet! Even so, as you begin to set up your computer system and attach various gizmos, ensure that those devices with on-off switches have the switches in the Off position.

This section covers the basics of connecting many popular items to the console. Use this information when you first set up the computer, as well as later when you expand or add to your computer system.

Unless you read otherwise, it's okay to plug in most computer gizmos while the computer is on. There are some exceptions to this rule, so carefully read this section!

Audio

Computer audio involves both output and input — the famous I/O you probably read about in Chapter 1 or maybe sang songs about when you went to computer camp as a child.

Know your computer cables

Unless your computer system is a wireless gizmo, the devices in it connect to the console by using a cable. The cable is known by which hole, or *port,* it plugs into, as well as the cable's length. For example, USB cables plug into USB ports and come in varying lengths.

The ends of a computer cable are configured so that you cannot plug the cable in backward. Generally, the connector for the console is one shape, and the connector for the gizmo is another shape. There are exceptions, in which case it doesn't matter which end of the cable plugs in where.

Some cables plug in snugly. The phone and network cables have little tabs on them that snap when the cable is properly inserted. You must press the tab to remove the cable. The video cable, as well as older printer and serial cables, have thumbscrews on the side, which help attach and tighten the cable to the connector.

Some cables are permanently attached to their devices: The mouse and keyboard have this type of cable, for example. Other cables are separate. That just means that you must remember to plug in both ends.

Extra cables, if you need them, can be purchased at any computer or office supply store or over the Internet. As a suggestion, measure the distance for which you need a cable and then double it to get a cable of the proper length. For example, if it's 2 feet between your console and where you want a microphone, get a 4-foot cable.

Audio input is supplied by a microphone. A microphone connects to the computer's microphone jack by using a standard audio *mini-DIN* connector. Audio output is supplied by either headphones, left-right speakers, or full-on-wake-up-the-neighbors surround sound. No matter how sophisticated the PC's sound system, audio connections are made by plugging things into the appropriate jacks in the console.

✔ Refer to Chapter 13 for more information on PC audio, including some speaker layout instructions.

✔ Both headphones and speakers use the Line Out, headphone, or speakers jack. Further, speakers may need to be plugged into the wall for more power; see the section "The Final Connection: Power," later in this chapter.

✔ Be sure to check the front of the console for another spot to plug in the headphones or microphone. It's much handier than using the connector on the back.

✔ The Line In connector is used to connect any non-amplified sound source, such as your stereo, VCR, or phonograph or a tiny dog waiting inside a parked car or another noise-generating device.

✔ Yes, the difference between the Line In and microphone jacks is that Line In devices aren't amplified.

✔ USB speakers plug into one of the PC's USB ports. Ditto for a USB headset, which is a combination of headphone and microphone. See "USB," later in this chapter.

✔ If your audio equipment lacks a mini-DIN connector, you can buy an adapter at any audio store or Radio Shack.

✔ Some PCs have special audio hardware, which you can determine by looking at the console's rear for audio connectors on an expansion slot cover. If your PC is configured that way, be sure to plug the speakers into the audio card's output jacks, not the standard audio output jacks on the I/O panel.

If your PC sports SPDIF connectors, you can optionally use digital audio devices for your computer sound. The digital audio devices must also have SPDIF connectors, and you must use special (and not cheap) fiber optic cable to connect these high-end toys.

✔ Plug optical audio input cables into the computer's SPDIF In connection. To use the computer's optical audio output, plug the cable into the SPDIF Out connector.

✔ Be careful not to bang, touch, or taunt the clear glass ends of the optical cable. Better cables come with little protective caps that you can keep on the ends when the cable isn't connected.

✔ SPDIF stands for Sony/Philips Digital Interconnect Format. It's also written S/PDIF or S/P-DIF.

IEEE, 1394, FireWire

On a PC, the IEEE port is used primarily for connecting audio or video devices to the console, most notably a digital video camera. There may also be a chance that an external scanner or disk drive uses the IEEE port. (See Chapter 7.)

You can plug any IEEE device into the computer at any time. The computer or the device can be on or off when you plug things in or remove them. Be sure to check with the device's documentation for any exceptions to this rule.

✔ There are two types of IEEE connectors: regular and mini. The smaller, mini connector is used specifically with digital video and is often labeled DV. Be sure to look for one of these in the secret panel on the front of the console (if the console has such a panel).

✔ IEEE devices require an IEEE cable, which may or may not come with the device.

✔ See Chapter 7 for more information on all things IEEE.

Joystick or gamepad

You're an old-timer if you call it a joystick any more. Nope, it's a *gamepad* or, often, *game controller*. Joysticks are so 1980s. Today's advanced video games need at least three joysticks, a hat switch, various fire buttons, control buttons — the whole enchilada. If you're a gamer and you have a favorite gamepad or controller to use with your PC, it's most likely a USB gizmo, and it plugs into any USB port on the console.

Keyboard and mouse

Set up the keyboard right in front of where you'll sit when you use the computer, between you and where the monitor goes. The mouse lives to the right or left of the keyboard, depending on whether you're right- or left-handed.

The PC keyboard plugs into the keyboard port on the back of the console. The mouse plugs into the mouse port. Note that the two ports look identical but are different. Don't plug the keyboard or mouse into the wrong port or else neither device works.

- ✔ If you're using a USB keyboard or mouse, plug the keyboard or mouse into any USB port.

- ✔ Some USB keyboards and mice come with a tiny adapter, designed to convert the USB port into a keyboard or mouse port connector.

- ✔ Don't plug the keyboard or mouse into the keyboard or mouse port while the computer is on. It may damage the keyboard, mouse, or computer. This warning doesn't apply when plugging a keyboard or mouse into a USB port.

Modem

A dialup modem connects to the phone company's wall jack by using a standard telephone cord. (The cord probably came with the PC.) It works just like plugging in a telephone, and you leave the cord connected all the time. (The modem "hangs up" after a connection, just like a telephone.)

You can use the modem's second phone jack, if available, to connect a real telephone to the computer so that you can use the phone when the computer isn't on the line. The second phone jack is labeled Phone and may have a telephone symbol by it. (The first jack is labeled Line.)

You may also have an external dialup modem, which connects to either the USB port or the serial port. You still need a telephone cord to connect the external modem to the phone company's wall jack. Note that external modems have on-off switches.

- ✔ Broadband modems — either cable, DSL, or satellite — plug into the computer's networking jack. See "Network," a little later in this chapter.

- ✔ Be careful not to confuse the modem's jack with the networking jack. They look similar, but the networking jack is slightly wider.

Monitor

Set the monitor atop your desk, generally back away from where you sit, to accommodate room for the keyboard.

The monitor plugs into the VGA, or graphics adapter, jack on the back of the console. The plug goes in only one way. If you have a digital monitor, find and use the digital jack. Some digital monitors come with a digital-to-VGA adapter if your console lacks a digital jack.

If the console has two VGA connectors, you want to use the one on an expansion card rather than the one on the console's I/O panel.

The monitor also requires power. See the section "The Final Connection: Power," later in this chapter.

Network

Plug the network, or Cat 5, cable into the network jack on the back of the console. This is how you connect your PC to a network, or how you connect to a broadband modem.

- ✔ Another name for the network jack is RJ-45. It's similar in size to the modem's jack, so try not to confuse them.

- ✔ Setting up a network involves more than just connecting the network cable to the console. Part IV of this book covers computer networking.

Printer

Set up the printer where it's within arm's reach of the console. This isn't a necessity; it's just handy to have the printer nearby so that you can reach over and get whatever it is you're printing.

The printer requires power, so you need to plug it into a wall socket. See the section "The Final Connection: Power," later in this chapter.

To get the printer and console talking, you need to formally introduce the two. No invitation is necessary; what you need is a cable, either a USB cable or the traditional printer cable. When you're blessed with a wireless printer, keep it close enough to the console to ensure that it's in range of the signal.

Whether you're using USB or a traditional printer cable, the cable has unique ends. One goes into the printer, the other goes into the console. You cannot plug the thing in backward.

✔ For printers with both printer and USB options, use the USB option.

✔ If you use a standard printer cable, be sure to get a bidirectional cable. It's often necessary for the printer software to work properly.

✔ Printers can also be accessed via the computer network. See Part IV of this book for more information on networking.

S-Video

The *S-Video* connector is designed to send video output from the computer to a monitor or television screen or to any video gizmo that has S-Video input. You can, for example, connect the console to a large-format TV to play a computer game. You can do this rather than hook up a standard monitor to your PC.

✔ S-Video is for video output only; it doesn't transmit any audio.

✔ See Chapter 10 for more information on computer monitors.

Serial

The serial, or COM, port isn't as popular as it once was, although you may still find external modems or mice that connect to this port. Otherwise, you can leave it alone.

✔ COM is short for *com*munications.

✔ When you have two serial ports, the first is COM1 and the second is COM2.

✔ Another term for the serial port is RS-232.

USB

USB devices plug into the USB port — any USB port. The USB cable may be attached directly to the gizmo, or you may have to use (or buy) a separate

USB cable. Fortunately, the USB cable has unique ends; you cannot plug in anything backward.

Examples of USB gizmos to attach to the console include the printer, scanner, digital camera, webcam or video camera, speakers, headset, disk drives, keyboard, mouse, and on and on.

Note that some USB devices must be attached directly to the console or to a powered USB hub. For example, an external disk drive or USB-powered device may need to be connected directly to the console, not "daisy-chained" to another USB device. See Chapter 7 for more information on this, as well as a general discussion of USB phenomena.

Wireless gizmos

Just because the gizmo says that it's wireless, don't think that it means wire-free. For example, a wireless keyboard or mouse may not connect to the console by using a wire, but a wireless transmitter *is* wired to the console, to either the USB or the keyboard/mouse ports. Beyond that point, however, you won't find any more wires.

Wireless networking is more or less truly wireless. The networking adapter on the console has a tiny antenna — no wires. But the rest of the network will, at some point, require a wire or two. See Chapter 19 for wireless networking nonsense.

The Final Connection: Power

The last thing you need to do, after plugging your computer components into the console and setting them all up, is to plug all those gizmos into the wall. The things need power!

The mighty power strip

You may have noticed that you have far many more devices that need to be plugged in than you have available sockets in the wall. No problem! That's why power strips were invented! The idea is to plug everything into a power strip and then plug that single power strip into the wall, as illustrated in Figure 3-1.

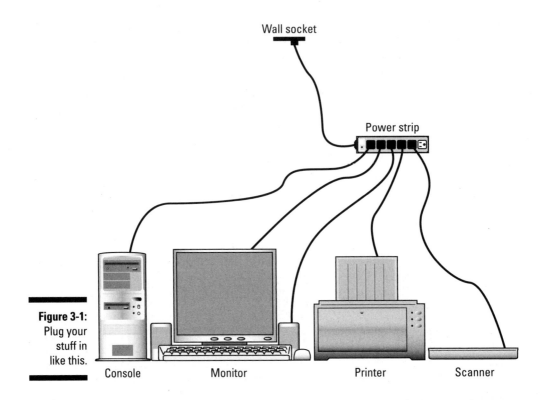

Wall socket

Power strip

Figure 3-1:
Plug your
stuff in
like this.

Console   Monitor   Printer   Scanner

Follow these steps:

1. **Ensure that all your gizmos with on-off switches are in the Off position.**

2. **Ensure that the power strip is in the Off position.**

3. **Plug everything into the power strip.**

4. **Turn your gizmos to the On position.**

Now you're ready to turn on the computer system, which is done by turning on the power strip. But not yet! The official on-off information is in Chapter 4. See that chapter for more information, although I highly recommend finishing this entire chapter before you plow ahead.

✔ Most power strips have six sockets, which is plenty for a typical computer system. If not, buy a second power strip, plug it into its own wall socket, and use it for the rest of your computer devices.

✔ Try to get a power strip with line noise filtering. Even better, pay more to get a power strip that has line conditioning! That's super nice for your electronic goodies.

✔ I recommend the Kensington SmartSockets power strip. Unlike cheaper power strips, the SmartSockets brand lines up its sockets in a perpendicular arrangement, which makes it easier to plug in bulky transformers.

✔ Don't plug one power strip into another power strip; it's electrically unsafe!

✔ Don't plug a laser printer into a power strip. The laser printer draws too much juice for that to be effective — or safe. Instead, you must plug the laser printer directly into the wall socket. (It says so in your laser printer's manual — if you ever get around to reading it.)

Surges, spikes, and lightning strikes

The power that comes from the wall socket into your computer isn't as pure as the wind-driven snow. Occasionally, it may be corrupted by some of the various electrical nasties that, every now and then, come uninvited into your home or office. Here's the lowdown:

Line noise: Electrical interference on the power line, most commonly seen as static on the TV when someone uses the blender.

Surge: A gradual increase in power.

Serge: Some guy from Europe.

Spike: A sudden increase in the power, such as what happens when lightning strikes nearby.

Dip: The opposite of a surge; a decrease in power. Some electrical motors don't work, and room lights are dimmer than normal. This is also known as a *brownout*.

Power outage: An absence of power coming through the line. People in the 1960s called it a *blackout*.

If possible, try to get a power strip with surge protection for your computer. You have a price to pay, but it's worth it. For an even better power strip, find one with both surge protection and noise filtering or line conditioning.

The most expensive form of protection is spike protection. That causes the power strip to lay down its life by taking the full brunt of the spike and saving your computer equipment.

Note that spikes come through not only the power lines but also the phone lines. So, if lightning strikes are a common occurrence in your area, get a power strip with phone line protection, as well as network protection if you're using a broadband modem.

For more information about nasty things that can walk into your house through your wall sockets, contact your electrical company. It may offer its own solutions to help you keep your valuable electronics safe, such as power protection right at the breaker box.

The UPS power solution

UPS stands for *u*ninterruptible *p*ower *s*upply, and it's the best thing to have for hooking up your computer system to the wall socket. Basically, a *UPS* is a power strip combined with a battery to keep your computer running when the power goes out.

The notion behind a UPS is not to keep computing while the power is out. Instead, the UPS is designed to keep your basic computer components — the console and monitor — up and running just long enough for you to save your work and properly shut down the computer. That way, you never lose anything because of a power outage.

Figure 3-2 illustrates the proper way to set up your computer system with a UPS and power strip. Not shown is a USB cable, which is used on some UPS systems to alert the computer about a power outage. Refer to Chapter 15 for information on how that works.

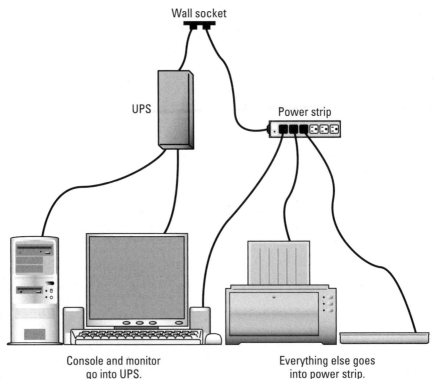

Wall socket

UPS

Power strip

Figure 3-2:
Hooking
up a UPS.

Console and monitor
go into UPS.

Everything else goes
into power strip.

✔ Ignore what it says on the box: A UPS gives you *maybe* five minutes of computer power. Be expedient and save your stuff to disk, and then shut down Windows and turn off the computer. You can print, scan, modem, or do whatever when the power comes back on.

✔ Some UPS systems also have non-battery-backed-up plugs so that you can plug everything into the UPS directly. Just be sure to plug the monitor and console into the battery-backed-up sockets.

✔ Leave the UPS on all the time. You need to turn it off only when the power is out and the computer has been properly shut down.

✔ In addition to providing emergency power, a UPS provides higher levels of electrical protection for your equipment. Many models offer surge, spike, and dip protection, which keep your PC running smoothly despite any nasties the power company may throw your way.

Using the UPS (a short play)

A thunder clap is heard. The lights flicker and then go out. ROGER *is left sitting in the dark, but his computer is still on. The UPS* beeps *once every few seconds.* FELICIA *rushes in.*

FELICIA: The power is out! The brioche I put in the toaster oven is ruined! Did you lose that urgent doodle you were creating in Paint?

ROGER: No, darling, I'm still working on it. See? Our UPS has kept the computer console and monitor on during this brief outage.

FELICIA: Oh! That explains the beeping.

ROGER: Yes, the UPS beeps when the power has gone out. It does that just in case I don't notice the pitch darkness we happen to be in.

FELICIA: Well, hurry up and print your doodle!

ROGER: Nay! I shan't print. Printing can wait, which is why I did not connect the printer to the UPS. It's as powerless as the toaster oven.

FELICIA: What can you do? Hurry! The UPS battery won't last forever!

ROGER: Relax, gentle spouse. I shall save to disk, thus. [Ctrl+S] Now I may shut down the computer, assured with the knowledge that my doodle file is safely stored on the internal hard drive. There. *(He turns off the computer and monitor. He shuts off the UPS and the* beeping *stops.)* Now we can weather the storm with peace of mind.

Two hours later, after the power is back on, FELICIA and ROGER are sipping wine:

FELICIA: Honey, you sure are smart, the way you used that UPS.

ROGER: Well, I'm just thankful I read Dan Gookin's book *PCs For Dummies,* published by Wiley Publishing, Inc. I think I shall buy more of his books.

FELICIA: Who knew that we could find such happiness, thanks to a computer book?

They canoodle.

Chapter 4

The Most Powerful Button (On-Off)

In This Chapter

▶ Starting your PC

▶ Introducing Windows

▶ Logging in to and out of Windows

▶ Locking the PC

▶ Using Sleep mode

▶ Hibernating the PC

▶ Restarting Windows

▶ Turning the computer off

▶ Setting the power button's function

▶ Keeping the PC on all the time

*T*he easiest way to tell whether your computer is evil is to note how it's turned on or off. Truly benevolent computers have a real on-off switch. When the thing goes all twisted on you, hellbent to take over the world, you can either casually or with dramatic aplomb turn the sucker off. Sadly, however, not every PC comes with a true on-off switch. Whether this implies that the computer is wicked depends, of course, on which version of Windows is running.

Seriously, many computers sold today lack a true on-off switch. Instead, the modern PC sports a *power button*. You use that button to turn the PC on, most definitely. The power button might also turn the computer off, but that's not a guarantee. Again, the purpose here isn't to allow the computer to begin a malevolent bender. No, thankfully, mankind is safe from your PC, and so will you be, if you follow the gentle power button advice offered in this chapter.

Turn On Your PC

When everything is plugged in and ready to go (refer to Chapter 3), you turn on the computer this way:

1. **Turn on everything but the console.**

2. **Turn on the console last.**

Or, if everything is plugged into a power strip, just turn on the power strip.

If the console and monitor are plugged into a UPS (which should be kept on all the time) and everything else is plugged into a power strip, do this:

1. **Turn on the power strip, which turns on all the computer's external devices, or *peripherals*.**

2. **Press the monitor's power button to turn it on.**

3. **Press the console's power button to turn it on.**

Success is indicated by your computer system coming to life; you can hear the fan whine and the disk drives warble into action, and various lights on the console, keyboard, and other devices may flash at you or glow softly. The scanner and printer may whir and grind their servos. Get ready to start computing!

✔ By turning the console on last, you allow time for the other devices in the computer system to initialize and get ready for work. That way, the console recognizes them and lets you use those devices in your computer system.

✔ Not all computer devices have their own on-off switches. For example, some USB devices (scanners and disk drives) use the USB port's power. To turn these devices off, you must unplug the USB cable (although that's not necessary unless the device is behaving improperly).

✔ You don't have to turn everything on when the computer starts. For example, if you don't plan on printing, there's no need to turn the printer on. In fact, you don't need to turn on most printers until you're ready to print, anyway.

✔ Some devices can be left on all the time. For example, your printer may have a special low-power mode that allows you to keep it on all the time, yet it uses very little (if any) energy. It's often better to keep such devices on all the time than to turn them on or off several times a day.

✔ It's generally a good idea to keep the DSL or cable modem on all the time. Ditto for the router or network switch.

✔ Also see the later section "Should You Leave the Computer On All the Time?" for information on keeping your computer on all the time.

✔ The largest button on the front of the monitor turns it on. Some older models may have the on-off switch in back. Indeed, many computer devices have their switches in the back, usually next to where the power cord attaches.

✔ When something doesn't turn on, check to see whether it's plugged in. Confirm that all the cables are properly connected.

The Setup program

At some point during the startup process, you see a message on the monitor about pressing a certain key, or keyboard combination, to enter the Setup program. *Pay attention to those keys!*

You don't always need to run or access the Setup program, but it's good to know how to get there when you do — for example, when you're adding more memory to the PC, updating some types of hardware, or disabling chipset features — technical stuff, and rare, but often necessary.

✔ Write down on this book's Cheat Sheet the keys used to access the Setup program.

✔ Common keys to press for getting into the PC Setup program include Del or Delete, F1, F2, F10, F11, and the spacebar.

✔ The Setup program is part of your computer's hardware. It's not part of Windows.

✔ The Setup program might also be known as the BIOS Setup utility.

✔ One feature of the Setup program is that you can apply a system password for your computer. Although I strongly recommend using passwords on the Internet and for your computer accounts, I recommend against setting a system password in the Setup program. Unlike with those other passwords, if you forget the system password, there's nothing you can do, and your computer is pretty much useless.

Trouble in Startup Land!

Hopefully, Windows starts right up and you get on with your work. You may experience a few unwelcome detours along the way. The most common startup error message refers to a missing file, something Windows was expecting to find but could not locate. To fix that type of startup error, as well as other errors, such as starting in the oddly named Safe mode, please refer to my book *Troubleshooting Your PC For Dummies* (Wiley Publishing, Inc.).

Here Comes Windows!

Starting a computer is a hardware thing. But the hardware is dumb, remember? It needs software to keep things hopping, and the most important piece of software is your computer's operating system. For most PCs, that operating system is *Windows.* So, after starting your computer's hardware, the next thing you have to deal with is Windows.

Who the heck are you?

The first time you run Windows on your PC, you do some extra setup and configuration. Part of the configuration involves creating a user on the computer.

The *user account* identifies who you are and keeps your information separate from anyone else who may be using the same computer. By adding a password, you ensure that your information on the computer stays safe and protected. I highly recommend that you create a password.

You configure Windows only once. After that, starting up your PC proceeds as described in the next section.

Log in, mystery guest

The first thing you must do in Windows is to *log in* and identify yourself. On a computer with several users, you must first choose your user account from a list. After that step, or when your computer has only one account, you must type your password when prompted, as shown in Figure 4-1. Here are the details:

1. **Choose your account from any multiple accounts listed on the screen.**

   This step is optional when you have only your own account on the computer. In that case, just skip to the next step:

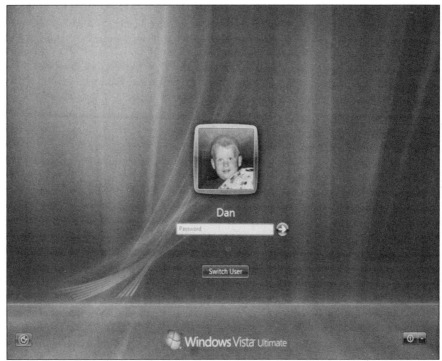

Figure 4-1:
Hello,
computer?
It's me!

2. **Enter your password into the box, if one appears.**

    Carefully type your password into the box.

3. **Click the blue arrow button or press the Enter key to have Windows check your password.**

If everything goes well, you next see the Windows *desktop*, which is where you can actually start using your computer. (See the next section.)

When you goof up typing your password, try again. You can use the Password Hint link to remind you of your password — but you must type a password to get into the system!

✔ The word *login* comes from the word *log,* as in a list of activities or experiences. The login is just like entering your name in a log.

✔ Get used to typing that password! You might have gotten by without a password in older versions of Windows, but Windows Vista focuses on security, and for security, you must have a password. I'm serious! No more whining about typing passwords!

Welcome to the desktop

The desktop is your home plate in Windows, the starting point, the main gate, the lobby, the vestibule. Chapter 5 discloses specific information about the desktop, stuff too explosive to reveal at this point in the book.

What you do next depends on the reason you bought your computer. This book has some ideas in it, but remember that this book is a *reference,* not a tutorial. As such, the reference for turning on your computer is all done.

Turning the Computer Off (Shutdown)

Common sense would dictate that the button you use to turn the computer off would logically be the same button you use to turn the thing on. But computers are not about logic, let alone common sense.

The PC proudly breaks with the strong tradition of electronic devices having an on-off switch. That's because there's more than one way to turn a computer off. In fact, the proper term isn't even "turn the computer off." No, you *shut down* the computer. As it turns out, turning the computer off is merely one of several ways you can shut down a computer.

Options for PC shutdown

Here are your choices for turning off the computer, er, I mean for computer shutdown:

Keep the computer on all the time: This option is viable, given the glut of other choices. See the section "Should You Leave the Computer On All the Time?" toward the end of this chapter.

Log Off: Tell Windows that you're done without having to turn the computer off and then on again.

Lock the computer: Use this quick way to suspend computer operations and present the login screen, but without actually logging off.

Switch User: Allow another user on the same computer to access their account without logging off from your own account.

Sleep Mode: The computer slips into a special, power-saving Sleep mode, like going into a low-power coma.

Hibernate: The computer turns itself off, but when you turn it back on again, it comes back to life much faster. Think "suspended animation."

Restart: You turn the computer off and on again in one step, mainly when installing or upgrading software or sometimes to fix minor quirks — like slapping Windows upside its head.

Shut Down: This is the one true option that turns the darn thing off.

Yank the power cord out of the wall: This method is satisfying, but not recommended.

Many of these options are found on the official Shutdown menu, located on the Start button's menu, as shown in Figure 4-2. To get at the Shutdown menu, follow these steps:

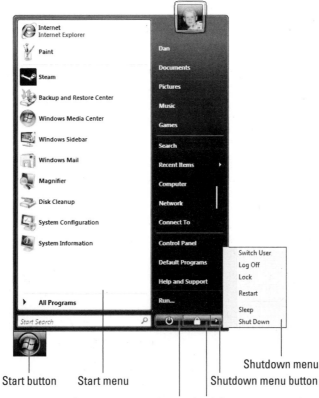

Figure 4-2: Where the Shutdown menu lurks.

Start button   Start menu

Start menu power button   Lock Computer

Shutdown menu button   Shutdown menu

1. **Pop up the Start button's menu.**

   You can pop up the menu by clicking the Start button with the mouse or by pressing the Windows key on the keyboard.

2. **Click the Shutdown menu's triangle button in the lower right corner of the Start button menu.**

Using the various options on the Shutdown menu are covered in the sections that follow.

Log yourself off

Logging off is an utter waste of time, especially when you're the only person using the computer. A better option when you just want a break is to lock the computer, as covered in the next section. But when several people have accounts on the same computer, you can log off to keep the computer on, toasty, and ready for someone else to use it. To do so, follow these steps:

1. **Click the Start button.**

2. **Click the Shutdown menu button on the Start menu.**

   Refer to Figure 4-2.

3. **Choose the Log Off command.**

As the computer logs you out, you're prompted to save any unsaved files, and any open programs or windows are closed. You're done for the day. Windows once again displays its initial screen, listing all available accounts on the computer. Time for someone else to use the PC.

Lock the computer

When you log out, you stop using Windows. Rather than fully log out, consider locking the computer instead.

To lock the computer, press the Win+L key combination, where Win is the Windows key on the computer keyboard and L is the L key. Immediately, you see the initial login screen; no one can access the computer at that point unless they have an account and know the account's password. The computer is locked.

✔ Locking the computer is a good, secure thing to do when you need to step away from your computer in an unsecured environment, such as any public place.

- ✔ You can also lock the computer by clicking the padlock button in the lower right corner of the Start button menu.
- ✔ Press Win+L, where L stands for *lock*.

Switch users

The Switch User command on the Shutdown menu, as shown in Figure 4-2, allows you to temporarily log out and allow another user on the same computer to log in. This option is faster than logging out because it doesn't require you to save your stuff or close your programs. When you return (log in again), all your stuff is waiting for you just as you left it.

Sleep mode

Sleep mode, once known as Stand By or Suspend mode, is an energy-saving way to not quite turn the PC off. In Sleep mode, Windows saves what you're doing and then puts the computer into a special low-power mode. The computer isn't exactly off, and it restores itself quickly, which makes Sleep mode more effective as a way to shut down the computer.

To put your PC to sleep, choose the Sleep command from the Shutdown menu, beautifully illustrated in Figure 4-2.

To wake the computer from its slumber, you can wiggle the mouse or press a key on the keyboard. Be patient! Sometimes it takes a few seconds for the PC to wake up. (The time lag is one major difference between the old Stand By mode and Windows Vista's Sleep mode.)

- ✔ You can also program the Start button menu's Power button to put the computer to sleep. See the section "Setting the Start menu's power button function," later in this chapter.
- ✔ Sleep mode is controlled in the Power Options window, which you can get to from the Windows Control Panel: Either open the Power Options button directly in Classic view, or from the Control Panel Home, choose System and Maintenance and then Power Options.

Hibernation

The most dramatic way to save power and not-quite-exactly turn the PC off is to use Hibernation. What Hibernation does is to save all the computer's memory — everything the system is doing — then turn the computer off (really turn it off, not just "sleep"). When you turn the computer on again, things return to the way they were before. So, hibernation not only saves electricity but also provides a faster way to turn the computer off and then on again.

To hibernate your computer, you must program one of the power buttons: the console's power button, the console's moon button (if it has one), or the Start menu power button. To program a power button to hibernate the computer, read the section "Power Button, What's Your Function?" later in this chapter. After you program one of those buttons, pressing (or clicking) it hibernates the computer.

To wake up a computer that's hibernating, you simply turn it on, just as you normally turn on the computer.

- ✔ Not every PC can hibernate.

- ✔ Hibernation saves electricity because the computer is really turned off, and it saves time because it takes less time to turn the computer on again. Also see Chapter 15 for more information on PC power management.

- ✔ If you have a PC with multiple operating systems — a *multiboot* system — you have to select Windows XP from that menu first. After that, Windows unhibernates and restores things to the way they were.

Restart Windows

You need to reset or restart Windows in two instances: Whenever Windows tells you to restart after you install something new or make some change or whenever Something Strange happens. For some reason, a restart clears the computer's head like a good nose blow, and things return to normal.

To restart Windows, choose the Restart command from the Shutdown menu, as shown in Figure 4-2. Windows shuts itself down — almost as though it were turning the computer off. But, just at the moment the system would have turned off, it starts back up again — a restart.

- ✔ If any files are unsaved, you're asked to save them before shutting down.

- ✔ Windows may initiate a restart on its own; or, when upgrading, you may have to click a button in a window to restart the computer.

Turn the darn thing off

Banish all doubt: You really can turn the computer off. Be in charge! From the Shutdown menu, choose the Shut Down command, as shown in Figure 4-2. After a spell and a fashion, the computer turns itself off.

If you had any unsaved documents or files, Windows asks you to save them before it fully shuts down.

After the console turns itself off, go ahead and turn off the other components in your computer system: monitor, scanner, and any other external devices. Or, if you have a power strip, simply flip its switch to turn everything off.

If you have a UPS, however, *do not* turn it off; you want to leave it on so that its battery remains charged.

> ✔ See? You don't need to press the power button to turn the computer off, but you can if you like. Refer to the next section.

> ✔ If the computer shuts down and then immediately restarts, you have a problem. Refer to your dealer or computer manufacturer for assistance, or check out my other PC book, *Troubleshooting Your PC For Dummies,* published by Wiley.

Power Button, What's Your Function?

It's called a power button and not an on-off switch because the power button is *programmable.* You can tell the computer what to do when you press the power button, from "do nothing" to "whistle an aria." The choice is up to you.

Setting the console's power button function

What does the console's power button do? To know for certain, as well as to change the power button's function, you need to access the Power Options, System Settings window, shown in Figure 4-3. Getting to that window depends on how you view the Windows Control Panel.

When you're using the Control Panel Home, choose System and Maintenance, and then in the next window, choose the item Change What the Power Buttons Do, found beneath the Power Options heading.

From the Control Panel Classic view, double-click the Power Options icon to display the Power Options window. On the left side of the window, click the link labeled Change What the Power Buttons Do.

Figure 4-3:
Change the
power
buttons'
functions in
this window.

Next to the option labeled When I Press the Power Button, you find a menu
button. From that button, you can choose what the console's power button
does when you press it. You have four choices:

✔ **Do nothing:** This option effectively disables the power button; press it
and nothing happens.

✔ **Sleep:** The computer goes into Sleep mode.

✔ **Hibernate:** The computer hibernates.

✔ **Shut down:** The computer shuts down.

For example, if you want the computer to just shut down when you press the
power button, choose the option that reads Shut Down.

After making your choice, click the Save Changes button. Then you can
optionally close the System Settings window.

✔ Regardless of how you program the power button, you can always use it
to turn off the PC in a panic: Simply press and hold the power button for
about two or three seconds, and the computer turns off. Although this is
a handy trick to know, you should use it only in times of desperation.
Otherwise, shut down the PC properly, as described in this chapter.

✔ Refer to Chapter 5 for more information on the Windows Control Panel.

Regarding that bonus power button (the secret one)

Some PC cases have a true on-off switch in addition to a power button. You can find the on-off switch on the back of the console, usually by the place where the power cord connects to the PC's power supply. The switch is often labeled | and O, for on and off, respectively. Use this button rather than the power button only in times of dire emergency. Also note that the on-off switch must be in the on position for you to turn on your computer (using the power button).

Setting the moon button's function

If your PC's console has a moon button, you can program its function just as you can program the console's power button. To program the moon button, walk through the process described in the preceding section but choose settings for the sleep (moon) button: use the menu button by the When I Press the Sleep Button option.

Setting the Start menu's power button function

The other power button you can program is the one found on the Start button's menu. That software power button can be programmed to sleep, hibernate, or shut down the PC. The steps are kind of technical, so follow closely:

1. **Open the Control Panel.**

   Refer to Chapter 5 for more information on the Windows Control Panel.

2. **Open the Power Options window.**

   Opening the window depends on how you view the Control Panel: From the Control Panel Home, choose System and Maintenance and then choose Power Options. From the Control Panel Classic view, open the Power Options icon.

3. **Choose any of the options that reads Change Plan Settings.**

   It doesn't matter which of the three Change Plan Settings options you click.

4. **Click the link labeled Change Advanced Power Settings.**

   The Power Options dialog box appears.

5. **Scroll through the list to find the Power Buttons and Lid option.**

6. **Click the plus sign (+) by the option Power Buttons and Lid to display its contents.**

7. **Click the plus sign (+) by the option Start Menu Power Button.**

8. **Click the option by the word *Setting* to display a menu button.**

9. **Use the Setting menu button to choose the Start menu power button's function.**

   The options are Sleep, Hibernate, and Shut Down.

10. **Click the OK button to confirm your choice and close the Power Options dialog box.**

11. **Close the Edit Play Settings window.**

The Start menu power button changes appearance and color depending on which option you programmed. But the appearance and colors are easy to forget. Instead, just point the mouse at the Start menu power button, and a pop-up information box appears, describing the button's function.

Should You Leave the Computer On All the Time?

I've been writing about computers for over 20 years now, and this debate has yet to be settled: Should you leave your computer on all the time? Does it waste electricity? Is it better for the PC to be on all the time — like the refrigerator or Spiderman night light? Will we ever know *the truth?* Of course not! But people have opinions.

"I want to leave my computer off all the time"

Hey, I'm with you.

"I want to leave my computer on all the time"

I say Yes. If you use your computer often, such as for a home business, or you find yourself turning it on and off several times during the day, just leave it on all the time.

The only time I ever turn my computers off is when I'll be away for longer than a weekend. Even then, I just hibernate the computers (well, those computers that have the Hibernation feature) rather than turn them off.

Does this method waste electricity? Perhaps, but most computers have Stand By mode and save energy when they're not being used. Modern PCs don't use that much electricity, especially when you have an LCD monitor (see Chapter 10), and having a PC on all the time doesn't raise your electrical bill significantly, not like a Jacuzzi or a Tesla coil.

Also, computers enjoy being on all the time. Having that fan going keeps the console's innards at a constant temperature, which avoids some of the problems that turning the system off (cooling) and on again (heating) cause.

- If you use your PC only once a day (during the evening for e-mail, chat, and the Internet, for example), turning it off for the rest of the day is fine.

- Most businesses leave their computers on all the time.

- Whatever you do with your PC, it's always a good idea to turn the monitor off when you're away. Some monitors can *sleep* just like PCs, but if they don't, turning them off can save some electricity.

- If you do leave your computer on all the time, don't put it under a dust cover. The dust cover gives the computer its very own greenhouse effect and brings the temperatures inside the system way past the sweltering point, like in a sweaty Southern courtroom drama.

- Another good idea: Turn off the computer during an electrical storm. Even if you have spike protection or a UPS, *don't* let that nasty spike of voltage into your computer during a lightning storm. Unplug the computer. And remember to unplug the phone line. You can't be too careful.

Chapter 5

Windows Rules

In This Chapter

▶ Visiting the desktop

▶ Finding the taskbar

▶ Using the Start button

▶ Viewing the Notification Area

▶ Getting to the Control Panel

▶ Finding Network stuff

▶ Locating important places in Windows

▶ Getting help

*T*hat hardware may look snazzy, and I'm sure you paid a pretty penny for it, but when it comes to being in charge of a computer, it's software that rules the roost. Of all your PC software, the Most Supreme One is the *operating system*. On a PC, that operating system is Windows.

This chapter provides a quick look into popular places in Windows, where to go to get things done, and some locations that are relevant to this book's contents. You see, this is not a Windows book; it's a PC book! But because no one can write a compelling PC book without at least mentioning Windows, a chapter like this one becomes necessary.

For more information on the various parts of Windows, please refer to this book's companion *PCs For Dummies Quick Reference*. You can also check out my tome *Find Gold in Windows Vista* (both published by Wiley) for a more detailed, loving look at your PC's prime piece of software.

The Smiling Face of Windows

Part of the operating system's job is to interface with you, the human. (See Chapter 1.) The way that interface is handled in the Windows operating system is via the desktop, or the main screen you see when Windows first starts, which is shown in Figure 5-1.

System Icons   Desktop   Shortcut Icons   Sidebar

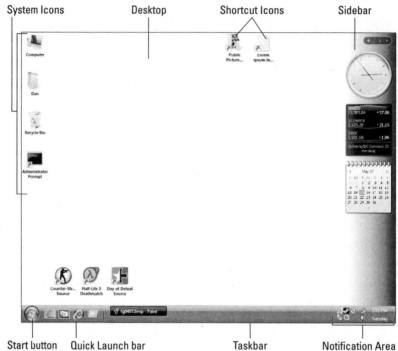

Figure 5-1:
The desktop
and all its
accoutre-
ments.

Start button   Quick Launch bar   Taskbar   Notification Area

Along with the desktop, you'll find several other major features of Windows, things you can use to get work done or to manage the computer. These include the Start button, the Start button's menu, the taskbar, and the notification area. The following sections illuminate each of these items.

The desktop

Windows main screen is the *desktop*. That's where the actual windows appear, those that frame the programs you run or show you a list of files or icons. The desktop can also have its own icons, such as shortcut icons to programs, files, or folders you often use. It can also be splashed with a fancy picture or background, such as the famous Vanilla Ice Cream in A Snowstorm picture shown in Figure 5-1.

Also shown in Figure 5-1 is the Windows Sidebar, a diversionary device displaying various tiny, informational programs, or *gadgets*. The Sidebar can be hidden or dwell on the left or right side of the desktop, and its gadgets can float on top the desktop. (Refer to a book specific to Windows for more information on the Sidebar.)

✔ The desktop is merely the background on which Windows shows you its stuff — like that pale blue bedsheet they use as a backdrop for any elementary school's production of *Eat Your Vegetables*.

✔ Icons are tiny pictures representing files or programs on your computer. See Chapter 24 for more information on icons.

✔ You can change the desktop background to any image. See Chapter 10.

✔ Also see Chapter 10 for information on changing the size of the desktop, or its *resolution*.

✔ The desktop is called a desktop for traditional reasons. Several generations of computers ago, it really did look like a desktop, complete with paper pad, clock, glue, scissors, and other desktop-y things.

The taskbar

The desktop is more like a corkboard where you pin icons than a place where you can grab hold of Windows and strangle it, if the desire is there. If you really want to wrap your paws around Windows, you must notice the taskbar.

The taskbar is typically located on the bottom of the desktop, as shown in Figure 5-2. Four important items are noted in the picture, although the Quick Launch bar may not be visible on your PC's taskbar.

Start button   Window buttons   Notification Area

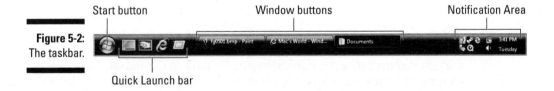

Figure 5-2:
The taskbar.

Quick Launch bar

You use the taskbar to control the windows on the screen; it allows you to quickly switch between those windows, or *tasks,* by clicking a window's button. The taskbar is also home to the Start button, which is where you *really* control Windows, as well as other doodads covered throughout the remainder of this chapter.

The Start button

The Start button is where you start a number of activities in Windows. It truly is the place to go when you want to start a program, start some activity, adjust the way Windows works, or even shut down the computer.

 The Start button lives on one end of the taskbar, usually in the lower left corner of the desktop. Clicking the Start button with the mouse displays the Start button menu. That's where the fun — or anguish — starts!

- ✔ Unlike in previous versions of Windows, the Start button does not have the word *Start* on it.

- ✔ You can also pop up the Start button menu by pressing the Win key on your computer's keyboard. If your computer doesn't have a Win key, press Ctrl+Esc to pop up the Start button menu.

- ✔ You make the Start button menu go away by pressing the Esc key on the keyboard.

The Start button menu

You use the Start button menu to start programs as well as get at key locations elsewhere in Windows. Figure 5-3 shows an example of what the menu may look like.

Important things to find on the Start button menu are listed in the figure. Note that the Start button menu can be customized, so what you see on your screen may look different from what's shown in the figure.

One of the most important items on the Start button menu is the All Programs menu. When you click the All Programs triangle (see Figure 5-3), the left side of the Start button menu is replaced with a list of programs and folders. You can either choose a program from the list to run the program or choose a folder to see additional programs. Chapter 27 offers more information on the All Programs menu.

- ✔ To customize the Start button menu, right-click the Start button and choose Properties from the pop-up menu. Click the Customize button in the dialog box that appears, and you can find many options for adjusting how the Start button menu looks and behaves.

- ✔ Figure 5-3 shows the Start button menu as it appears in the Windows Vista Aero interface. A classic Start menu is available, which looks similar to the way the Start menu looked in previous versions of Windows.

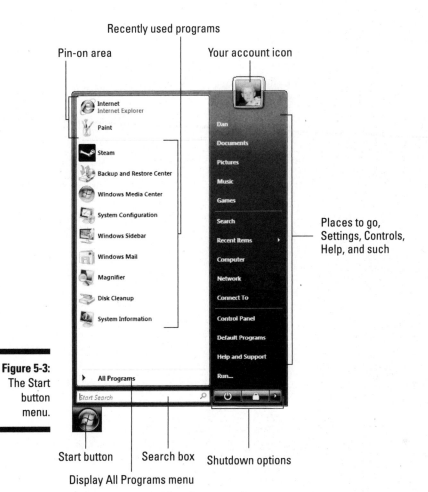

Recently used programs

Pin-on area

Your account icon

Places to go,
Settings, Controls,
Help, and such

Figure 5-3:
The Start
button
menu.

Start button   Search box   Shutdown options

Display All Programs menu

The Notification Area

The tiny tab on the opposite end of the taskbar from the Start button (refer to Figure 5-2) displays the current date and time, and also wee little icons that represent special programs running in Windows. That location is the *notification area*.

✔ You can see more information about the special programs by clicking, double-clicking, or right-clicking the wee icons.

✔ Some icons display pop-up bubbles with messages in them as various things happen in Windows.

✔ Once upon a time, the notification area was known as the *system tray*. You may still find it referred to that way in various documentation.

The Control Panel

One important place to know in Windows, especially in regard to your PC hardware, is the Control Panel window. The *Control Panel window* lists various parts of Windows and grants you access to other, specific windows and dialog boxes where you can make adjustments to Windows and control how the computer operates. That's the good news.

The bad news is that there are *two* ways of viewing the Control Panel. Shown in Figure 5-4 is the Control Panel Home window, which lists all the activities and locations by topic. Choose a topic to see additional topics or click a link to perform a specific activity.

Figure 5-4:
The Control
Panel
Home.

The second way to view the Control Panel is the Control Panel Classic view. In that window, you see all Control Panel items displayed as icons. Classic view is preferred by old-timers as well as by advanced users, who find it quicker to use than the Control Panel Home.

To display either Control Panel window, follow these steps:

1. **Click the Start button.**

2. **Click the Control Panel menu item on the right side of the Start button menu.**

After displaying the Control Panel window, follow the directions (for either the Control Panel Home or Classic view) to get at whatever window or dialog box you need in order to modify your computer's hardware, software, or configuration.

✔ To switch between Classic view and the Control Panel Home, you click the appropriate link from the left side of the Control Panel window.

✔ You can also access the Control Panel window from any folder window: Click the triangle on the far right side of the Address Bar. From the drop-down menu that appears, choose Control Panel.

Network Control

Networking is more a part of using a PC than it ever has been, especially with the popularity of broadband Internet connections. Fortunately, Windows Vista has perhaps the easiest possible way of managing the network. But it helps to know where two key locations are within Windows: the Network and Sharing Center and the Network window.

Also see Part IV of this book, which covers networking specifically.

The Network and Sharing Center

The main control window for networking in Windows Vista is the Network and Sharing Center, and it's shown in Figure 5-5. The window visibly describes your computer network, lists any and all wireless connections, and contains all the various networking options in a collapsible format.

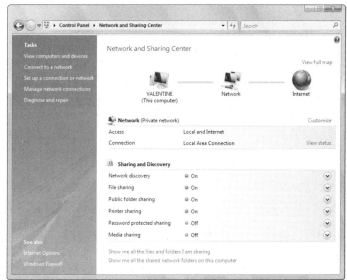

Figure 5-5:
The Network and Sharing Center.

You access the Network and Sharing Center window from the Control Panel. Because the Control Panel has two faces, there are two ways to access the window:

From the Control Panel Home, beneath the title Network and Internet, click the View Network Status and Tasks link.

 From the Control Panel Classic view, open the Network and Sharing Center icon.

The Network window

 Another networking place to know is the Network window, which can be accessed by opening the Network icon on the desktop (if it exists) or by choosing Network from the Start button menu. The Network window displays various computers available on the network, as well as other networking devices. More information on this window is provided in Part IV.

Places for Your Stuff

Windows provides special folders where you can store the things you create and keep on the computer — files and folders. Files are covered in Chapter 24, but for now, a few specific locations are worthy of note:

 Computer: This main icon details all the long-term storage in your computer, which includes disk drives, CD/DVD, media storage, as well as any network drives you're using. You display the Computer window by opening the Computer icon on the desktop or accessing it from the Start button menu.

 User Profile: The main folder for your stuff is named after your account, and it's officially called the User Profile folder. I prefer to call it your account folder. Within this main folder, you find various subfolders to help you organize your stuff. The subfolders include

Documents: For general files and stuff

Music: For audio and musical files

Pictures: For your digital photographs and graphics

Video: For digital video and animations

Plus, the user Profile folder has many other specific and useful folders — including any folders you create yourself.

 Recycle Bin: This icon represents the place where files go after they're deleted — kind of like File Hell but nondenominational. Normally, this icon is found on the desktop.

Windows Help

Microsoft abandoned the practice of including a manual with Windows eons ago. In fact, Windows never came with a full manual, merely online help — or help that you can get from the computer itself. The result of that evolution is the Windows Help system, which is kind of a cross between an online manual and a really vapid robot.

To access the Windows Help system, you press the F1 key on the keyboard. I know: "F1? What's up with that?" Felp? "F any 1 can help me?" I just don't get it, but that's the key to use.

Pressing F1 in the midst of doing anything in Windows displays helpful information about what you're doing.

To get general help, choose the Help and Support command from the Start button menu, and you see the Help and Support Center. There, you can type a question or pick a topic to search for help, as shown in Figure 5-6.

Figure 5-6:
Help?

Note that Windows may dial in to the Internet to complete your help request. This is normal (and you notice it only if you have a dialup Internet connection).

The Help engine is its own program. When you're done using Help, remember to quit: Click the X Close button in the upper left corner of the window.

Part II
Computer Guts

The 5th Wave   By Rich Tennant

"Well, here's your problem. You only have half the ram you need."

In this part . . .

Social commentator and comic George Carlin is quoted as saying he's not afraid of heights — he's afraid of *falling* from those heights. I believe something similar applies to high tech. You see, technology involves lots of electronics — the guts of your computer. You have nothing to fear from electronics, but it helps to be afraid of being electrocuted.

Fortunately, using a computer does not involve directly touching anything electrical. Your odds of death by PC electrocution are moderately low. But that doesn't excuse you from knowing the names of those electronic tidbits that make your PC do its thing. In this part of the book, you'll find out how to name, use, adjust, and abuse all the stuff that makes your PC work. It can be shocking, but that's merely your reaction to the prices.

Chapter 6

Mysteries of the Console

· ·

In This Chapter

▶ Studying the console's insides

▶ Examining the motherboard

▶ Understanding the microprocessor

▶ Working with expansion cards

▶ Setting the clock

▶ Knowing about the chipset

▶ Supplying the console with power

· ·

*B*eneath the console's sleek, futuristic exterior lies a tangled chaos of electronic entrails. It's a tropical jungle of twisty, vine-like cables connecting various circuit boards to power supplies and disk drives, tossed in with a high-tech salad of circuits, transistors, capacitors, resistors, and other components, many of which are sharp and pointy. Scary? Not really, but it isn't exactly inviting.

Despite the complex nature of the console's innards, it's not a forbidden place. Most computer consoles open easily, and that's for a reason: Sometimes, you need to get in there to add new stuff to your PC. It's rare, but it happens. But even when you never venture into the computer's case, it helps to be familiar with those mysteries found inside the console. This chapter helps explain that stuff.

A Look Inside the Console

Despite expansion options available inside the console, most folks use a computer for its full lifetime and never pop the lid. Even so, "out of sight" shouldn't imply "out of mind." Some items inside the console are worth knowing about. It helps you to become a better computer user to know official names and duties, even of things you never see with your own eyes.

Discovering your PC's inner guts

Figure 6-1 highlights the important things to note inside your PC's console. The figure shows a sideways view of a typical mini-tower PC, as though you removed the right side of the console and looked inside. (In the figure, the left side represents the front of the console.)

Missing from Figure 6-1 are the myriad cables that festoon the console's interior space; the typical PC's console is a lot less roomy. And, if you've owned the computer for a while, some dust is in there too — maybe even cat hair!

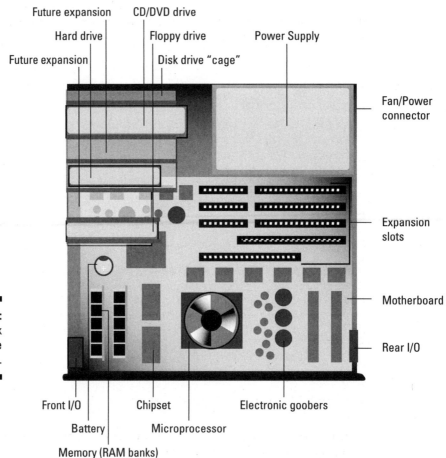

Figure 6-1:
A peek inside the console.

The three main parts of the console's tummy are

- The disk drive cage
- The power supply
- The motherboard

The *disk drive cage* is a contraption used to hold internal disk drives, an optical (DVD) drive, a hard drive, plus maybe a floppy drive. The cage also has room for even more disk drives (the so-called "future expansion"), usually right behind some knockout panels on the console's front.

The *power supply* feeds the console that all-important stuff called electricity. You can read more about the power supply in the section "The Source of PC Power," at the end of this chapter.

Finally, the *motherboard* is the computer's main circuitry board. It's important, so it's talked about later in this chapter, starting with the section "The Mother of All Boards."

Everything inside the PC's case is a *modular* component: Individual pieces can be replaced without having to toss out the entire console. Modularity is one of the keys to the PC's success over the years.

Opening the case (if you dare)

It's rare for anyone to open the PC's console these days; few options require internal expansion, especially with new PCs. I don't recommend opening the console just to casually poke around. About the only time you must open the console is when performing some type of upgrade. Especially when you don't know a screwdriver from a butter knife, or when your life insurance isn't paid up, I strongly recommend having a professional do the upgrade. Otherwise, here are the general steps I recommend for opening the console:

1. **Turn off the computer.**

   Refer to Chapter 4.

2. **Unplug the console; remove the power cord.**

   Turning the console off isn't enough. You really need to unplug the power cord. Unplugging other cables isn't necessary unless you need to do so to move the console around.

3. **Move the console out from the wall or locate it in a place where you have room to work.**

4. **Open the console's case.**

    The steps for opening the case depend on the case. Some cases require a screwdriver and the removal of several screws. Other cases may just pop up, slide off, or swing open.

When the case is open and the computer's guts are visible, you're ready to work inside the console. Use Figure 6-1 as a general reference — but mind the cables!

- ✔ Never plug in the console when the case is open. If you need to test something, close up the case!

- ✔ Typically, you open the case to do one of three things: Add more memory; add an expansion card; or replace the PC's battery.

- ✔ While you work in the console, try to keep one hand touching the case or, preferably, something metal, like the disk drive cage. That way, your electric potential is the same as the console's, and you reduce the chances of generating static electricity — which can damage your computer.

Closing the case

When you finish doing whatever motivated you to open the console, close it up! Heed these cautious steps:

1. **Check to ensure that all the wires and cables have been properly reconnected.**

2. **Confirm that no tools or parts are left loose inside the case.**

3. **Reattach the lid or console cover.**

4. **Reattach the power cord to the console.**

5. **Turn the computer on.**

6. **Pray that it still works.**

    This step is optional in case you don't believe in a higher, divine being. But why take chances now?

The Mother of All Boards

The computer's largest circuitry board is the *motherboard*. It's where the computer's most important electronics exist. The motherboard is home to the following essential PC components, many of which are illustrated earlier in this chapter, in Figure 6-1:

- ✔ Microprocessor
- ✔ Chipset
- ✔ Memory
- ✔ Battery
- ✔ Expansion slots
- ✔ I/O connectors
- ✔ Electronic goobers

The microprocessor, chipset, battery, and expansion card items all have their own sections in this chapter. Refer to them for more information. Computer memory is a big deal, so it's covered exclusively in Chapter 8.

The *I/O connectors* are simply places on the motherboard where various internal options plug in and communicate with the rest of the computer system. For example, on the motherboard, you find an I/O connector where the internal disk drives plug in and an I/O power connector for electricity from the power supply.

The electronic goobers are those miscellaneous pieces of technology that engineers put on the motherboard to look impressive.

The Microprocessor Is Not the Computer's Brain

No, the microprocessor is *not* the computer's brain. Software is the brain. The microprocessor is just hardware, and it does only what the software tells it to do. Despite that, the microprocessor is quite a significant part of your computer system. In fact, the microprocessor is your PC's main chip. Just about everything else on the motherboard exists to serve the microprocessor.

Despite its importance, what the microprocessor does is really rather simple: Beyond basic math (addition, subtraction, division, multiplication), the microprocessor can fetch and put information to and from memory, and it can do basic input/output (I/O) stuff. That doesn't seem very impressive, yet the key to the microprocessor's success is that, unlike your typical brooding teenager, the microprocessor does things very fast.

- ✔ When your jaw is tired, you can refer to the microprocessor as the *processor.*
- ✔ Another term for a microprocessor is CPU. *CPU* stands for *central processing unit.*

✔ Modern PC microprocessors run very hot and therefore require special cooling. If you ever look inside the PC console, you'll notice that the microprocessor wears a tiny fan as a hat. That helps keep the thing cool.

Name that microprocessor!

Once upon a time, computer microprocessors were named after famous numbers, like 386 and 8088. The trend now is toward microprocessor names, but not human names, like John or Mary, or even dog names like Fluffy and Chomps. No, now microprocessors are named after potential science fiction heroes, pharmaceuticals, or sounds made by a baby rhinoceros in distress.

Seriously, the primary microprocessor is the Pentium, developed by industry leader Intel. Other microprocessor names include Celeron, Athlon, Opteron, Duron, and Xenon. (Six more names and you have a galactic pantheon.)

The number-name thing is difficult for the computer industry to completely break with, so you also see microprocessor names followed by numbers and other strange words. Honestly, the microprocessor name and number matter only when you first buy the computer, and even then the only numbers that truly matter are the dollars you plunk down for the thing.

Beyond the name, the truly important yardstick used to judge a microprocessor (aside from price) is its speed, which is covered in the next section.

✔ The two most popular types of Pentium chips now sold are the Pentium 4 and the Pentium dual core, or Core 2 Duo. Between the two, the dual-core chips are better.

✔ Intel is the world's leading manufacturer of computer microprocessors. The company developed the 8088, which dwelt in the bosom of the first IBM PC.

✔ Another way to describe a microprocessor is by which type of socket on the motherboard it plugs into. This information is important only to those folks who choose to build their own PCs.

✔ Little difference exists between a true Intel and a non-Intel microprocessor. As far as your PC's software is concerned, the microprocessor is the same no matter who made it. I must note, however, that computer gamers prefer AMD microprocessors.

Microprocessor muscle and speed

Microprocessors are gauged by two factors: their muscle power and how fast they go.

Microprocessor muscle is measured in bits — specifically, how many bits at a time the chip can toss around. The more bits a microprocessor can deal with at once, the better. For a typical PC microprocessor, that's 32, 64, or 128 bits, with 64 bits the most common.

It helps to think of bits in a microprocessor like cylinders in a car: The more you have, the more powerful the engine. Or, a better example is lanes on a freeway: The more you have, the quicker larger chunks of data (traffic) can move around.

Current microprocessor speed is measured in *gigahertz (GHz),* or billions of cycles per second. The higher the value, the faster the microprocessor, with average speeds between 2.0 GHz (slower) and 4.0 GHz (faster).

Sadly, speed isn't really a realistic gauge of how fast a microprocessor does its microprocessing. Speed is a relative measurement when it comes to computers, but even so, a Pentium running at 2.4 GHz is slower than a Pentium running at 3.0 GHz — not that you would notice.

Which microprocessor lives in your PC?

It's not easy, after you get home, to confirm that your PC has the micro-processor you bought. Even if you crack open the case, you can't really see the microprocessor because it's wearing that little fan hat — and even if you peeled off the hat, the numbers and names printed on the chip may not be of any use to you.

One way to discover which type of microprocessor dwells in your PC's bosom is to use Windows. The System window shows a brief microprocessor and RAM summary, similar to the one shown in Figure 6-2.

To summon the System window, press Win+Break on your keyboard (that's the Windows key plus the key labeled Break or Pause Break). You can also open this dialog box by right-clicking the Computer icon on the desktop and then choosing Properties from the pop-up menu.

In Figure 6-2, you can see that the PC sports a Pentium D microprocessor run-ning at 3.00 GHz. The computer sports 1022MB of RAM. That jibes with what I paid for, so my dealer is off the hook.

> ✔ Not every System window displays information as complete as that shown in Figure 6-2. When Windows doesn't really know, it may say something vague, as in "x86 Family."

> ✔ See Chapter 8 for more information on RAM.

Figure 6-2:
The System
window.

Expansion Slots

The success of the original IBM PC was due to its openness. Part of that openness was the ability to expand the computer internally by adding additional circuitry boards. Those boards, or *expansion cards*, plugged directly into *expansion slots* on the motherboard. The idea is that you can expand your computer system by adding options not included with the basic PC.

Sadly, whereas most PCs still come with expansion slots, the need for expansion cards is waning. The modern PC comes with just about any option you need already available on the motherboard. Other options can be added via the USB port (see Chapter 7). Expansion cards are still available, but they're not as much of a requirement as they once were.

✔ The number and type of slots available in your computer depend on the size of the console's case as well as on the motherboard's design. Small-footprint PCs have the fewest expansion slots. Some home systems (and nearly all laptops) lack expansion slots. Tower computer models have the most, sometimes up to eight expansion slots!

✔ Expansion cards are sometimes called *daughterboards*. Get it? Motherboard, daughterboard? I'm looking forward to *auntboard* or perhaps *secondcousinboard*.

✔ Most expansion cards come squirming with cables. This mess of cables makes the seemingly sleek motherboard look more like an electronic pasta dish. Some cables are threaded inside the PC; others are left hanging limply out the back. The cables are what make the internal upgrading and installation process so difficult.

✔ The backsides of most expansion cards stick out the rear of the consoles; the card's back replaces the metallic slot cover to reveal special connectors or attachments for the expansion card.

The PCI Express

The best type of expansion slot to have in your PC is the PCI Express, also written as PCIe. Without boring you, the PCI Express type of expansion slot communicates with the motherboard, and therefore with the microprocessor, both quickly and efficiently. That makes it an ideal way to add extra circuitry to your computer.

✔ When your PC has PCI Express expansion slots, you must be sure to buy only PCI Express expansion cards. For example, if you choose to add an internal TV adapter, you have to buy a PCI Express TV adapter.

✔ A common type of PCI Express card to add to a PC is a high-end graphics card. See Chapter 10 for more information on graphics.

✔ PCI stands for Peripheral Component Interconnect. As if you care.

Older expansion slots

In addition to PCI Express, or in its stead, your PC may sport one of the older yet still popular expansion slots. These slots come in many delicious flavors:

PCI: The PCI slot is the most common form of internal expansion for a PC (for a Macintosh too, but that's not the subject here). Some PCs have a mixture of PCI and PCI Express slots. If so, go with PCI Express when you have that option.

AGP: This type of expansion slot was specifically designed to deal with graphics adapters. In fact, AGP stands for Accelerated Graphics Port. Older PCs may sport this expansion slot, but the best video cards use PCI Express.

ISA: The most ancient type of expansion slot is the ISA, which stands for (get this) Industry Standard Architecture. That's because it never really had a name until another, better type of expansion slot came along. ISA slots hang around to be compatible with older expansion cards.

Other standards no longer available, but listed here for humorous reasons, include MCA, VESA Local Bus, NuBus, EISA, and Lego. What you can derive from this is that new expansion slot standards come and go quite frequently in the computer world.

The PC's Ticker

Your computer is secretly a very expensive and questionably accurate time-piece. Indeed, just about every computer comes with an internal clock, even the primitive computers of the early steam-powered age, back in the 1970s. Today's computers keep the time circuitry on the motherboard. A special battery keeps track of the date and time whether the PC is plugged in. And Windows itself maintains the clock, displaying the time or letting you set the time when the computer clock is (often) woefully off.

- ✔ The computer clock is displayed by Windows in the Notification Area (see Chapter 5).

- ✔ Computers need clocks just like humans do: to keep track of time. Computers use clocks for scheduling, to determine when files are saved, to track information, and generally to prevent everything from happening all at once.

- ✔ The date-and-time format is based on your country or region, which was set when you first configured Windows. The date/time format can be changed by using the Control Panel: From the Control Panel Home, click Clock, Language, and Region, and then find the link Change the Date, Time, or Number Format. From the Control Panel Classic view, double-click to open the Regional and Language Options icon.

"My clock is all screwy!"

Computers make lousy clocks. A typical PC loses about a minute or two of time every day. Why? Who knows!

Generally speaking, the clock runs slow or fast because of all the various things going on inside the computer. The more that stuff goes on, the more the clock is wrong. Especially if you put your computer to sleep, or "hibernate" it, the clock can get really nuts. (Refer to Chapter 4 for more hibernation information.)

On the positive side, the computer's clock is well aware of daylight savings time: Windows automatically jumps the clock forward or backward, and does so without having to know the little ditty "Spring forward, fall back." Or is it the other way around? Whatever — the computer knows and obeys.

What do you do if the clock is wrong? Why, set it, of course. Keep reading!

Set the clock

To set the date and time on your PC, heed these steps:

1. **Right-click the time display in the Notification Area: Click-click.**

2. **From the pop-up menu, choose the command Adjust Date/Time.**

   The Date and Time Properties dialog box appears.

3. **Click the button Change Date and Time.**

   Changing the time requires administrator approval.

4. **Grant administrator approval: If you're logged in as an administrator, click the Continue button; otherwise, type an administrator password to continue.**

   The Date and Time Settings dialog box appears, as shown in Figure 6-3.

Figure 6-3:
The Date
and Time
Settings
dialog box.

5. **Manipulate the controls in the Date and Time Properties dialog box to change or set the date or time.**

   For example, type **10:00 AM** if it's 9:58 AM or so. Then, when the telephone time lady (or whoever) says that it's 10 o'clock, click OK to set the time instantly.

6. **Click OK when you're done.**

Internet time to the rescue!

One way to tame the wild computer clock is to have the computer itself automatically synchronize the time with one of the many worldwide time servers. A *time server* is a computer designed to cough up accurate time information for any computer that checks in on the Internet.

To configure your PC to use a time server and synchronize itself with time on the Internet, open the Date and Time Properties dialog box, as described in the preceding section. Then follow these steps:

1. **Click the Internet Time tab in the Date and Time Properties dialog box.**

   The current Internet time settings are displayed in the dialog box.

2. **Click the Change Settings button.**

   Administrator approval is required in order to continue.

3. **Click the Continue button or type an administrator's password to continue.**

4. **Put a check mark by the option Synchronize with an Internet Time Server.**

5. **(Optional) Choose a time server from the drop-down list.**

6. **Click the Update Now button to ensure that everything works.**

   When a problem occurs, repeat Steps 5 and 6 by choosing another time server.

7. **Click OK, and then OK again to close up all the dialog boxes.**

With Internet time, Windows automatically adjusts the PC's clock whenever you're connected to the Internet. There's nothing else you need to do — ever!

About the PC's Battery

All PC's have an internal battery, which is part of the motherboard. Its primary purpose is to help the PC's clock keep time even when the computer is off or unplugged.

A typical PC battery lasts for about six years, possibly more. You'll know when it dies because the computer's date and time are way off, or perhaps the PC even has a message telling you that the motherboard's battery needs replacing. You can get a replacement at any Radio Shack.

✔ Yes, you have to open the console's case to get at the battery. Don't expect it to be easy to find, either!

✔ The PC's battery may also be used to back up special system information, such as the number of disk drives, memory configuration, and other trivia the computer needs to know all the time, but may not remember otherwise.

✔ The motherboard's battery is in addition to any other batteries in the computer, such as the main battery used to power a laptop.

The Chipset

Rather than refer to the various and sundry computer chips on the motherboard as The Various and Sundry Computer Chips on the Motherboard, computer scientists have devised a single descriptive term. All those chips comprise the *chipset.*

The chipset is what makes up your computer's personality. It contains instructions for operating the basic computer hardware: keyboard, mouse, networking interface, sound, and video, for example.

Different chipsets are available depending on what types of features the computer offers. For example, some motherboards may come with advanced graphics in the chipset or maybe wireless networking. Sadly, there's no easy way to tell based on the chipset's weirdo names or numbers; you must refer to the chipset's documentation to see what you're really getting. (Even then, the info is really only interesting to diehard computer nerds.)

✔ Different PCs use different chipsets, depending on which company manufactured the motherboard.

✔ An older term for the chipset, particularly the main ROM chip in a PC, is BIOS. *BIOS* stands for Basic Input/Output System. There's a BIOS for the keyboard and mouse, one for the video system, one for the network, and so on. Altogether, they comprise the *chipset.* (See Chapter 8 for more info on ROM.)

The Source of PC Power

Lurking inside your PC's console is something that does no thinking and isn't used for data storage. That's the *power supply.* It does several wonderful things for Mr. Computer:

✔ Brings in electricity from the wall socket and converts the electricity from wild AC current into mild DC current

✔ Provides electricity to the motherboard and everything living on the motherboard

✔ Provides juice to the internal disk drives

✔ Contains fans that help keep the inside of the console cool

✔ Contains or is directly connected to the PC's power button

The power supply is also designed to take the brunt of the damage if your computer ever suffers from electrical peril, such as a lightning strike or power surge. In those instances, the power supply is designed to die, and to sacrifice itself for the good of your PC. *Don't panic!* You can easily replace the power supply and discover that the rest of your PC is still working fine.

✔ Thanks to the fans, the power supply is the noisiest part of any PC.

✔ Power supplies are rated in *watts*. The more internal hardware stuff your PC has — the more disk drives, memory, and expansion cards, for example — the greater the number of watts the power supply should provide. The typical PC has a power supply rated at 150 or 200 watts. More powerful systems may require a power supply upward of 300 watts.

✔ One way to keep your power supply — and your computer — from potentially going Poof! (even in a lightning strike) is to invest in a surge protector, or UPS. Refer to Chapter 3 for details.

Chapter 7

Jacks on the Box

· ·

In This Chapter

▶ Understanding ports

▶ Praising the USB port

▶ Adding USB gizmos

▶ Removing USB gizmos

▶ Adding even more USB ports

▶ Making use of the IEEE port

▶ Hanging on to older PC ports

· ·

*O*ne key to the PC's success over the past quarter-century is its expand-ability. You can not only expand a computer on the inside of the console (via the expansion slots), but you can also add a nearly infinite number of gadgets to your computer system on the outside of the console. That's done by plugging the gizmo into one of the many connectors found on the computer console.

This chapter is about those connectors, as well as about the smattering of devices, or *peripherals,* you can use to expand your computer system.

Is It a Port, a Jack, or Just a Hole?

If it's found on a computer, you must assume that the spot where you plug something in has an official name. Relax. It does. Rather than say "that spot where you connect a cable," you have many options.

The first option is *hole.* This choice is bad because there are many holes in a computer console, several of which are unsuitable for attaching anything.

Another option is *connector,* but that's a vague term.

From the audio industry, the term *jack* is often used. Happily, the location where you plug audio equipment — headsets, speakers, and microphone, for example — into the PC is a jack. But that's still not computer-y enough.

Finally, there's the term *port*. Yes, port is the official term used to describe not only the connection being made but also the technology that makes the connection work.

For technological as well as historical reasons, the typical PC has a variety of ports. It has legacy ports, originally designed for specific devices, such as the printer, mouse, and keyboard. But modern ports are more versatile and support a variety of devices. These include the USB, and IEEE 1394 FireWire ports. The rest of this chapter covers what's what and how each port is best used.

- ✔ Officially, a *port* is a place on the computer where information can be sent or received or both. Often, it's called an *I/O port* because it's used for both input and output. Information flows out of the computer through the port, and into the computer from whichever gizmo is attached to the port.

- ✔ Also refer to Chapter 3 for information on plugging things into the various PC ports.

All Hail the USB Port

The most versatile port on your PC is the USB, where the U stands for *universal* and means that this port can be used to plug in an entire universe of peripherals, often replacing the function of many other individual ports on the computer.

The variety of USB devices is legion. Here's just a sampling of what you can plug into a USB port: speakers, headsets, joysticks, scanners, digital cameras, video cameras, webcams, floppy drives, keyboards, CD and DVD drives, hard drives, flash drives, media card readers, networking gizmos, pointing devices, tiny fans, lamps, tanning beds, time machines — and the list goes on and on. More and more USB devices are appearing every day.

The best news about USB? It's *easy.* Just plug in the gizmo. Often, that's all you need to do!

- ✔ USB stands for Universal Serial Bus. Say "you S bee."

- ✔ USB ports, as well as USB devices, sport the USB symbol, as shown in the margin.

- ✔ Refer to Chapter 2 for information on finding the USB port on your PC's console.

Hanging around USB cables

Whereas a few USB devices attach directly to the computer, such as USB thumb or keychain drives, most USB devices need cables. The name of the cable is, surprising, *USB cable*.

USB cables are judged by their length and the type of connector on each end.

As far as length goes, you can get a USB cable up to 3 or 4 meters long. Any longer and the signal may be compromised.

The standard USB cable has two different ends, dubbed A and B. The A end is flat, and it plugs into the console or a USB hub. The B end has a trapezoidal shape and plugs into the USB device. Special A-A extension cables are also available, so try not to confuse them with the standard A-B cable.

Connecting a USB device

One reason the USB port took over the world is that it's smart. Dumb things never take over the world. Witness the Tablet PC. But I digress.

Adding a USB device to your computer is easy: Just plug it in. You don't need to turn off the computer first, and often times you don't even need to install special software. When you plug a USB device into the console, Windows instantly recognizes it and configures the device for you.

Of course, it pays to read the directions! Some USB gizmos require that you first install software before connecting the device. The only way to tell is to read the quick setup information or dive right into the manual that came with the USB device.

Where's the power cord?

Another advantage of USB is that many types of USB devices don't require a separate power cord. Instead, they use the power supplied by the USB ports themselves. These are known as *USB-powered* devices.

Some folks are uncomfortable that a USB-powered device lacks an on-off switch. That's okay; it's fine to leave the device on, as long as you keep the computer on. But, if you really, *really* want to turn the gizmo off, simply unplug the USB cable.

  ✔ USB devices that require lots of power, such as printers and certain external disk drives, also have their own power cords.

✔ USB gadgets that require power may insist on being plugged into a USB-powered hub. That means the USB connection must be made either directly to the computer itself or to a USB hub that supplies power. See the section "Expanding the USB universe," later in this chapter, for information on powered versus unpowered hubs.

Removing a USB device

This is cinchy: To remove a USB device, just unplug it. That's it! Well, unless that device is a disk drive or media storage device. In that case, you must officially *unmount* the gizmo before you unplug it. Refer to Chapter 9 for information on removing a USB disk drive or storage media.

Expanding the USB universe

There never seems to be enough USB ports when you need them. Fortunately, when you need more USB ports, you can quickly add them by plugging a USB hub into your computer system.

A USB *hub* allows you to greatly expand your PC's USB universe. A typical expansion hub, as shown in Figure 7-1, connects to your PC's USB port. But then it turns around and instantly provides even more USB ports for the devices that need them.

✔ If one hub isn't enough, buy another! You can connect hubs to hubs, if you like. As long as the cables fan out from the PC and nothing loops back on itself, it all works.

✔ Sometimes, you don't have to buy a separate USB hub. Some USB devices act as hubs, providing connectors for plugging in additional USB devices.

✔ Using hubs, you can expand your PC's USB universe to the maximum 127 USB devices. You'll probably run out of desk space before that.

✔ Some USB devices prefer to be plugged directly into the console. These types of devices say so on their boxes and in their manuals.

✔ A hub that also plugs into the wall socket is known as a *powered* USB hub. (The console is also a powered USB hub.) This type of hub is necessary for some USB devices to operate.

✔ An example of an unpowered hub is a keyboard that has USB ports on it. Those ports are designed to connect non-USB powered devices, such as mice.

✔ The first hub (your PC) is the *root* hub.

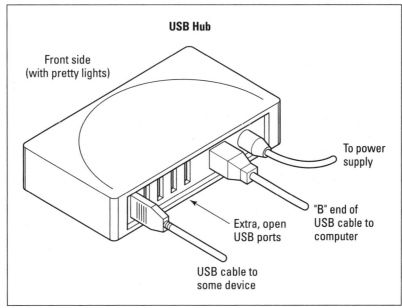

USB Hub

Front side
(with pretty lights)

To power
supply

"B" end of
USB cable to
computer

Extra, open
USB ports

USB cable to
some device

Figure 7-1:
Add more
USB ports
with a
USB hub.

The Port of Many Names, IEEE

About the time the USB port was taking over the computer world, a second "universal" computer port standard appeared. This *IEEE port* works similarly to USB, can be plugged and unplugged like USB, and has hubs like USB. Once upon a time, IEEE was faster than USB, which made it ideal for high-speed devices, like disk drives and video cameras.

Today, the IEEE port isn't taking a back seat to USB. With the new USB 2.0 standard, USB devices are now just as fast as IEEE devices. In fact, the only time you'll see IEEE used on a PC is for connecting certain high-speed digital imaging devices, such as video cameras. Beyond that, the world of computer peripherals is dominated by USB.

✔ The IEEE 1394 port is often called IEEE or 1394. Another term is *FireWire*, although that term is primarily used for Macintosh computers. Regardless, it's the same port.

✔ The IEEE port comes in two sizes: regular and Mini DV. Refer to Chapter 2 for information on the different connector sizes.

✔ Many PCs do not come with an IEEE port. Don't be disappointed if your PC lacks one; IEEE can be added by installing an expansion card in the console. See Chapter 6.

✔ When your PC has both IEEE and USB ports and the gizmo you're installing uses both IEEE and USB connectors, choose USB. I find that USB is more reliable than IEEE, at least on the external disk drives where I find both options available.

✔ IEEE uses its own, unique cables, which aren't the same as USB cables. Also, unlike USB cables, IEEE cables have the same type of connector on both ends.

✔ Unlike USB cables, IEEE cables are quite expensive. Maybe that's when you pronounce it "Ieeeee"?

✔ Some IEEE ports are marked by the FireWire symbol, as shown in the margin.

✔ Another term for IEEE is I.Link. Officially, the standard is known as the High Performance Serial Bus.

Legacy Ports

When the PC was first designed, external thingamajigs were attached to the console by using specific and aptly named ports. If you wanted to attach a keyboard, mouse, or printer, for example, you would use a specific keyboard, mouse, or printer port.

Since that time, those older, or *legacy,* ports have been gradually phased out on PCs and replaced by the versatile USB port. For example, you can now have a PC where the mouse, keyboard, and printer plug into the USB port. But on most PCs, those older ports still exist and are still used just as they were on the first IBM PC.

The magical KVM switch

KVM is an acronym for *keyboard, video, and mouse.* The *KVM switch* is a box you can use to attach a single keyboard, monitor, and mouse to two (or more) computers. That way, you can use two computers without having to buy each one its own keyboard, monitor, or mouse. Often, people use the KVM switch so that they can use their current computers as well as access older computers or second computer systems.

Alas, there's no inverse-KVM switch, or a device that lets a single computer have two keyboards, monitors, and mice attached so that two people can use a single computer at the same time. That is possible with the Linux and Unix operating systems, but not with Windows.

The mouse and keyboard

The mouse and keyboard ports are designed specifically for what they do: The mouse plugs into the mouse port, and the keyboard into the keyboard port. And, despite the fact that both ports look alike, they're unique, and strange things happen when you connect things improperly.

Some wireless keyboards and mice still use the traditional keyboard and mouse ports. You plug the wireless base station into the keyboard or mouse port (or both), and then you can use the wireless keyboard and mouse.

The printer port

It should be no surprise that the computer's printer can plug into the printer port. But you probably didn't know that the port was originally called the LPT port. LPT was an IBM acronym-thing for Line Printer. It may also be called a PRN port, which is how the word *printer* looks when the keyboard is broken.

✔ I highly recommend using the USB connector (covered later in this chapter) rather than the traditional printer port and printer cable, to connect your PC's console to a printer. It's just better.

✔ Folks with two computers often use something called an A-B switch to share a single printer between those two computers. A-B switches are still available, although the better solution is to *network* the computers and the printer, which also works better in sharing a high-speed Internet connection. See Part IV of this book for information on networking.

The serial port

The original PC's serial port was at one time the *versatile* port. Unlike with the other legacy ports, you could plug in a variety of devices to the serial port: printer, mouse, modem, and scanner, for example. Sadly, serial devices still required extra setup, and communication was slow. Therefore, although versatile, the function of the PC's serial port has been taken over by the superior USB port.

✔ The serial port is also known as the COM or COM1 port. Some old-timers may call it the RS-232C port.

✔ The serial port connector is about the same size as the standard video connector on a PC's rump. The difference is that a serial port has 9 holes in it and the video connector has 15. Be careful not to confuse the two!

Chapter 8

Temporary Storage (Memory)

· ·

In This Chapter

▶ Understanding memory

▶ Using chips and dips (and SIMMs)

▶ Measuring memory quantity

▶ Discovering how much memory is in your PC

▶ Understanding virtual memory

▶ Adding memory to your computer

· ·

Memory is one of the computer's basic resources: temporary storage. The more memory you have, the happier the computer seems to be. Not having enough memory is like trying to put too many people into a bus: It's cramped, hot, and smelly; nothing gets done quickly; and you can really tell who had the kimchi for lunch. But, when you have enough memory, it's like swimming in the ocean — with no jellyfish or sharks. And free tacos. But, I digress. More memory is better. This chapter tells you why.

Why Memory?

If your computer were a sport, memory is the field on which competition would take place. Memory is where the action is.

Software is in charge. It tells the microprocessor what to do. But the microprocessor is only a minicalculator. It's fast, but, like the absent-minded professor, the microprocessor doesn't remember much. It has some storage, but not a lot.

To provide those Elysian Fields upon which the microprocessor can dance and play, your computer needs vast swaths of memory. The microprocessor uses that memory for storage, but it can also manipulate the contents of memory. That's basically how your programs work with data: The data is stored in memory, and the microprocessor manipulates the contents of memory.

Memory is temporary storage because it requires electricity to maintain its contents. This is why you save information to long-term storage (a disk drive or storage media) when you're done creating something in memory. The disk drives or storage media provide safe, long-term storage. When you need to access the information again, it's opened up and loaded back into memory from disk. After the information is there, and the microprocessor can again work on it.

- ✔ All computers need memory.

- ✔ Memory is where the microprocessor does its work.

- ✔ The more memory in your PC, the better. With more computer memory, you can work on larger documents and spreadsheets, enjoy applications that use graphics and sound, and boast about all that memory to your friends.

- ✔ The term *RAM* is used interchangeably with the word *memory*. They're the same thing. (In fact, RAM stands for random access memory, in case you have been working any crossword puzzles lately.)

- ✔ Turning off the power makes the *contents* of memory go bye-bye. The memory chips themselves aren't destroyed, but the chips require electricity in order to maintain their contents.

- ✔ Computer memory is *fast.* The microprocessor can scan millions of bytes of memory — the equivalent of Shakespeare's entire folio — in fractions of a second, which is far less time than it took you to even trudge through *Hamlet* in the 11th grade.

- ✔ The PC's disk drives provide long-term storage for information. This type of storage is necessary because computer memory is lost when the power is turned off or when you restart Windows. See Chapter 9.

- ✔ *Saving* a file is the process of copying information from memory to long-term (disk) storage.

- ✔ *Opening* a file is the process of copying information from long-term storage into memory. This copying is necessary because the microprocessor can only work on information in memory; it cannot access information stored on a disk drive or media card.

- ✔ Memory is reusable. After creating something and saving it to disk, the computer wipes memory clean and lets you start afresh.

Delicious Chocolate Memory Chips

Physically, memory dwells on the PC's motherboard, sitting very close to the microprocessor for fast access and ready dispatch. Memory comes in the form of tiny wafers called *DRAM* chips. On the PC, DRAM chips are used in groups of nine, and those nine chips are permanently attached to teensy-weensy memory expansion cards, called *DIMMs*.

Figure 8-1 shows what a DIMM might look like, although in real life a DIMM is slightly smaller than what's shown in the figure and often covered by a piece of metal. A DIMM also has chips on both sides, which is why it's a DIMM, or *Dual* Inline Modular Memory thing, and not a SIMM, or Single Inline Modular Memory thing.

Figure 8-1: A semi-sweet DIMM.

Each DIMM card contains a given chunk of RAM measured in one of the magical memory values of 1, 2, 4, 8, 16, 32, 64, 128, 256, or 512 megabytes or gigabytes (see the later sidebar "Why the magical numbers?").

Each of those memory slots that the DIMM cards are plugged into is a *bank* of memory. So, a PC with 2GB of RAM may have four banks of 512MB DIMMs installed or two banks of 1GB DIMMs. Don't let the numbers and abbreviations drive you nuts; these things are explained in the next section.

✔ DRAM stands for *d*ynamic *r*andom *a*ccess *m*emory. It's pronounced "dee-ram," and it's the most common type of memory chip installed in a PC.

✔ Other types of memory chips exist, each with a name similar to DRAM, such as EDORAM or NIFTYRAM or DODGERAM. And then there's DDR2 and GDDR2 and WRAM and on and on. Most of these are merely marketing terms, designed to make one type of memory sound spiffier than another.

✔ Yes, I'm just kidding about the "chocolate" part of RAM. Memory has no flavor, although it has been reported on the Internet that memory chips are hard to chew, are generally bitter, and often taste like blood.

TECHNICAL STUFF

Boring details on RAM, ROM, and flash memory

RAM, which stands for *random access memory*, refers to memory that the microprocessor can read from and write to. When you create something in memory, it's done in RAM. RAM is memory and vice versa.

ROM stands for *read-only memory*. The microprocessor can read from ROM, but it cannot write to it or modify it. ROM is permanent. Often, ROM chips contain special instructions for the computer — important stuff that never changes. For example, the chipset on the motherboard is in ROM (refer to Chapter 6). Because that information is stored on a ROM chip, the microprocessor can access it. The instructions are always there because they're not erasable.

Flash memory is a special type of memory that works like both RAM and ROM. Information can be written to flash memory, like RAM, but it isn't erased when the power is off, like RAM. Sadly, flash memory isn't as fast as RAM, so don't expect it to replace standard computer memory any time soon.

Here a Byte, There a Byte, Everywhere a Byte-Byte

Memory is measured by the byte. A *byte* can store a single character. For example, the word *oboe* is 4 characters long and requires 4 bytes of computer memory storage. The word *goober* is 6 characters long and requires 6 bytes of memory to store. How many letters in your name? That's how many bytes of storage your name would occupy in computer memory.

Bytes, however useful, are puny. Back in the microcomputer days of the 1970s, having a few thousand bytes was *really something*! Today, most PCs need *billions* of bytes just to run the operating system. That's okay for many reasons, the first of which is that computer memory is now relatively cheap. More importantly, it's easy to reference large quantities of memory, thanks to handy and confusing computer jargon, as shown in Table 8-1.

Table 8-1		Memory Quantities	
Term	*Abbreviation*	*About*	*Actual*
Byte		1 byte	1 byte
Kilobyte	K or KB	1 thousand bytes	1,024 bytes

Term	Abbreviation	About	Actual
Megabyte	M or MB	1 million bytes	1,048,576 bytes
Gigabyte	G or GB	1 billion bytes	1,073,741,824 bytes
Terabyte	T or TB	1 trillion bytes	1,099,511,627,776 bytes

Although it's handy to say "kilobyte" rather than mouth out "1,024 bytes," it's hard to visualize how much data that really is. For comparison, think of a kilobyte (KB) as about a page of text from a novel. One *megabyte* (MB) of information is required in order to store one minute of music on a CD or as much text information as in a complete encyclopedia.

The *gigabyte* (GB) is a huge amount of storage — 1 billion bytes. The *terabyte* (TB) is 1 trillion bytes, or enough RAM to dim the lights when you start the PC.

A *trilobite* is an extinct arthropod that flourished in the oceans during the Paleozoic era. It has nothing to do with computer memory.

Each memory term indicates a magnitude of approximately 1,000 times. So, 1,024KB equals 1MB, and 1,024MB equals 1GB. Also see the following sidebar, "Why the magical numbers?"

Other trivia:

- ✔ The term *giga* is Greek, and it means *giant.*

- ✔ The term *tera* is also Greek. It means *monster!*

- ✔ A specific location in memory is an *address.*

- ✔ Hard disk storage is also measured in bytes.

- ✔ A PC running Windows Vista requires at least 1GB of memory in order to work well.

- ✔ A typical hard drive now stores between 50 and 400 *gigabytes* of data. At the high end, some hard drives hold 1,024GB, or one terabyte of information. Gadzooks!

- ✔ Bytes are composed of 8 bits. The word *bit* is a contraction of *bi*nary digi*t*. Binary is base 2, or a counting system that uses only ones and zeroes. Computers count in binary, and their bits are grouped into clusters of eight, for convenient consumption as bytes.

Why the magical numbers?

Computer memory comes in given sizes. You see the same numbers over and over:

1, 2, 4, 8, 16, 32, 64, 128, 256, 512, 1024, 2048, 4096, and so on.

Each of these values represents a *power of two* — a scary mathematical concept that you probably slept through in high school. To quickly review: $2^0 = 1$, $2^1 = 2$, $2^2 = 4$, $2^3 = 8$, and up to $2^{10} = 1024$, and so on, until you get a nosebleed.

These specific values happen because computers count by twos — ones and zeros — the old

binary counting base of song and legend. So, computer memory, which is a binary-like thing, is measured in those same powers of two. RAM chips come in quantities of 256MB or 512MB, for example, or maybe 2GB.

Notice that, starting with 1024, the values take on a predictable pattern: 1024 bytes is really 1K; 1024K is really 1M, and 1024M is 1G. So, really, only the first 10 values, 1 through 512, are the magical ones.

Some Memory Q&A

It doesn't matter where I am — shopping at the liquor store, working off my community service, or leaving the local strip bar — people still stop and ask me questions about computer memory. Over the years, I've collected the questions and have distilled the lot into the several subsections that follow. This section should cover up any loose ends or random access thoughts you may have about computer memory.

"How much memory is in my PC right now?"

This information may be a mystery to you, but it isn't a secret to your computer. The System window shows you how much memory lives inside the beast: Press Win+Break on the computer keyboard to summon the System window (refer to Figure 6-2, over in Chapter 6).

The amount of memory (RAM) appears right beneath the type of microprocessor (processor) that lives in your PC. In Figure 6-2, it says that the computer has 1022MB of RAM — about half of what I prefer to have in Windows Vista (but I'm cheap). Close the System window when you're done checking your PC's memory.

"Do I have enough memory?"

It depends on whether you're answering questions before or after the subpoena.

"Does my PC have enough memory?"

Knowing how much memory is in your PC is one thing, but knowing whether that amount is enough is entirely different!

The amount of memory your PC needs depends on two things. The first, and most important, is the memory requirement of your software. Some programs, such as photo-editing programs, require lots of memory. It says right on the box how much memory is needed. For example, the Photoshop photo-editing program demands 512MB of RAM.

To test your PC's memory, you need to make the computer *very* busy. You do this by loading and running several programs simultaneously. I'm talking about *big* programs, like Photoshop or Word or Excel. While all those programs are running, switch between them by pressing the Alt+Esc key combination.

If you can easily switch between several running programs by using Alt+Esc, your PC most likely has plenty of memory. But, if you press Alt+Esc and the system slows down, you hear the hard drives rumbling, and it takes a bit of time for the next program's window to appear, your PC could use more memory.

Close any programs you have opened.

- ✔ Generally speaking, all PCs should have at least 512MB of RAM, which is what you need, at minimum, to run Windows Vista (but not run it well).

- ✔ One sure sign that your PC needs more memory: It slows to a crawl, especially during memory-intensive operations, such as working with graphics.

- ✔ Not enough memory? You can upgrade! See the section "Adding More Memory to Your PC," at the end of this chapter.

"Will the computer ever run out of memory?"

Nope. Unlike the hard drive, which can fill up just like a closet full of shoes and hats, your PC's memory can never really get full. At one time, back in the dark ages of computing, the "Memory full" error was common. That doesn't happen now, thanks to something called virtual memory.

"What is virtual memory?"

Windows uses a clever technique to prevent your computer's memory from ever becoming full: It creates virtual memory.

Virtual memory is a fake-out. It lets the computer pretend that it has much more memory than it has physical RAM. It does that by swapping out vast swaths of memory to the hard drive. Because Windows manages both memory and hard drive storage, it can keep track of things quite well, by swapping chunks of data back and forth. *Et, voila!* — you never see an "Out of memory" error.

Alas, there's trouble in paradise. One problem with virtual memory is that the swapping action slows things down. Although it can happen quickly and often without your noticing, when memory gets tight, virtual memory takes over and things start moving more slowly.

- ✔ The solution to avoiding the use of virtual memory is to pack your PC with as much RAM as it can hold.

- ✔ Windows never says that it's "out of memory." No, you just notice that the hard drive is churning frequently as the memory is swapped into and out of the disk drive. Oh, and things tend to slow down dramatically.

- ✔ You have no reason to mess with the virtual memory settings in your computer. Windows Vista does an excellent job of managing them for you.

"What is video memory?"

Memory used by your PC's video system is known as *video memory.* Specifically, memory chips live on the video adapter card. Those memory chips are used specifically for the computer's video output and help you see higher resolutions, more colors, 3-D graphics, bigger and uglier aliens, and girlie pictures that your husband downloads from the Internet late at night but says that he doesn't.

As with regular computer memory, you can upgrade video memory if your PC's video card has room. See Chapter 10 for more information on video adapters.

Shared video memory is used on some low-end computers to save money. What happens is that the computer lacks true video memory and instead borrows some main memory for use in displaying graphics. This is fine for simple home computers but not nearly good enough to play cutting-edge games or to use photo-editing software.

"What are kibi, mebi, and gibi?"

Seeing how the world loves standards, there's an international attempt to standardize what K, M, G, and so on mean when it comes to numbers. Specifically, according to the standard, KB should refer to 1,000 bytes, not the actual 1,024 bytes it more accurately references. To differentiate between 1,000 and 1,024, the standards people are proposing that *kibi,* or *Ki,* be used to refer to 1,024 bytes. Ditto for *mebi* and *Mi* and *gibi* and *Gi;* for example:

1MB = 1,000,000 bytes

1Mi = 1,048,576 bytes

Both these values are correct, according to the standard. One megabyte (MB) is one million bytes. But on a computer, they want us to use one *mebibyte* (*Mi*) to refer to the actual value, which is 1,048,576 bytes.

Weird? You bet! And you can probably guess why this change is slow to happen and why many in the computer industry are reluctant to adopt the new terms. Don't fret! If and when it happens and knowing about it becomes important, you'll read about it in a future edition of this book.

Adding More Memory to Your PC

The best thing you can do for your PC is to add more memory. It's like adding garlic to spice up a salad. *Bam!* More memory provides an instant boost to the system.

Adding memory to your computer is LEGO-block simple. The only difference is that the typical LEGO block set, such as the Medieval Castle or Rescue Helicopter set, costs less than $100. Your computer, on the other hand, may cost 5 to 20 times that much. Adding memory isn't something to be taken lightly. Unless you're comfortable upgrading your PC, I highly recommend that you have a dealer or computer expert do the work for you.

Before you run amok buying RAM, you need to know a few things about your computer — specifically, how memory is handled on the motherboard. You need to know how many memory banks, or DIMM slots, the motherboard has and the maximum memory capacity. It also helps to know how your PC's current memory is configured.

Suppose that your computer has 512MB of RAM and you want to upgrade to 1GB. That isn't as easy as just adding a 512MB DIMM to your computer. Consider Figure 8-2.

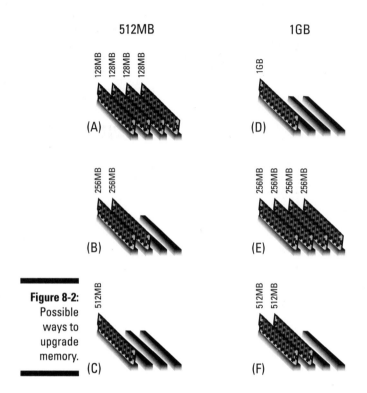

512MB   1GB

Figure 8-2:
Possible
ways to
upgrade
memory.

If your memory is configured as shown in Figure 8-2, Example A, you must toss out all that RAM and upgrade using any of the options D, E, or F.

If your 512MB memory is configured as shown in Example B, you can cheaply upgrade using Example E, although Examples D and F are both still available (but more expensive).

Finally, if you have 512MB memory configured as shown in Example C (the best), you upgrade using option F.

If you find any of this confusing, again, refer to your computer dealer for upgrading help. (This also explains why sometimes you must toss out all the computer's existing RAM to add more.)

✔ Before you buy memory, check to see how the memory is configured on the motherboard. Open, or empty, memory banks are a *good thing*.

✔ My favorite place to get memory chips online is Crucial, at www.crucial.com. The Web site asks a series of questions and then provides memory solutions to solve your problems exactly.

✔ If you want to try upgrading memory yourself, go ahead. I know that Crucial, as an example, provides a well-written booklet for doing the upgrade as part of the memory it sells. When you're in doubt, however, I strongly recommend having someone else do it.

An Homage to Gilbert and Sullivan

Of all hardware computable

One thing is indisputable

To make things go

And fast, not slow

Your PC needs some RAM

With memories undeniable

And DRAM chips quite reliable

Your programs fly

The disks won't die

On a PC full of RAM

The programs load in graphics mode

With the colors bright and more;

The look and feel are quite unreal

With a gigabyte or four!

Now the fact is indisputable

And the data's irrefutable

You can multitask

Things are running fast

'cause the PC's full of RAM!

Chapter 9

Permanent Storage (Disks and Media)

In This Chapter

▶ Understanding permanent storage

▶ Discovering how a disk drive works

▶ Recognizing the hard drive

▶ Using the DVD drive

▶ Ignoring the floppy drive

▶ Working with memory cards

▶ Adding external storage

▶ Using storage media in Windows

*P*ermanent, or long-term, storage is a relatively new concept when
it comes to computer science. In the olden days, computers were
programmed by hand, wired specifically to run one program. Temporary
memory was available, although it was scarce. As computers evolved, scientists observed that it was rather silly for them to keep reprogramming their
computers every time the system was turned on. So, to save time, and to
reduce the number of cranky scientists, permanent computer storage was
developed.

By using permanent storage, your computer can remember things long after
the power is turned off. Rather than type a program you want to run (and at
11 million lines of code, you'd have to be awfully desperate to run Excel), you
simply *load* the program into memory from permanent storage. And all that
stuff you create? It's safe and sound, saved to the computer's permanent storage. This chapter covers almost everything you need to know about permanent storage.

Storage for the Long Haul

All the action may happen in temporary storage (memory), but when you want to avoid doing the same things over and over again — let alone having to reprogram your computer every time you start it — you need some permanent storage.

Permanent storage provides a place for the computer to put stuff that will still be there when the power is turned on again. This includes not only all the stuff you create and keep, but also all the computer software (programs) plus the operating system. Indeed, loading the operating system — transferring it from permanent storage into temporary storage — is one of the first things a computer does when it starts.

- ✔ Permanent storage is used to keep all the stuff you create, stuff you collect from the Internet, songs, videos, all your computer software, as well as the operating system itself.

- ✔ The microprocessor works only with temporary storage, or memory. To use information that's stored long term, that information must be transferred into computer memory. In Windows, transferring information from permanent storage into memory is known as *opening* the information.

- ✔ When you're done working on something in memory, you *save* the contents of memory to a file on permanent storage. Also see Chapter 22 for more information on *files*.

Storage media roundup

The PC has available to it many gizmos to provide permanent storage. These gizmos fall into two categories:

Disk drives: These devices provide the traditional type of PC storage media. There are three popular types: hard disk drive, CD/DVD drive, and floppy disk drive.

Memory cards: These gizmos provide solid-state storage; the memory card has no moving parts. Memory cards are typically used in digital cameras and other portable gizmos, but can also be read by the PC and used for long-term storage.

Sections later in this chapter go into detail on these various forms of storage, where to find them in Windows, and how to use them.

All storage media is measured by its capacity in bytes. Refer to Chapter 8 for more information on bytes, megabyte, gigabyte, and other related terms.

Ask Mr. Science: How does a disk drive work?

Glad you asked, Billy!

A *disk drive* is really several things:

- ✔ Media, on which information is recorded (the *disk* part of disk drive)
- ✔ Drive, which spins the disk and reads information from and writes information to the disk
- ✔ Interface, which communicates information between the disk drive and the computer's motherboard

Disk media varies, depending on the type of drive. For a hard drive, the media is a metal disk coated with magnetic oxide — the same stuff used to record on cassette tape or videotape. The magnetic oxide stores electronic impulses by orienting its magnetic particles in one direction or another.

For a CD or DVD drive, the media is the disc itself, which unlike a hard drive, is removable. The actual media consists of a thin, metal foil sandwiched between two plastic disks. The metal has tiny pits in it, which are detected by a laser beam.

The drive mechanism spins the disk so that data can be read or written using a special mechanism. On the hard drive, the mechanism is a *read-write head.* A CD or DVD drive uses a laser to read the disk. For creating a CD or DVD, a secondary and more powerful laser is used to burn tiny pits into the recordable disc's surface.

The final part of the disk drive is the *interface,* or wires through which information is sent to and from the computer's motherboard and the microprocessor. The PC currently uses the popular Serial ATA interface to connect disk drives inside the console. Externally, the USB interface can be used.

- ✔ Hard drives secretly contain more than one disk. Most hard drives contain multiple disks, or *platters.* They're all hermetically sealed — in an airtight environment. That way, the hard drive can be extra precise without having to worry about contaminants or nasty particles in the air.
- ✔ Floppy disks are composed of Mylar coated with magnetic oxide, essentially the same material as videotape but smooshed flat like a pancake. The disk is contained inside a hard plastic shell.
- ✔ Serial ATA is also known as SATA.
- ✔ Another internal disk drive interface is ATA, or Advanced Technology Attachment. It's also known by the acronym IDE or ATAPI. Most modern motherboards use Serial ATA, older motherboards were ATA only, and many motherboards feature both interfaces.

The Hard Disk Drive

The *hard disk* is the primary place for storing stuff on your PC. It's your main source of permanent storage. That's because the hard drive is capable of storing the greatest amount of information and accessing it in the quickest manner possible.

There are two measuring sticks for hard disk drives. One is capacity, the other is speed. Because the speed specifications are rather nerdy, I don't bother mentioning them here. Suffice it to say, all hard drives are fast but some are faster (and more expensive) than others.

For capacity, hard drive storage is measured like computer memory, in bytes. The typical hard drive now stores gigabytes of information, typically between 40GB and 300GB or more. The main consumers of hard drive space are media files: music and video.

Unlike other types of storage media, the hard drive cannot be removed from the computer. You can add another hard drive to your PC, but you cannot remove a hard drive and quickly replace it as you can with other media. For this reason, your PC must have plenty of hard drive storage.

- Most PCs have one physical hard drive installed inside the console.

- On nearly every PC, the hard drive is given letter C and referred to as "drive C" or "the C drive." See the section "Permanent Storage ABCs," later in this chapter, for more information.

- The hard drive is where Windows lives, where you install software, and where you keep the stuff you create or save on your computer. That's what the hard drive is designed for.

- Extra hard drives can be added to your PC, to give you even more storage. You can generally add a second internal hard drive to the console, plus nearly unlimited external hard drives via the USB port. See the section "External Storage," later in this chapter.

- A single physical hard drive can be divided into multiple logical hard drives. This division is done by *partitioning* the drive. For example, a single 350GB hard drive can be partitioned into a 300GB drive C and a 50GB drive D. Many PC manufacturers use this scheme, by dedicating drive D as a "recovery" drive, to be used in case of disk disaster.

- Note that partitioning is *not* a beginner's duty, and it's generally done only when installing a new hard drive or setting up a secondary hard drive.

TECHNICAL STUFF

Which disk is the *boot* disk?

The PC requires software — specifically, an operating system — in order to run. The operating system dwells in permanent storage and must be loaded into memory each time the PC starts. To find the storage media, or *boot disk,* the PC first looks on the hard drive, and then to the DVD drive, and then perhaps to the floppy drive or a USB drive for an operating system. Whichever drive is used to load the operating system then becomes the boot disk.

Originally, the PC was configured to look for an operating system first on the floppy drive and then on the hard drive. That order could not be changed. But when CD-ROM drives became

popular, manufacturers altered the PC's startup, or boot, process so that an operating system could be loaded from a CD or from the hard drive or floppy drive. Also altered was the order in which the drives were searched; a user could, for example, specify to search the CD drive first and then the hard drive, or direct the computer *not* to even boot from a floppy disk.

Modern PCs continue the tradition of letting you select not only the first boot disk but also the order in which various storage media are searched for an operating system. To set the boot disk or change the order, use the Setup program as described in Chapter 4.

The DVD Drive

The PC's primary form of removable storage is the DVD drive. Only a DVD drive is needed because DVD drives can read both CDs and DVDs.

The DVD drive is used for two main purposes. First, you install most software on your PC from CDs or DVDs. Second, you'll most likely use the media on those discs — music CDs or video DVDs — to entertain yourself while you use the PC.

The typical DVD drive is *read-only.* Information can only be read from a read-only drive; you cannot use a read-only drive to create a CD or DVD. You may find the drive labeled by using the acronym ROM, where the RO stands for *read-only.* (The M is for *memory,* but it should really be S, for *storage.*)

Most DVD drives sold today can not only read discs but create them as well. Such drives are usually labeled DVD–/+/R/W, which is a fancy way of specifying which types of disc formats the drive can write to. Further, many DVD drives are also *combo* drives that can also create CDs. More information on all this disc-creating stuff can be found in Chapter 28.

- ✔ The typical PC has at least one DVD drive installed.

- ✔ DVD is an acronym for *digital versatile disc*. Or, it may be *digital video disc*.

- ✔ CD stands for *compact disc*.

- ✔ A DVD drive features the DVD logo. If you don't see the DVD logo, your PC has a mere CD-ROM drive.

- ✔ It's possible to start the PC from an operating system stored on a CD or DVD. To do so, insert a boot disc into the DVD drive and restart the PC (see Chapter 4). When the computer starts up again, look for an on-screen prompt asking whether to start, or boot, the computer from the disc in the DVD drive. Also see the nearby sidebar "Which disk is the *boot* disk?"

- ✔ The British spelling of *disc* is used for historical reasons, mainly that Handel was rumored to have recorded the *Messiah* on an early type of CD.

Disc capacity

As with all computer storage, DVDs and CDs measure their capacity in bytes.

- ✔ A typical CD holds up to 640MB of information.

- ✔ A typical music CD can store up to 80 minutes of music.

- ✔ Typical DVD technology is capable of storing 4GB of information on a disc.

Variations are available, such as smaller-diameter disks, double-sided discs, and high-capacity, dual layer discs, not to mention HD and Blu-ray discs. Until these types of discs become popular on the PC, there's no point in waxing poetic about them here.

About the speed rating (the X number)

DVD and CD drives have speed ratings measured in *X*. The number before the *X* indicates how much faster the drive is than the original PC CD-ROM drive (which plays as fast as a musical CD player). So, a 52X value means that the drive is 52 times faster than the original PC CD-ROM drive.

It's common to list a CD-R/RW drive with three Xs in its rating:

- ✔ The first X represents the drive's write speed, or how fast a CD-R can be written to.

- ✔ The second X specifies how fast the drive can rewrite to a CD-RW.

- ✔ The final X indicates how fast the drive can be read from.

DVD drives, especially combo drives that can write a variety of disc formats, come with multiple X ratings, one for each of the various types of discs they create.

Inserting a disc

Generally speaking, the disc is always inserted label side up. Aside from that, how you stick the disc into the drive depends on how the drive eats discs:

Tray type: The most popular type of DVD drive uses a slide-out tray to hold the disc. Start by pressing the drive's eject button, which pops out the tray (often called a *drink holder* in computer jokes). Drop the disc into the tray, label side up. Gently nudge the tray back into the computer. The tray slides back in the rest of the way on its own.

Slide-in type: Another type of disk drive works like the CD player in most automobiles; the drive is merely a slot into which you slide the disc: Pushing the disc (label side up) into the slot causes some gremlin inside the drive to eventually grab the disc and suck it in all the way. Amazing.

After inserting the disc, you may see an AutoPlay dialog box displayed. Use the dialog box to choose a special way to view the disc's contents, or just press the Esc key to dismiss the AutoPlay dialog box.

When the disc is in the drive, you use it just like any other disk in your computer.

- ✔ When you insert the disc upside down (label side down), the drive can't read it and most likely simply ejects the disc automatically.

- ✔ An exception to the label-side-up rule is a DVD with data recorded on both sides. For example, some DVD movies have the TV version on one side and the widescreen, or letterbox, version on another. If so, make sure to put the proper side up in the drive.

- ✔ Some CDs are clipped. That is, they aren't round discs but, rather, are business card size or some other odd shape. These discs work fine in the tray type of CD-ROM/DVD drive, but don't insert them into the slide-in type of drive.

Ejecting a disc

Follow these steps to eject a disc from a DVD drive:

1. **Open the Computer window.**

   Refer to Chapter 5 for directions on opening this window.

2. **Click to select the DVD drive icon.**

3. **Click the Eject button on the toolbar.**

   The disc spits from the DVD drive.

You may be tempted to eject the disc by punching the eject button on the front of the drive. Don't! If Windows is using the drive, you see an ugly error message on the screen when you try to eject a disc this way.

In times of urgency, such as when the computer is locked up (or turned off), you can manually eject a disc by pushing a straightened paper clip into the tiny hole (the "beauty mark") on the front of the DVD drive. That action manually ejects the disc when the computer is too stupid to do it by itself.

The Floppy Disk Drive

There's no reason for you to use floppy disks with a PC any more. They're too pathetic to hold data and, generally, are way too unreliable for me to recommend them for backups or anything else.

✔ If you're using a floppy disk with your computer, consider using a memory card instead. See the next section.

✔ If your computer has a floppy disk, it's always drive A.

✔ The floppy disk holds only 1.4MB of information, which is not a lot of capacity for today's large files.

✔ This book's companion, *PCs For Dummies Quick Reference* (from the Wiley Publishing empire), contains more information on floppy disks, if you *really* need to know.

Other weird disk drives

The PC's history is dotted with various and sundry alternative forms of disk drives. There's a veritable salad bar of options and choices, depending on which part of computer history you're looking at.

For the longest time, removable hard drives were popular. Before the CD-R appeared, the magneto-optical (MO) disk was popular. Various removable cartridge drives came and went, such as the Bernoulli disk, Zip disk, and Jaz disk. The SuperDrive and its high-capacity SuperDisk were popular for a while. Many of these alternative disk drives tried to replace the standard PC floppy disk, but none succeeded.

Memory Cards

The most recent form of permanent computer storage technology to appear on the scene is the *memory card*. I use the general term memory card to apply to all the different types of solid-state storage devices. These cards vary in size from a stick of gum to a poker chip, albeit a rectangular poker chip.

Like other storage media, memory card capacity is measured in bytes. Smaller-capacity cards store a few megabytes, although 256MB seems to be the smallest memory card available now. At the high end, top-price memory cards can hold up to 8GB of data — or more!

To read a memory card, your PC must come equipped with a memory card reader. Most modern PCs come with a combination card reader, a series of four separate slots into which each type of memory card can be inserted (see Figure 2-2, in Chapter 2). Older PCs can use a memory card reader peripheral, which attaches to the PC by using a USB cable.

✔ A memory card isn't the same thing as a *flash drive*. Both devices are similar in that they're solid-state, but a flash drive connects to the PC by using a USB port, not a memory card slot. Flash drives are also known as *thumb drives* because many of them are about the same size as a human thumb.

✔ Technologically, memory cards exist in the weird space between traditional computer RAM and disk storage. The memory cards themselves lack the high capacity of disk storage. Therefore, they won't be replacing the PC's hard drive any time soon. And although memory cards do not require electricity in order to maintain their contents, they're still too slow to replace traditional computer memory (RAM).

Memory card roundup

Sadly, there isn't one standard type of memory card. Instead, there are six main types:

✔ CompactFlash

✔ Memory Stick

✔ MultiMediaCard (MMC)

✔ Secure Digital (SD)

✔ SmartMedia

✔ xD

Each memory card has its own variations. For example, there are two types of CompactFlash memory cards: Type I and the thicker Type II. Likewise, there are several sizes and types of Memory Sticks and Secure Digital cards as well as other differences in the other card types — nothing worth memorizing.

Generally speaking, a PC memory card reader needs only four slots to read the six memory card types. That's because many of the cards can use the same type of slot: the Secure Digital card and MultiMediaCard both fit into the same size slot, as well as the SmartMedia and xD cards, which also fit into identical slots.

Inserting a memory card

To use a memory card, just plug it into the proper card slot, either located directly on the PC's console or via a memory card adapter attached to a USB port. Windows instantly recognizes the card and *mounts* it into the computer system, making whatever information is on the card instantly available.

After inserting the memory card, you may see the AutoPlay dialog box displayed. Use the dialog box to choose how to view the card's contents, such as choosing the View Pictures option to view images stored on the card from a digital camera.

The information on a memory card is accessed through the Computer window. The memory card is given a letter, just like any other permanent storage device in Windows. See the section "Permanent Storage ABCs," later in this chapter.

- ✔ Do not force a memory card into a slot! If you cannot get the memory card into one slot, try another.

- ✔ Memory cards are inserted label side up. For vertically mounted memory card readers, try label-left (although this may not always work).

- ✔ Yes, the quickest way to get images from your digital camera is to yank out (well, gently yank out) its memory card and plug that card into your PC. See Chapter 16.

Ejecting a memory card

You cannot just yank out a memory card. I know: It's tempting. And often, there's nothing to prevent you from being naughty and yanking out the card. But if you do so, you run the risk of damaging the card or destroying the information stored on the card. Be proper! Follow these steps to remove a memory card the safe, happy way:

1. **Open the Computer window.**

   Chapter 5 discusses how to open this window if you're unfamiliar with Windows.

2. **Click to select the memory card's icon.**

   It's found in the part of the window labeled Devices with Removable Storage.

3. **Click the Eject button on the toolbar.**

   You may notice the memory card's icon change or turn gray, which is a sign that it's okay to remove the card.

4. **Pull the memory card from the card reader.**

Be sure to store the memory card in a safe, static-free location when you're not using it.

When the memory card is canceled

Just like other types of storage media, memory cards wear out. Memory cards use flash memory to store information, and flash memory is limited in how many times it can be written to and read from. The limitation is quite high, and the memory cards are manufactured to use storage as efficiently as possible, to put off that inevitable death date. Even so, eventually the memory cards will err and stop working. When that happens, dispose of the memory card properly and buy another one.

External Storage

Your PC's permanent storage isn't limited to what's available inside the console. Using the smarts of the USB port, you can expand your computer system externally, by adding peripheral hard drives, DVD drives, flash drives, or memory card readers to your heart's content.

Oh, you can also use the IEEE port to add external storage, although on a PC it's more common to use the USB port.

Adding external storage

To add another storage media to your computer, an external disk drive or flash drive, simply plug it in. The drive attaches to the console by using a USB connector. It may also require power, so plug the drive into the wall — or better, into a UPS. (See Chapter 3.)

When you plug the drive into the USB connector, and assuming that the drive has power and is turned on, Windows instantly recognizes the drive and adds it to your computer's list of permanent storage devices, found in the Computer window. You can then immediately start using the drive.

One major bonus for external storage devices is that they can survive your current computer setup. For example, my external USB hard drive may outlive my current computer and end up plugged into next year's model. That way, I don't have to copy over my software; instead, I just plug in the USB drive.

Removing external storage

Although you can easily unplug any USB device from your computer at any time, I do not recommend doing so for external storage. Because the computer may be using the storage, it's always best to properly remove the external drive *logically* before you remove it physically.

Another sticking point is an external drive with removable storage, such as an external DVD drive or memory card reader. In that case, you must properly eject the storage media *before* you remove the drive. To do so, refer to the sections "Ejecting a disc" and "Ejecting a memory card," earlier in this chapter.

After the media has been ejected, or for external storage that doesn't have removable media, you must properly remove external storage by following these steps:

1. **Open the Computer window.**

   See Chapter 5 for more information on finding the Computer window.

2. **Right-click the external storage device's icon.**

3. **From the pop-up menu, choose the command Safely Remove.**

   Windows displays a message (in the Notification Area), informing you that the device can be safely removed.

4. **Unplug or detach the external storage device.**

If you see an error message, the disk drive is either busy or being used. You have to wait and try again. If the error is persistent, you should turn off the computer. Detach the device. Then restart the computer.

Permanent Storage ABCs

Windows lets you view all permanent storage devices in the computer in one central location: the Computer window. That window is configured to display storage devices in categories, as shown in Figure 9-1. The categories Hard Disk Drives and Devices with Removable Storage are shown in the figure.

Figure 9-1:
Assorted
disk drive
flavors.

Beyond the categories, each storage device in the computer is given an icon, a name, and a drive letter.

Unique icons are used to represent the various disk types. In Figure 9-1, you can see different icons for hard drives, the DVD drive, as well as the various memory card drives. Note that the boot disk is shown with a Windows flag.

Drive names are assigned by Windows and can be changed, but the name is used only in the Computer window. What's more important than the name is the *drive letter*, A through Z, used by Windows to identify the various storage media.

On all PCs, the first three letters are consistently assigned:

  ✔ Drives A and B represent the PC's first and second floppy drives, whether the computer has any floppy drives or not.

  ✔ Drive C is always the computer's primary hard drive, the one from which Windows was started.

After drive C, the drive letters can be wildly inconsistent from PC to PC. Basically, Windows assigns the drive letters according to these rules:

- ✔ If any additional hard drives are in the console, they're given drive letters D, E, and onward, one letter for each extra hard drive beyond drive C. For example, in Figure 9-1, the second hard drive, Recovery, is given drive letter D.

- ✔ Any internal CD or DVD drive is given the next drive letter after the last hard drive has been given a letter.

- ✔ After the CD or DVD drive, any internal memory card readers are given the next few drive letters, as shown in Figure 9-1.

- ✔ After all internal storage has been assigned drive letters, Windows begins assigning letters to external storage devices in the order in which they're found. Each new storage device is given the next letter in the alphabet.

- ✔ Any external devices added after the computer starts, such as a flash memory drive, are given the next available letter of the alphabet.

The point to remember here is that not every PC will have the same drive letter assignments. For example, on your PC, drive D may be the DVD drive, but that doesn't mean that drive D on *all* PCs is the DVD drive.

- ✔ Disk drives on the network can be added to your computer system. When you add the network drive, however, you get to choose which drive letter it uses, from any of the available (unused) drive letters.

- ✔ It's possible to reassign letters to any drive except for the first hard drive, which must be drive C. Any good medium-level Windows book should tell you how to do this. Look under Computer Management for the proper information.

- ✔ Yes, sometimes Windows gets confused and may assign a different letter to a storage device than it did the last time you used your computer. This is especially true for external storage devices. Don't ask me why this happens.

- ✔ Make a note of your PC's disk drive assignments on this book's Cheat Sheet (in the front of this book).

Chapter 10

Glorious Graphical Goodness

In This Chapter

▶ Understanding PC graphics lingo

▶ Learning about the monitor

▶ Discovering the graphics adapter

▶ Adjusting the display

▶ Personalizing windows

▶ Changing the background

▶ Using a screen saver

▶ Adjusting the resolution

*A*lthough the console is where all the action takes place, it harbors no jealousy that you spend most of your time looking at the computer's monitor. I don't blame you. The console is rather boring to look at. Sure, some newer consoles have that eerie blue or red glow to them. And the console's case looks like it could have been designed in an alien laboratory. Perhaps it's about to sprout arms and legs and go on a killing spree? Everybody panic!

Relax. There's no need to feel that the computer's monitor is distracting you from anything evil that the console might be doing. In fact, the monitor is made to be your focus of attention on purpose. (Unless you can't type, in which case you spend most of your computer time looking at the keyboard.)

The monitor is the main way the computer has to communicate with you, the human. It shows you text and glorious graphics. But the monitor itself is only part of your PC's graphics system. This chapter divulges the details.

Proper Jargon Department

It just doesn't pay to know anything about graphics on a PC until you separate and identify the three confusing terms used to describe the TV-set-like-thing part of a computer. Allow me to illuminate:

- ✔ The *monitor* is the box.
- ✔ The *screen* is the part of the monitor on which information is displayed.
- ✔ The *display* is the information that appears on the screen.

Despite these differences, most people continue to misuse the terms. They'll say, "The screen says that the computer doesn't like me" or "The monitor shows something about how the computer hates me with a hot passion" or even "The display is showing how much the computer despises the intestinal portion of my corporeal being." They all describe the same thing: that the computer basically hates your guts.

The PC's Graphics System

The monitor may get all the attention, but it's really only the visible half of what I call your computer's graphics system. It has two components:

- ✔ The monitor
- ✔ The graphics adapter

The monitor is the dumb part. All it does is display information. The monitor lives outside the console, so it gets more attention than the true brains of the operation, the graphics adapter.

It's the graphics adapter that tells the monitor what to display and where, plus how many colors to use and the overall resolution of the image. It's the graphics adapter that determines your PC's graphics potential.

Figure 10-1 illustrates the monitor/adapter relationship. The graphics adapter can be a separate expansion card, as shown in the figure, or more often than not its circuitry is found on the motherboard. A cable then connects the monitor to the console. The monitor, of course, plugs into the wall for power.

- ✔ Your PC needs both a monitor and a graphics adapter.
- ✔ The graphics adapter is also known as a *video card*.

✔ If your PC has more than one monitor (and it can, you know), it must have one graphics adapter for each monitor or a special graphics adapter that supports multiple monitors. (The dual-monitor thing is possible only with those more expensive versions of Windows Vista.)

Two types of monitors: LCD and CRT

PC monitors come in two different flavors, each of which is known by a popular TLA (*three-letter acronym*): LCD and CRT.

✔ The *LCD* monitor is the newer, flatter type of computer screen.

✔ The *CRT* monitor is the traditional, glass-screen, television-set-like monitor.

Between the two, the LCD monitor is more popular. The prices on LCD monitors have dropped dramatically in recent years, not to mention that the monitors are easy on the eyes and use less electricity than their glass-based counterparts. As time goes on, it's getting more and more difficult to find a CRT monitor.

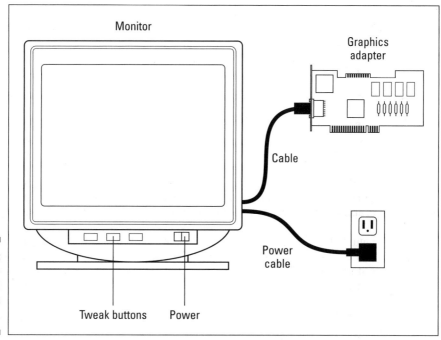

Figure 10-1:
The monitor and graphics adapter.

In two instances, however, a CRT monitor is better than an LCD monitor. The first comes with computer graphics. A CRT monitor is better able to emulate true colors than is an LCD. The second exception is computer games, where CRT monitors update faster than LCDs.

- ✔ CRT stands for *cathode ray tube*. Note that it's *cathode* ray tube, not *catholic* ray tube.

- ✔ LCD stands for *liquid crystal display*. It isn't a hallucinogenic.

- ✔ Be aware that some CRT monitors are advertised as "flat screen." This term isn't misleading: The glass on the front of the monitor is indeed flat, and it provides a better viewing surface than the traditional convex glass. But it's *not* an LCD monitor.

- ✔ All LCD monitors are flat.

Adept graphics adapters

The most important half of the computer's graphics system is the graphics hardware itself, known as the *graphics adapter*. It's the circuitry that runs the monitor and controls the image that the monitor displays.

Graphics adapters come in various price ranges and have features for artists, game players, computer designers, TV junkies, and regular Joes like you and me and guys named Joe. You should look for three key things in a graphics adapter:

- ✔ The amount of memory

- ✔ The type of GPU

- ✔ The type of interface

PC graphics require special memory that's separate from the computer's main memory. This memory is known as *video RAM,* or, often, *VRAM.* The more memory, the more colors and high resolutions and fancier tricks the graphics adapter is capable of.

Graphics adapters can have from 0M (no memory) up to 768MB and beyond. In the case of graphics adapters, more isn't necessarily better. Only if your applications demand more memory, or can take advantage of the extra video memory, is the price worth it. Otherwise, a typical PC has between 32MB and 512MB of video RAM.

Another measure of a graphics adapter's muscle is made by judging its own microprocessor, or graphics *processing unit* (GPU). That microprocessor is specially geared toward graphical operations, and, by having it, the graphics adapter takes a load of work away from the PC's main microprocessor, and things really fly on the screen. Two common models of GPU are available: the ATI Radeon and the NVIDIA GeForce. Both are approximately equal in power and popularity.

Finally, there's the interface, or how the graphics adapter plugs into the motherboard. The best models use the PCI Express slot, which is the most efficient. Other models use the AGP port, which gives them direct access to the microprocessor and system memory. Note that some graphics adapters built into the motherboard still use PCI Express or AGP even though the graphics adapter isn't on a separate expansion card.

Low-end graphics adapters are often included with a PC's chipset. Even so, you can install a better graphics adapter and use the PC Setup program to disable the cheesy adapter that's built into the motherboard.

- ✔ The more memory the graphics adapter has, the higher the resolutions it can support and the more colors it can display at those higher resolutions.

- ✔ Some video adapters "share" memory with main memory, such as adapters listed with 0MB of memory. Obviously, for anyone interested in playing games or creating computer graphics, it's a bad deal.

- ✔ Another term for GPU is VPU, or *visual processing unit*.

- ✔ Refer to Chapter 6 for more information on expansion slots.

- ✔ Many graphics adapters are advertised as supporting 3-D graphics. That's okay, but they work only if your software supports the particular 3-D graphics offered by that graphics adapter. (If so, the side of the software box should say so.)

- ✔ Graphics adapters may also be judged on their ability to capture or process standard television signals. See Chapter 17 for more information on computers and television.

- ✔ Graphics adapters were once known by various acronyms in the PC world. The most popular acronym was VGA, which stands for Video Gate Array (not Video Graphics Adapter, as is commonly believed). Other acronyms exist, with some incorporating the letters VGA into their alphabet soup. The names are primarily for marketing reasons and have no significance for PCs in general.

Love Your Monitor

A PC's monitor is really a *peripheral*. It's separate from the console. In fact, you don't need to have the same brand of computer and monitor. You can mix and match. You can even keep your old PC's monitor with a new console you may buy — as long as the monitor is in good shape, why not?

Despite all the features and technical mumbo jumbo, all monitors serve the same function: They display information that the computer coughs up.

The physical description

Monitors are judged by their picture size, measured on a diagonal, just like a TV set. Common sizes for PC monitors are 15, 17, 19, and 21 inches. The most common sizes are 17 and 19 inches. Some monster-size monitors, dubbed widescreen or cinema monitors, go up to 23 inches or larger. Oooooooo! (That's me swooning.)

Each monitor has two tails (refer to Figure 10-1). One is a power cord that plugs into the wall. The second tail is a video cable that connects to the graphics adapter port on the back of the console (see Chapter 3).

The most important part of the monitor is perhaps the on-off button, found near the lower-right front corner of the monitor. Additional buttons adorn the front of the monitor, which you use to control the monitor's display. These buttons may be visible, like a row of ugly teeth, or they may be hidden behind a panel. The following section, "Adjust the monitor's display," discusses what they do.

✔ Monitors display a message when the monitor is turned on and the PC is not (or the monitor isn't receiving a signal from the PC). The message may read `No Signal` or something like that, or it may urge you to check the connection. That's okay. The monitor pops to life properly when you turn on the console and it receives a video signal.

✔ Other features that have optionally found their way onto modern PC monitors include integrated stereo speakers as well as integrated cameras. Generally, these devices are adequate; better options for speakers and PC video exist.

Adjust the monitor's display

If you have the time, you can spend the better part of a day adjusting various features of your computer monitor. But although the features you can adjust are numerous, the knobs used to make the adjustments are not. Typically, you use between three and five buttons to adjust all your monitor's technical features.

The key to adjusting the display is locating a main button, sometimes labeled Menu. Pressing that button pops up an on-screen display, such as the one shown in Figure 10-2. You then use additional buttons — plus, minus, up, down — to select items from the menu and use possibly even more buttons to adjust values.

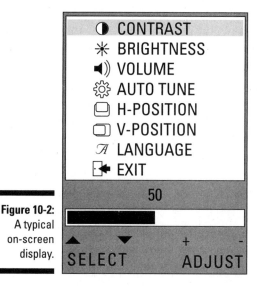

Figure 10-2:
A typical
on-screen
display.

If you're lucky, your monitor may not use the on-screen menu system but, ideally, have a row of buttons that control individual monitor settings, such as those shown in Figure 10-3. The idea is to use these buttons to adjust what the icons represent. Sometimes, you have to press more than one button to make a specific adjustment.

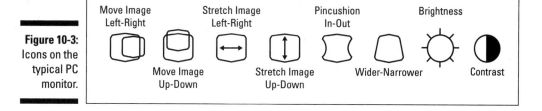

Figure 10-3:
Icons on the
typical PC
monitor.

✔ This is one area of the PC that I really wish they would standardize.

✔ The on-screen information appears over any other image displayed on the monitor. Don't let it freak you out.

✔ Use the buttons to adjust the image size to make full use of the monitor's display area.

✔ Most monitors also have a Save or Store button, which remembers the settings you have entered and makes them permanent. Use it.

Windows and Your Monitor

The graphics adapter controls the monitor, and software rules over the graphics adapter. Which software? Specifically, a *video driver* thingie controls the graphics adapter. But lording it over the video driver is the operating system. Windows gives you plenty of options for adjusting the display and what you see on the screen. This section mulls over several interesting and useful examples.

Summoning the Personalization window

One of the many things Windows lets you personalize in the Personalization window is the display. To view the Personalization window, follow these steps:

1. **Right-click the desktop.**

2. **Choose Personalize from the pop-up menu.**

   The Personalization window appears.

The Personalization window lists seven categories of things you can personalize in Windows. Four of those categories relate directly to the display: Window Color and Appearance, Desktop Background, Screen Saver, and the last item, Display Settings.

Additional control over your display may be available by using custom software that came with your PC's display adapter. For example, ATI adapters come with a special control center that you can access from the Notification Area. NVIDIA adapters have a control panel you can access from a command shown when you right-click the desktop.

Going for a new look

Windows lets you mess with the way its windows appear on the screen. You can change the basic color scheme, transparency and other effects, and other time-wasting endeavors. Follow these steps:

1. **From the Personalization window, choose Window Color and Appearance.**

   The Window Color and Appearance window shows up, as depicted in Figure 10-4, good buddy.

2. **Choose a new color from the palette that's displayed, or use the Show Color Mixer button to fashion your own, custom color.**

3. **Put a check mark by Enable Transparency if you like that see-through look.**

4. **Click OK to set the colors.**

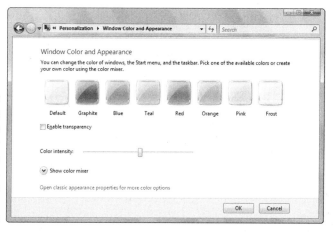

Figure 10-4: Change your monitor's resolution and colors here.

To make more specific adjustments, click the link at the bottom of the window, Open Classic Appearance Properties for More Color Options. You can use the Appearance Settings dialog box to adjust just about every aspect of Windows. For example, you can choose the Windows Classic option to make Windows Vista look as dumb as Windows 98.

Changing the background (wallpaper)

The desktop background, commonly called *wallpaper,* is what you see when you look at the desktop. It can be a solid color, or it can display any graphics image stored on your hard drive or found on the Internet. This process is all handled by the Desktop Background window, as shown in Figure 10-5.

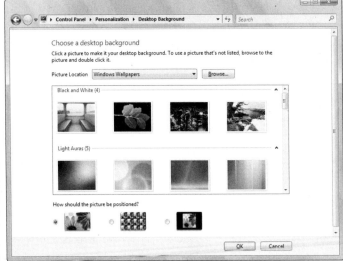

Figure 10-5:
Select
desktop
wallpaper
here.

Here's how to use that window:

1. **From the Personalization window, choose Desktop Background.**

2. **Select a main picture category from the Picture Location menu button.**

   The Windows Wallpapers category lists some preset pictures that come with Windows: landscapes, abstract images, animals, fat guys mowing the lawn, and so forth.

   The Pictures, Sample Pictures, and Public Pictures categories list images found on your PC's hard drive. You can also use the Browse button to locate images not stored in the traditional Pictures folder (or folders).

   The Solid Colors category lists solid colors. You can also click the More button to mix up your own color.

3. **Choose a picture or solid color.**

   For a picture, you can optionally select whether the image is to be centered, stretched, or tiled — whichever option best splays out the picture on the screen.

4. Click the OK button to set your choice.

You can also optionally close the Personalization window.

- ✔ The Browse dialog box works just like the Open dialog box. See Chapter 25.
- ✔ To set an image from the Web as your wallpaper, right-click the image in Internet Explorer and choose the Set As Background command from the pop-up menu.

- ✔ Creating your own wallpaper is easy. You can do so in the Windows Paint program, or you can use a scanned image or a shot from a digital camera. After that image is saved in the Pictures folder, you can access the image from the Desktop Background window to set it as the desktop background.

Saving the screen

The *screen saver* is an image or animation that appears on the monitor after a given period of inactivity. After your computer sits there, lonely and feeling ignored, for 30 minutes, for example, an image of a fish tank appears on the monitor to amuse any ghosts in the room.

To set up your computer to display a screen saver, obey these steps:

1. From the Personalization window, choose Screen Saver.

The Screen Saver Settings dialog box appears, as shown in Figure 10-6.

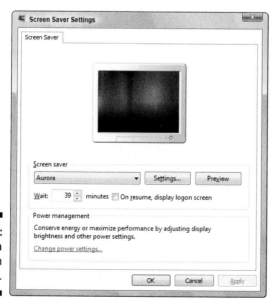

Figure 10-6: Select a screen saver here.

Making things easier to see

If you have trouble seeing small things, adjust your display so that they appear as big as possible: Choose a low resolution, such as 800 x 600 or even 640 x 480. Take advantage of the various View⇨Zoom commands available in applications, which greatly enlarge the text or subject matter.

You can also direct Windows to use larger icons on the display: Right-click the desktop and choose View⇨Medium Icons or View⇨Large Icons from the pop-up menu.

---

2. **Choose a screen saver from the menu button.**

    The screen saver is previewed in the tiny monitor window.

3. **Click the Settings button to adjust any options for the individual screen saver you chose.**

    The options vary, depending on the screen saver.

4. **Enter the number of minutes to wait before the screen saver kicks in.**

    Or, if you're impatient, click the Preview button to see the full-screen screen saver. (Click the mouse to end the screen saver.)

5. **Click the OK button.**

After you haven't touched the mouse or keyboard for a given length of time, the screen saver appears on your monitor. To return to Windows, press a key on the keyboard or jiggle the computer mouse.

✔ To disable the screen saver, choose (None) from the screen saver menu button.

✔ Beware of downloading screen saver files from the Internet. Although some of them are legitimate screen savers, most of them are invasive ads or programs that are impossible to uninstall or remove. If you download this type of screen saver, you're pretty much stuck with it. Be careful!

✔ You may never see the screen saver, especially if you're using the PC's power management system to put the monitor to sleep. See Chapter 15 for more information.

✔ For extra security, in the Screen Saver Settings dialog box, put a check mark by the option On Resume, Display Logon Screen.

✔ The problem the original screen savers tried to prevent was known as *phosphor burn-in*. It can still happen on monitors now, but only if the same image is displayed for months. LCD monitors aren't susceptible to phosphor burn-in.

Adjusting the display size (resolution) and colors

The monitor's physical dimensions cannot change, but you can set the amount of stuff you see on the screen by adjusting the screen *resolution.* That's the number of dots, or *pixels,* the monitor displays, measuring horizontally by vertically.

To set the screen's resolution, follow these steps:

1. From the Personalization window, choose Display Settings.

The Display Settings dialog box appears, as shown in Figure 10-7.

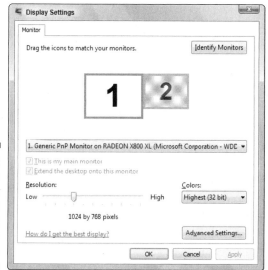

Figure 10-7: Change your monitor's resolution and colors here.

2. Use the Resolution slider in the Display Settings dialog box to set the monitor's resolution.

The Screen Resolution slider sets the display resolution, measured in pixels horizontally and vertically. The larger the numbers, the more information is displayed. Smaller values yield less information but make everything appear bigger.

The preview window in the upper center of the dialog box gives you an idea of how the new resolution affects the display.

TIP

Take a picture of the screen

Say "pixel!" Click. You can take a picture of the display on your PC without using a digital camera or mounting the monitor atop a photocopy machine. It's simple. The key is a key on the keyboard: Print Screen.

Yes, in the olden days, the Print Screen key did send a printed copy of all text on the screen (it was all text in those days) to the computer's printer. Now, however, pressing the Print Screen key captures everything you see on the screen, saving it to the Windows Clipboard. From there, the screen image can be pasted into any graphics application, such as Windows Paint.

You can also use the Alt+Print Screen key combination to capture the topmost window on the screen.

For real sophistication, you need to use a new Windows Vista utility: the Snipping Tool. That program lets you capture all or part of the screen, use a timer to grab a future screen shot, plus modify the screen image in a variety of ways. The Snipping Tool is far more versatile and useful than the old Print Screen key screen-capture trick.

3. **Set the Colors value by using the menu button; choose the highest colors value available for the resolution you chose.**

   The Colors value determines how many colors are available at a specific resolution. The values are Medium (16 bit) and Highest (32 bit). The Medium value is your only option for certain high resolutions.

4. **Click the Apply button to preview the new resolution.**

5. **Click the Yes button if the new resolution is acceptable; you're done. Otherwise, click No and repeat Steps 2 through 4 until you're happy.**

   You can also just click the Cancel button at any time to dismiss the Display Settings dialog box.

The maximum number of resolution and color settings depends on the graphics adapter and not on the monitor size. The more video RAM the graphics adapter has, the more options are available.

- ✔ Note that many LCD monitors have preferred resolutions, such as 1024 by 768 or 1280 by 1024. Try to stick with the standard resolutions recommended by the monitor's manufacturer.

- ✔ Pixel is a contraction of *pic*ture *el*ement. On a computer display, a pixel is a single dot of color.

- ✔ Higher resolutions work best on larger monitors.

- ✔ Some computer games automatically change the monitor's resolution to allow the games to be played. This change is okay, and the resolution should return to normal after you play the game.

Chapter 11

Input Buddies: Keyboard and Mouse

In This Chapter

▶ Understanding the keyboard

▶ Using specific keys

▶ Controlling the keyboard in Windows

▶ Sitting and typing properly

▶ Getting to know the mouse

▶ Working with the mouse in Windows

▶ Fixing various mouse problems

R emember those classic comic duos? Laurel and Hardy. Abbott and Costello. Martin and Lewis. Both people serve to entertain, but note that each individual in the pair is different. There's the straight man and the wise guy, the fat one and the skinny one, the clever one and the fool. In many ways, your computer's primary input devices share these comic attributes: The keyboard is long and flat, the mouse is squat round. The keyboard deals with text, the mouse is for graphics. Oh, the comedy you could have with the keyboard and mouse. Imagine the adventures: *PC Keyboard and Mouse in Asia!*

But I digress. The keyboard and mouse are a famous duo, but only electronically. The keyboard is the traditional computer input device. The mouse is relatively new on the scene, but utterly necessary for the graphical fun and folly of today's PCs. This chapter covers 'em both.

Push the PC Keyboard's Buttons

Until they perfect talking with a computer, you're going to have to use the keyboard. Yes, the mouse can do a lot, but computers are still all about typing. Therefore, it helps to know a little bit about the device you'll paw the most when you use Mr. Computer.

✔ The keyboard is the computer's standard input device. Refer to Chapter 1 for more information on computer input.

✔ Although you can talk to the computer, it doesn't work as smoothly as you see on those science fiction TV shows. See Chapter 18.

The basic PC keyboard

PC keyboards are anything but standard. Customized keyboards, adorned with special buttons and features, seem to be the rule, not the exception. Still, the basic PC keyboard layout, showing the 104 keys common to all PC keyboards, is shown in Figure 11-1.

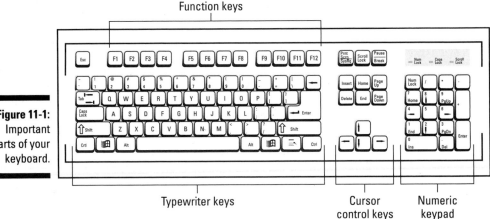

Figure 11-1: Important parts of your keyboard.

There are four main areas on your PC's keyboard, as illustrated in Figure 11-1:

Function keys: These keys are positioned on the top row of the keyboard. They're labeled F1, F2, F3, and on up to F11 and F12.

Typewriter keys: These keys are the same types of keys you would find on an old typewriter: letters, numbers, and punctuation symbols.

Cursor-control keys: Often called *arrow keys,* these four keys move the text cursor in the direction of their arrows. Above them are more cursor-control keys — the six-pack of Insert, Delete, Home, End, Page Up, and Page Down.

Numeric keypad: Popular with accountants, bank tellers, and airline ticket agents, the numeric keypad contains calculator-like keys. This keypad also doubles as a cursor keypad; the Num Lock key determines its behavior.

"Must I learn to type to use a computer?"

The short answer: No, you don't need to learn to type to use a computer. Plenty of computer users hunt and peck. In fact, most programmers don't know how to type, but that brings up an interesting story: A computer software developer once halted all development and had his programmers learn how to touch-type. It took two whole weeks, but afterward, they all got their work done much faster and had more time available to break away and play those all-important computer games.

As a bonus to owning a computer, you can have it teach you how to type. The Mavis Beacon Teaches Typing software package does just that. Other packages are available, but I personally enjoy saying the name Mavis Beacon.

In addition to the basic keyboard layout, your PC's keyboard may have *even more* buttons, or it may be ergonomically designed or whatever. The various and sundry keyboard options are covered throughout the following sections.

- ✔ Wireless keyboards are also available. They operate off batteries that seemingly must be changed every day or two.

- ✔ The *cursor* is the blinking goober on the screen that shows you where the characters you type appear. As though *cursor* isn't weird enough, the blinking doodad is also called an *insertion pointer.*

- ✔ See the section "The Lock sisters," later in this chapter, for more information on the numeric keypad's duplicity.

Shifty keys

Four keys on your keyboard are *modifier* keys. These keys work in combination with other keys to do various interesting and unbelievable things:

- ✔ Shift
- ✔ Ctrl or Control
- ✔ Alt or Alternate
- ✔ Win or Windows

Strange keyboard abbreviations

The keys on the keyboard are only so big. Therefore, some words have to be scrunched down to fit on the key cap. Here's your guide to some of the more oddly named keys and what they mean:

Print Screen is also known as PrScr or Print Scrn.

Page Up and Page Down are written as PgUp and PgDn on the numeric keypad.

Insert and Delete appear as Ins and Del on the numeric keypad.

SysRq means System Request, and it has no purpose.

You hold down a modifier key and then press another key on the keyboard. What happens then depends on the keys you press and how the program you're using reacts to the key combination.

- The Shift key is used to make capital letters or to access the punctuation and other symbols on the number keys and other keys. This is how you can create the %@#^ characters that come in handy for cursing in comic strips.

- Yes, Ctrl is pronounced "control."

- The Ctrl and Alt keys are used in combination with other keys as short-cuts for menu commands. For example, if you hold down the Ctrl key and press S (Ctrl+S), you activate the Save command. Holding down the Alt key and pressing the F4 key (Alt+F4) closes a window on the desktop. You press and hold the Ctrl or Alt key, tap the other key, and then release both.

- When pressed by itself, the Win key pops up the Start button menu. Otherwise, the Win key can be used in combination with other keys to do various things on the desktop. For example, Win+E summons the Windows Explorer program, and Win+D displays the desktop.

- Even though you may see Ctrl+S or Alt+S with a capital *S,* it doesn't mean that you must press Ctrl+Shift+S or Alt+Shift+S. The S is written in uppercase simply because Ctrl+s looks like a typesetting error.

- Don't be surprised if these shift keys are used in combination with each other. I have seen Shift+Ctrl+C and Ctrl+Alt+F6. Just remember to press and hold the Shift key first and then tap the other key. Release all the keys together.

- Some manuals use the notation ^Y rather than Ctrl+Y. This term means the same thing: Hold down the Ctrl key, press Y, and release the Ctrl key.

The Lock sisters

The three Lock sisters are special keys designed to change the way other keys on the keyboard behave:

Caps Lock: This key works like holding down the Shift key, but it works only with the letter keys. (Think *Caps* as in *cap*ital letters.) Press Caps Lock again, and the letters return to their normal, lowercase state.

Num Lock: Pressing this key makes the numeric keypad on the right side of the keyboard produce numbers. Press this key again, and you can use the numeric keypad for moving the text cursor.

Scroll Lock: This key has no purpose in life. Some spreadsheets use it to reverse the function of the cursor keys (which move the spreadsheet rather than the cell highlight). Scroll Lock does little else celebratory.

When a lock key is on, a corresponding light appears on the keyboard. The light may be on the keyboard or on the key itself. That's your clue that a lock key's feature is turned on.

- ✔ Caps Lock affects only the keys A through Z; it doesn't affect any other keys.

- ✔ If you type This Text Looks Like A Ransom Note and it appears as tHIS tEXT lOOKS lIKE a rANSOM nOTE, the Caps Lock key is inadvertently turned on. Press it once to return everything to normal.

- ✔ If you press the Shift key while Caps Lock is on, the letter keys return to normal. (Shift kind of cancels out Caps Lock.)

Know your ones and zeros

On a typewriter, the lowercase letter *L* and the number 1 are often the same. In fact, my old Underwood upright lacks a 1 key altogether. Unfortunately, on a computer, a big difference exists between a one and a little *L*.

If you're typing 1,001, for example, don't type l,00l by mistake — especially when you're working with a spreadsheet. The computer gags.

The same holds true for the uppercase letter *O* and the number 0. They're different. Use a zero for numbers and a big *O* for big O things.

Sometimes, zero is displayed with a slash through it, like this: Ø, or maybe with a dot in the middle. That's one way to tell the difference between O and 0, but it's not used that often. A better indication is that the letter O is often fatter than the zero character.

Specific keys from Any to the bizarre

Your computer keyboard is a virtual playground of buttons — some famous, some mysterious, and some non-existent. Here's a list of what's important and what's not:

 Ha-ha. There is no Any key on the keyboard. The infamous message once read "Press any key to continue" and the programmer thought he was being generous, but people still looked for that elusive Any key. Surprise! When the computer asks you to press the Any key, press *any key* on the keyboard. Specifically, press the spacebar.

 The Break key does nothing. Why is the key named Break? Why not call it the Brake key? Wouldn't that make sense? Who wants a computer to break, anyway? The Break key is the same as the Pause key. In fact, Break is really the Alt+Pause key combo. See the Pause key description later in this section.

 Enter is the keyboard's most popular key. It's so popular that there are *two* Enter keys on the keyboard, one by the typewriter keys and the second by the Numeric keypad. Both Enter keys work identically; you can use either one. Specifically, you press Enter to end a paragraph in a word processor, but in Windows pressing the Enter key is also the same as clicking the OK button in a dialog box.

 The one key that says "Hey! Stop it!" to Windows is the Escape key, labeled Esc on your keyboard. Pressing the Esc key is the same as clicking Cancel or No Way in a dialog box.

 Don't bother looking on the keyboard: It has no Help key. Instead, whenever you need help in Windows, whack the F1 key. F1 equals help — there's no way to commit that to memory.

 Honestly, the Pause key doesn't work in Windows. Some games may use it to pause the action, but it's not a consistent thing.

 This is the forward slash key. It's used as a separator and also to denote division, such as 52/13 (52 divided by 13). It's also used as a separator in Web page and other Internet addresses. Don't confuse it with the backslash key.

 The backslash (\) leans to the left. This character is used in *pathnames,* which are complex and not discussed in this book.

 From the computer's typewriter past comes the Return key. (The Enter key is from the computer's calculator lineage.) PCs lack a Return key, although if they had one, it would do the same thing as the Enter key.

 The System Request key shares its roost with the Print Screen key but by itself does nothing. Ignore it.

This booger is the Context key. It lives between the right Windows and Ctrl keys. Pressing this key displays the shortcut menu for whatever item is selected on the screen. It's the same as right-clicking the mouse when something is selected. Obviously, this key is next to useless.

 The Tab key is used in two different ways on your computer, neither of which generates a diet cola beverage. In a word processor, you use the Tab key to indent paragraphs or line up text. In a dialog box, you use the Tab key to move between the various graphical gizmos.

- Use Tab rather than Enter when you're filling in a form in a program or dialog box or on the Internet. For example, press the Tab key to hop between the First Name and Last Name fields.

- The Tab key often has two arrows on it — one pointing to the left and the other to the right. These arrows may be in addition to the word *Tab,* or they may be on there by themselves to confuse you.

- The arrows move both ways because Shift+Tab is a valid key combination. For example, pressing Shift+Tab in a dialog box moves you "backward" through the options.

- The computer treats a tab as a single, separate character. When you backspace over a tab in a word processing program, the tab disappears completely in one chunk — not space by space.

Special keys on special keyboards

The trend today is for your computer keyboard to sport even more buttons, specific keys not among the standard 104 PC keyboard keys. Usually, you find a row of special buttons along the top of the keyboard, but it may have buttons down the sides as well.

Those special buttons can do a variety of wondrous things. Some may adjust the PC's volume or play a song using Windows Media Player. Some buttons may assist with Web navigation, summon your e-mail program, open special folders in Windows, or run specific programs. The buttons can do anything because, again, they're nonstandard.

When you have a nonstandard keyboard, you most likely also have a special program that came with your computer. That special program controls the keyboard's special buttons, sometimes allowing you to reassign their functions. Look for the special program on the Start menu's All Programs menu, or it might be found in the Control Panel.

TECHNICAL STUFF

Scary math and your PC keyboard

Clustered around the numeric keypad, like yuppies lurking near Starbucks, are various keys to help you work with numbers. Especially if you're dabbling with a spreadsheet or other number-crunching software program, you find that these keys come in handy. Take a look at your keyboard's numeric keypad right now, just to reassure yourself.

What? You were expecting a × or ÷ key? Forget it! This is a computer. It uses special oddball symbols for mathematical operations:

✔ + is for addition.

✔ – is for subtraction.

✔ * is for multiplication.

✔ / is for division.

The only strange symbol here is the asterisk, for multiplication. Don't use the little *x!* It's not the same thing. The / (slash) is okay for division, but don't waste your time hunting for the ÷ symbol. It's not there.

Control the Keyboard in Windows

After pressing and holding a key for a given time, that key repeats. So when you press and hold the A key, eventually you see a whole slew of AAAAAAAAAAAA. . . . (That's so that you can easily type dialogue when your characters are falling off a cliff.) The pause before the key repeats is the *repeat delay.* The rapidity at which the key's character (or function) repeats is the *repeat rate.* Both these items are set by using the Keyboard Properties dialog box (see Figure 11-2).

Figure 11-2: Control the keyboard here.

Keyboard Properties

Speed | Hardware

Character repeat

Repeat delay:
Long ——————————O————— Short

Repeat rate:
Slow ————————————O— Fast

Click here and hold down a key to test repeat rate:

Cursor blink rate

| None ————————O———— Fast

OK | Cancel | Apply

To open the dialog box, from the Control Panel Home choose Hardware and Sound and then Keyboard. Or, from the Control Panel Classic view, open the Keyboard icon.

Within the Keyboard Properties dialog box, use the mouse to manipulate the sliders in the dialog box to set the rates, and then test out the rates in the text box that's provided. Click the OK or Apply button only when you're happy.

Proper Typing Attitude

Until Windows comes with a Virtual Nun simulator, it's up to you (and only you) to assume proper typing posture while you use the computer. Watch your wrists! Don't let them droop! It's important to observe proper posture and sitting position, especially to avoid the risk of something called repetitive stress injury (RSI).

Here are several things you can do to avoid RSI and keep your computing experience a pleasant one:

Get an ergonomic keyboard: Even if your wrists are as limber as rubber tree plants, you may want to consider an *ergonomic* keyboard. That type of keyboard is specially designed at an angle to relieve the stress of typing for long — or short — periods.

Use a wrist pad: Wrist pads elevate your wrists so that you type in a proper position, with your palms *above* the keyboard, not resting below the spacebar.

Adjust your chair: Sit at the computer with your elbows level with your wrists.

Adjust your monitor: Your head should not tilt down or up when you view the computer screen. It should be straight ahead, which doesn't help your wrists as much as it helps your neck.

✔ Ergonomic keyboards cost a little more than standard keyboards, but they're well worth the investment if you type for long hours, or at least want to look like you type for long hours.

✔ Some mouse pads have built-in wrist elevators. They're great for folks who use mouse-intensive applications.

✔ Many keyboards come with adjustable legs underneath for positioning the keys to a comfortable angle. Use these legs.

You and Your PC Mouse Go Hand in Hand

Your computer's mouse is an *input* device. Although the keyboard (another input device) can do almost anything, you need a mouse in order to control graphics and graphical whatnots on the screen — especially in an operating system like Windows.

- ✔ Your PC may have come with a specific mouse, but you can always buy a better replacement.
- ✔ The plural of computer mouse is *mice.* One computer has a mouse. Two computers have mice.

The basic computer mouse

The mouse finds its home to the right of the keyboard (for more right-handed people). It needs a clear swath of desk space so that you can move the mouse around; an area about the size of this book is typically all you need.

A typical computer mouse is shown in Figure 11-3, although what you see there is only one style of mouse. The variety is truly endless. Even so, nearly all computer mice have the same basic parts.

Right button

Wheel button   Mouse body

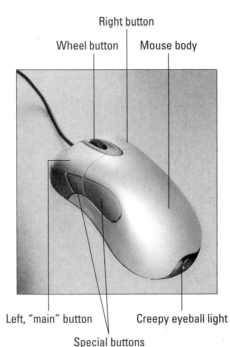

Figure 11-3:
A typical
computer
mouse.

Left, "main" button   Creepy eyeball light

Special buttons

Left (main) button: The left button, which falls under your right hand's index finger, is the *main* button. That's the button you click the most.

Wheel button: The center, or wheel, button can be pressed like the left and right buttons, and it can be rolled back and forth. Some wheels can even be tilted from side to side.

Right button: The right button is used for special operations, although right-clicking mostly pops up a shortcut or context menu.

Mouse body: The mouse is about the size of a bar of soap. You rest your palm on its body and use your fingers to manipulate the mouse buttons.

Special buttons: Some mice come with special buttons, which can be used for Internet navigation or assigned specific functions by using special software (see "Dink with the Mouse in Windows," later in this chapter).

Optical versus mechanical

The movement of the mouse on your desktop is detected internally by the mouse, either mechanically or optically.

The *mechanical* mouse houses a hard rubber ball that rolls as the mouse is moved. Sensors inside the mouse body detect the movement and translate it into information that the computer interprets.

The *optical* mouse uses an LED sensor to detect tabletop movement and then sends off that information to the computer for merry munching.

Of the two types, optical mice are better. They last longer and they're easier to clean. Also, optical mice don't need a mouse pad, which is necessary for a mechanical mouse's ball to get proper traction. An optical mouse can work on any nonreflective surface.

Cordless mice

Long before the farmer's wife wielded that carving knife, wireless computer mice have existed. There are two types:

- Infrared (IR)
- Radio frequency

With both types, the mouse relays a signal to a base station wired to the computer's mouse port. The cordless mouse requires power, which comes in the form of batteries. They must be replaced or recharged occasionally, or else the mouse doesn't work.

✔ Of the two types of wireless mice, radio frequency is preferred. It doesn't require a line of sight between the mouse and the wireless adapter, which can be a problem on the typically cluttered computer desk.

✔ The best solution for wireless mouse batteries is to use a mouse with a recharging cradle; the cordless mouse is stored in the cradle when it isn't being used. That makes the mouse easier to find and keeps the thing charged.

Other mouse species

Computer mice seem to sport a variety far greater than most PC peripherals. The most common alternative mouse is one with more buttons on it. The extra buttons can be programmed to do specific things, such as navigate the Web or turn pages when you're reading a document. How many buttons? The typical button-ified mouse may have five buttons. The most I've ever seen, however, is 57 buttons. (I kid you not.)

A popular mouse variation is the *trackball,* which is like an upside-down mouse. Rather than roll the mouse around, you use your thumb or index finger to roll a ball on top of the mouse. The whole contraption stays stationary, so it doesn't need nearly as much room and its cord never gets tangled. This type of mouse is preferred by graphic artists because it's often more precise than the traditional "soap-on-a-rope" mouse.

Another mouse mutation enjoyed by the artistic type is the *stylus* mouse, which looks like a pen and draws on a special pad. This mouse is also pressure sensitive, which is wonderful for use in painting and graphics applications.

Finally, those *cordless 3-D* mice can be pointed at the computer screen like a TV remote. Those things give me the willies.

Basic Mouse Operations

The computer's mouse controls a graphical mouse pointer or mouse cursor on the screen. When you move the mouse around by rolling it on your desk, the pointer on the screen moves in a similar manner. Roll the mouse left, and the pointer moves left; roll it in circles, and the pointer mimics that action; drop the mouse off the table and your computer sneezes. (Just kidding.)

Here are some of the more basic mouse operations:

Point: When you're told to "point the mouse," you move the mouse on the desktop, which moves the mouse pointer on the screen to point at something interesting (or not).

Click: A *click* is a press of the mouse button — one press and release of the main button, the one on the left. This action makes a clicking sound, which is where this maneuver gets its name. Clicking is often done to select something or to identify a specific location on the screen.

Right-click: This action is the same as a click, although the right mouse button is used.

Double-click: This one works just like the single click, although you click twice in the same spot — usually, rather rapidly. This is most commonly done in Windows to open something, such as an icon. Both clicks must be on (or near) the same spot for the double-click to work.

Drag: The drag operation is done to graphically pick up something on the screen and move it. To do that, you point the mouse at the thing you want to drag and then press and hold the mouse's button. Keep the mouse button down, which "picks up" the object, and then move the mouse to another location. As you move the mouse (and keep the button down) the object moves. To release, or *drop,* the object, release the mouse button.

Right-drag: This action is the same as a drag, but the mouse's right button is used instead.

Many of these basic mouse operations can be combined with keys on the keyboard. For example, a Shift+click means pressing the Shift key on the keyboard while clicking the mouse. A Ctrl+drag means pressing and holding the Ctrl key while you drag an object with the mouse.

✔ The best way to learn how to use a computer mouse is to play a computer card game, such as Solitaire or FreeCell (both of which come with Windows). You should have the mouse mastered in only a few frustrating hours.

✔ You don't need to squeeze the mouse; a gentle grip is all that's necessary.

✔ Press *and release* the mouse button to click.

✔ If you double-click your mouse and nothing happens, you may not be clicking fast enough. See the section "'Double-clicking doesn't work!'" later in this chapter.

Dink with the Mouse in Windows

In Windows, the mouse is controlled, manipulated, and teased by using the Mouse Properties dialog box, as shown in Figure 11-4. To display that dialog box, open the Control Panel Home and choose the Mouse link beneath the Hardware and Sound heading. From the Control Panel Classic view, double-click the Mouse icon to see the Mouse Properties dialog box.

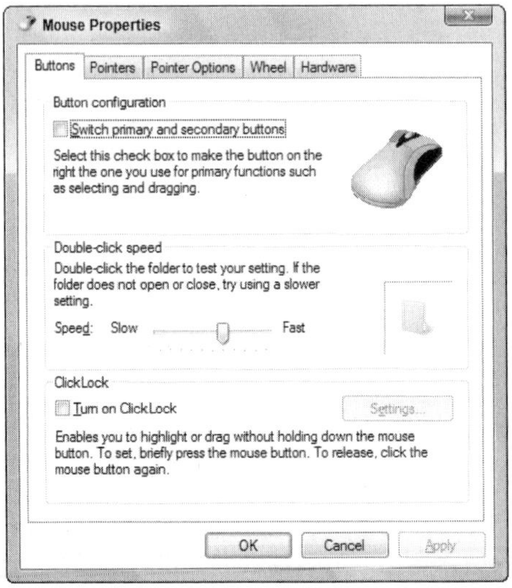

Figure 11-4:
The Mouse
Properties
dialog box.

> **Mouse Properties**
>
> Buttons | Pointers | Pointer Options | Wheel | Hardware
>
> Button configuration
>
> ☐ Switch primary and secondary buttons
>
> Select this check box to make the button on the right the one you use for primary functions such as selecting and dragging.
>
> Double-click speed
>
> Double-click the folder to test your setting. If the folder does not open or close, try using a slower setting.
>
> Speed: Slow ———|——— Fast
>
> ClickLock
>
> ☐ Turn on ClickLock   Settings...
>
> Enables you to highlight or drag without holding down the mouse button. To set, briefly press the mouse button. To release, click the mouse button again.
>
> OK   Cancel   Apply

Note that the Mouse Properties dialog box may look different from Figure 11-4 and what you see elsewhere in this book. It all depends on which mouse your PC uses. Although some tabs are generically the same, some are specific to the mouse hardware, such as assigning functions to any special mouse buttons.

"I can't find the mouse pointer!"

The Pointer Options tab in the Mouse Properties dialog box, as shown in Figure 11-5, contains a number of options to help you locate a lost mouse pointer. These options can come in handy, especially on larger displays or when the mouse pointer is floating over a particularly busy desktop.

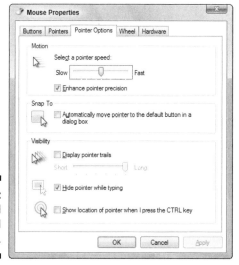

Figure 11-5:
Ways to find
a wayward
mouse.

✔ The Display Pointer Trails option displays a comet trail of mouse point-ers as you move the mouse about. Jiggling or circling the mouse makes lots of visual racket, which allows you to quickly locate the mouse pointer.

✔ The Ctrl key location option allows you to find the mouse pointer by tapping either Ctrl key on the keyboard. This action makes a radar-like circle appear, by zeroing in on the cursor's location.

✔ You can also employ the Snap To option, which specifically jumps the mouse pointer to the main button in any dialog box that appears. (I find this option annoying.)

"Double-clicking doesn't work!"

If you can't seem to double-click, one of two things is happening: Either you're moving the mouse pointer a little bit between clicks, or the double-click *rate* is set too fast for human fingers to manage.

The *double-click rate* is set in the Mouse Properties dialog box, on the Buttons tab in the Double-Click Speed area. Practice your double-clicking on the tiny folder icon off to the right. Use the Slow-Fast slider to adjust the double-click speed to better match your click-click timing.

"I'm left-handed, and the buttons are backward!"

What's so sinister about being left-handed, anyway?

In Windows, you can adjust the mouse for southpaw use on the Buttons tab, as shown earlier, in Figure 11-4. Put a check mark by the box labeled Switch Primary and Secondary Buttons. That way, the main mouse button is under your left index finger.

✔ This book and all manuals and computer books assume that the left mouse button is the main button. *Right-clicks* are clicks of the right mouse button. If you tell Windows to use the left-handed mouse, these buttons are reversed. Keep in mind that your documentation doesn't reflect that.

✔ Left-handed mice are available that are sculpted to fit your left hand better than all those biased, right-hand-oriented mice on the market.

✔ No setting is available for ambidextrous people, wise guy!

Chapter 12

The Printer's the Thing

In This Chapter

▸ Understanding computer printers

▸ Comparing inkjet versus laser printing

▸ Taking the printer offline

▸ Ejecting a page

▸ Giving the printer more ink

▸ Buying paper

▸ Installing a new printer

▸ Setting margins

▸ Printing in reverse order

▸ Stopping a printer run amok

*C*omputers and printers go back farther than you think. The first computer terminals were often teletype machines. Everything the computer scientist input to the computer was instantly printed on the teletype. The teletype tradition is why computers on TV and in film make noise when they print characters on the screen. In fact, the abbreviation for *teletype*, *tty*, is still used in computer science to refer to the standard I/O devices: the keyboard and monitor.

Eventually the teletype morphed into three unique computer peripherals: the keyboard, the monitor, and the printer. All three gizmos are still required now in order to complete the basic computer system. Although you may not purchase a printer when you buy your PC, it's still something worth looking into, and definitely something worth having. This chapter covers everything associated with computer printers and printing.

Behold the Printer

The printer's job is to print stuff, to get a *hard copy* of information stored in the computer. Yeah, the printer may also scan, copy, and Swiffer sweep the floor. But, at the heart of the thing is a gizmo that puts ink to paper and gives you something you can show the world.

Types of computer printer

Computer printers are categorized by how the ink gets splattered on the paper. Other subcategories are based on the printer's features. Here's the short list:

- ✔ Inkjet
- ✔ Photo
- ✔ All-in-one
- ✔ Laser
- ✔ Impact

The inkjet, photo, and all-in-one printers all use the same basic method for putting ink on paper: Tiny balls of ink are lobbed directly on the paper. Because the teensy-tiny ink balls stick to the paper, this type of printer needs no ribbon or toner cartridge; the ink is jetted out directly, which is how the printer gets its name.

Laser printers are found primarily in the office environment, where they can handle the high workload. The printer uses a laser beam to create the image, similar to a photocopier, which uses an image reflection. The result is crisp and fast output, but not as inexpensive as the inkjet type of printer.

Impact printers are few and far between these days, although once they were the dominant type of computer printer. These printers are slower and noisier than the other types of printers. They use a ribbon and some device that physically bangs the ribbon on the paper. Because of that, impact printers are primarily used now in printing invoices or multicopy forms. They're not practical for home use.

- ✔ Inkjet printers are by no means messy. The ink is dry on the paper by the time the paper comes flopping out of the printer.

- ✔ A laser printer that can print in color is known as a color laser printer. The regular (noncolor) laser printer uses only one color of ink — usually, black.

✔ Low-end inkjet printers cost less because they're dumb; they contain no internal electronics to help create the image. Instead, the computer is required to do the thinking, which slows things down a tad. When you pay more for an inkjet printer, the smarts are usually included with the printer.

✔ High-priced printers offer a higher-quality output, faster speed, more printing options, the ability to print on larger sheets of paper, and other amazing options.

A look around your printer

Take a moment to examine your printer and look for some handy items, as labeled in Figure 12-1:

Paper feed: The paper feed is where you store the paper that the printer eventually prints on. For more information, see the section "Feed your printer, Part II: Paper," later in this chapter.

Manual/envelope feeder: Fancier printers may have a special slot, tray, or foldout-thing used to manually feed special papers or envelopes. It may be hidden on your printer, and it's not shown in Figure 12-1, so look around a bit to see whether your printer has such a deal.

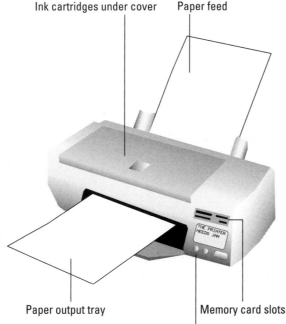

Ink cartridges under cover   Paper feed

Figure 12-1:
Notable
places on
the printer.

Paper output tray   Memory card slots

Control panel

Ink/toner replacement: Printers don't go on printing forever. At some point, you need to feed the thing more ink. Be sure that you know how to open the printer to find where the ink goes. Also see the section "Feed your printer, Part I: Ink," later in this chapter.

Control panel: Refer to the next subsection for the details.

Memory card reader: Many photo printers have a place where you can directly plug in your digital camera's memory card.

Paper output tray: The printed paper comes out and is stacked up in the output tray. If the paper comes out face up, be sure to see the section "Printing in reverse order," later in this chapter.

The mighty printer control panel

Every printer has a control panel somewhere on its body. The fancy models have LCD screens that display text or preview and select photos for printing. Less fancy printers may have only a couple of buttons. Either way, two important buttons to find or features to access on the control panel are

- ✔ On-Line or Select
- ✔ Form Feed

The purpose of On-Line or Select is to tell your printer whether to ignore the computer. When the printer is offline or deselected, the computer can't print. The printer is still on, which is good because you may need to access features, unjam the printer, or do things that you otherwise cannot do while the thing is printing.

The Form Feed button ejects a page of paper from the printer. For example, if you stop printing and only half a page is printed, you can use the Form Feed button to eject the rest of that page. Or, you can press the Form Feed button whenever you want the printer to spit a blank page at you.

- ✔ The computer can print only when the printer is online or selected.
- ✔ If your printer seems to lack a control panel, it's probably controlled via a software control panel in Windows. This is the printer's feature and not a part of Windows, so refer to the printer's manual for details.
- ✔ Printers with LCD control panels often use menu buttons to help you choose the online or form-feed options.
- ✔ All-in-one printers have additional buttons on the control panel — for example, buttons for making copies and scanning. A companion program in Windows probably allows for even greater control over the printer's abilities. Note that such programs are specific to your printer and not a part of Windows itself.

✔ Keep your printer's manual handy. For example, I put my printer's manual right beneath the printer, where I can always find it. You may never read the manual, but if your printer suddenly pops up and displays `Error 34`, you can look up `Error 34` and read how to fix it. (The voice of experience is talking here.)

Feed your printer, Part 1: Ink

This may be the 21st century, but mankind is still printing with ink and paper, just like the Chinese were hundreds of years ago. The type of ink and how it's stored depend on which type of printer you're using.

Inkjet printers, which include photo and all-in-one models, use *ink cartridges*. Laser printers use *toner,* a powdery ink substance that also comes in a cartridge. Either way, you spend lots of money replacing the ink in your printer.

All printers use black ink or toner. Color printers also use black, plus three other inks or toners: magenta, cyan, and yellow. Photo printers add two more colors: another flavor each of magenta and cyan.

Replacing a cartridge generally goes like this:

1. **Carefully unwrap the foil or wrapper around the new cartridge.**

2. **Remove any tape or covering, per the package's instructions.**

3. **Insert the cartridge into the printer, again following the instructions for your specific ink printer.**

4. **Put the old cartridge into the new cartridge's box and properly dispose of it or have it recycled.**

Some manufacturers sell their cartridges with return envelopes so that you can send the old cartridge back to the factory for recycling or proper disposal.

✔ Make sure that you don't breathe in the dust from a laser toner cartridge or else you'll die.

✔ Sometimes, the colors in an inkjet printer come three to a cartridge. Yes, that means that if only one color of ink goes, you must replace the entire cartridge even though the other two colors are still available.

✔ Yes, they make money by selling you ink. That's why the printer is cheap. It's the old "Give away the razor and sell them the blade" concept all over again.

✔ Make a note of which type of inkjet cartridges your printer uses. Keep the catalog number somewhere handy, such as taped to your inkjet printer's case, so that you can always reorder the proper cartridge.

✔ Always follow carefully the instructions for changing cartridges. Old cartridges can leak and get messy ink all over. Buy rubber gloves (or those cheap plastic gloves that make you look like Batman) and use them when changing an ink or toner cartridge. I also suggest having a paper towel handy.

✔ CYMK is an abbreviation for *c*yan, *y*ellow, *m*agenta, and blac*k,* the common ink colors used in inkjet printers.

✔ You don't always have to print in color! You can also just print in black ink, which saves the (often spendy) color cartridge from running low. The Print dialog box (covered later in this chapter) often has an option that lets you choose whether you want to print with color or black ink.

✔ When the laser printer first warns you that `Toner [is] low,` you can get a few more pages from it by gently rocking the toner cartridge: Remove the cartridge and rock it back and forth the short way (not end to end), which helps redistribute the toner dust.

✔ Rather than buy new cartridges, consider getting ink cartridge refills or toner cartridges recharged. Be sure that you deal with a reputable company; not every type of ink or toner cartridge can be reused successfully.

✔ Never let your printer cartridges go dry. You may think that squeezing every last drop of ink saves you money, but it's not good for the printer.

Feed your printer, Part II: Paper

Next to consuming ink, printers eat paper. Fortunately, paper isn't as expensive as ink, so it doesn't bankrupt you to churn through a ream or two. The only issue is where to feed in the paper. Like feeding a baby, there's a right end and a wrong end.

The paper goes into a feeder tray either near the printer's bottom or sticking out the top.

Laser printers require you to fill a cartridge with paper, similar to the way a copy machine works. Slide the cartridge all the way into the printer after it's loaded up.

Confirm that you're putting the paper in the proper way, either face down or face up. Note which side is the top. Most printers have little pictures on them that tell you how the paper goes into the printer. Here's how those symbols translate into English:

✔ The paper goes in face down, top side up.

✔ The paper goes in face down, top side down.

✔ The paper goes in face up, top side up.

✔ The paper goes in face up, top side down.

Knowing proper paper orientation helps when you're loading things such as checks for use with personal finance software. If the printer doesn't tell you which way is up, write *Top* on a sheet of paper and run it through the printer. Then draw your own icon, similar to those shown above, that help you orient the pages you manually insert into the printer.

Always make sure that you have enough printer paper. Buying too much isn't a sin.

Types of paper

There's really no such thing as a typical sheet of paper. Paper comes in different sizes, weights (degrees of thickness), colors, styles, textures, and, I assume, flavors.

The best general-purpose paper to get is standard photocopier paper. If you want better results from your inkjet printer, getting specific inkjet paper works best, although you pay more for that paper. The higher-quality (and spendy) inkjet paper is really good for printing colors; the paper is specially designed to absorb the ink well.

At the high end of the spectrum are specialty papers, such as photographic papers that come in smooth or glossy finishes, transparencies, and iron-on T-shirt transfers. Just ensure that the paper you get is made for your type of printer, ink jet, or laser.

✔ Some printers are capable of handling larger-size paper, such as legal or tabloid sizes. If so, make sure that you load the paper properly and tell your application that you're using a different-size sheet of paper. The File➪Page Setup command is responsible for selecting paper size.

✔ Avoid thick papers because they get jammed inside the printer. (They can't turn corners well.)

✔ Avoid using erasable bond and other fancy dusted papers in your printer. These papers have talcum powder coatings that gum up the works.

✔ Don't let the expensive paper ads fool you: Your inkjet printer can print on just about any type of paper. Even so, the pricey paper *does* produce a better image.

✔ My favorite type of inkjet paper is *laser paper.* It has a polished look to it and a subtle waxy feel.

Printer Set Up

Printers are one of the easiest devices to set up and configure. After freeing the printer from its box, and from various pieces of tape and evil Styrofoam, locate the printer's power cable. Then locate the printer cable, the one that connects the printer to the console.

Aha! The printer didn't come with a printer-to-console cable, did it? It never does. You have to buy the printer cable separately. I recommend getting a USB cable if the printer is USB-happy. Otherwise, buy a standard, bidirectional PC printer cable. Refer to Chapter 3 for information on plugging things in.

Before jumping the gun, read the printer's instruction sheet to see whether you need to install software before turning the printer on. Otherwise, turn the printer on. A USB printer is instantly recognized and configured by Windows. Life is good.

Printers using the traditional printer cable, or network printers, require more work. See the section "Manually adding a printer," later in this chapter.

Most printers, like computers, can now be left on all the time. The printer automatically slips into a low-power sleep mode when it's no longer needed. However, if you don't print often (at least every day), it's perfectly fine to turn off your printer.

- ✔ I recommend placing the printer near the console, about an arm's length away.

- ✔ Some USB printers demand to be directly connected to the computer, not plugged into a USB hub.

- ✔ You can connect a number of printers to a single computer. As long as the computer has a second printer port or uses another USB port or even the network, multiple printers work fine.

Windows and Your Printer

The printing action in Windows happens inside the Printers and Faxes window (see Figure 12-2). To get there, choose Printer from beneath the Hardware and Sound heading in the Control Panel Home or open the Printers icon in the Control Panel Classic view.

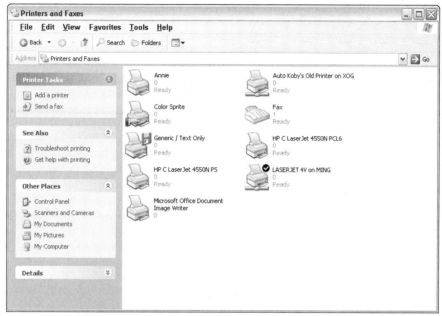

Figure 12-2:
The Printers
and Faxes
window.

The Printers and Faxes window lists all printing devices attached or available to your computer, including any fax modems. Here's a smattering of what you may see:

 The default printer: This printer is the one Windows uses automatically — the primary, or first, printer — which Windows calls the *default* printer. You can always spy this printer because of the check mark in a circle.

 The fax machine: This icon represents your PC's fax modem — if you have one. Sending a fax works just like printing.

 A shared printer: Printers with the sharing-friends icon are connected to your PC, but are available for use by others on the network.

 A network printer: Printers with plumbing beneath them exist elsewhere on the network. You can use them just like any other printer, but it's a walk to get your document after it prints.

All types of printer appear in the Printers window and use the same generic icon, so you cannot really tell which type of printer it is by looking at its icon in the window.

Manually adding a printer

Your printer was probably set up when you first ran your computer. Windows asks about the printer, and you answer a few questions, and then it's done. But when you need to add another printer, especially a non-USB printer, more work is involved.

The key to adding a non-USB printer, or any printer that stubbornly refuses to show itself in the Printers window, is to click the Add a Printer toolbar button found in the Printers window. When you click the Add a Printer toolbar button, you run the Add Printer Wizard, which quizzes you about the type of printer you're adding. Simply follow the wizard's directions to locate and set up the printer.

Here are some advice tidbits to help you work through the Add Printer Wizard:

- Let the network administrator worry about connecting network printers.
- Don't bother with the Plug and Play option; Windows has already recognized any Plug and Play printers.
- The printer is most likely connected to the first printer port, code-named LPT1.
- I recommend printing the test page just to ensure that the operation was successful.
- If your printer came with its own CD, you may need to install programs from that CD to begin or finish the printer installation. Refer to the documentation that came with the CD.

When the printer is connected properly and everything is up to snuff, you see that gratifying test page print. You can then start using that printer. Its icon appears in the Printers and Faxes window.

Setting the default printer

When your PC is connected to, or has access to, multiple printers, you can pick and choose which one you want to use as the main printer. The main, or default printer, is the one Windows uses automatically, for example, when you click a Print toolbar button.

To set a printer as the default, follow these steps:

1. **Open the Printers window.**

2. **Select the printer you plan to use most often.**

3. **Click the Set As Default button on the toolbar.**

The tiny check mark on the printer's icon confirms that you set the default printer.

You can change the default printer at any time by repeating these steps.

Basic Printer Operation

Under Windows, printing is a snap. All applications support the same Print command: Choose File⇨Print from the menu, or press Ctrl+P, to see the Print dialog box (see Figure 12-3). Make any necessary adjustments, and then click the Print button to print your masterpiece.

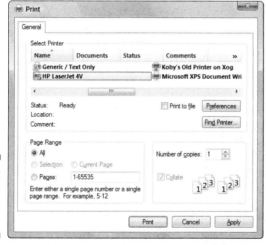

Figure 12-3:
A typical Print dialog box.

The Print dialog box shown in Figure 12-3 is typical for most programs. To print the entire document, just click the Print button. Otherwise, you can use the settings in the dialog box to change what and how you print.

For example, you can choose another printer from the list of available printers. Or, you can set the page numbers to print (Page Range) and the number of copies printed.

The Print dialog box may sport a Properties, Settings, or Options button that lets you set other, more specific aspects of printing and control how the printer works. For example, options to set whether printing happens in color or grayscale, determine how to render graphics, and choose which paper tray to use can be found by clicking an Options or Properties button.

- ✔ The common keyboard shortcut for the Print command is Ctrl+P.

- ✔ Rather than waste paper, consider using the File⇨Print Preview command instead. That command displays a sneak peek of what's to be printed so you can examine the printer's output before wasting a sheet of paper.

- ✔ In Microsoft Office 2007, the printing commands are kept on the Office Button menu. (There's no File menu.)

- ✔ Many applications sport a Print toolbar icon. If so, you can click that button to quickly print your document.

- ✔ The Print toolbar icon doesn't summon the Print dialog box. It just prints the entire document. To summon the Print dialog box, you must use Ctrl+P or choose File⇨Print from the menu.

"Where do I set my margins?"

The Print dialog box is concerned only with printing, not with formatting. Setting margins, paper size, and other aspects of what is to be printed is handled elsewhere in a program, usually in a Page Setup dialog box, as shown in Figure 12-4.

Figure 12-4:
The Page
Setup dialog
box.

To access the Page Setup dialog box, choose File⇨Page Setup from the menu. As with the Print dialog box, each application's Page Setup dialog box is different, with commands not always in the same location.

- ✔ The Page Setup dialog box is where you set things like margins, paper size, and so forth — not in the Print dialog box.

- ✔ Two options worth looking at in the Page Setup dialog box are Portrait and Landscape. *Portrait* is the normal way documents print; *Landscape* is printing "sideways," or with the long edge of the paper on top.

- ✔ Use the Page Setup dialog box to choose between Letter, Legal, and a number of other paper sizes. Be sure to stock the printer with that same size of paper as well.

- ✔ In Office 2007, the Page Setup dialog box is summoned by clicking the Dialog Box Launcher (button) found in the lower right corner of the Page Setup group on the Page Layout tab.

- ✔ Note that printers cannot print on an entire sheet of paper. There's usually a small margin around the sheet or just on one end of the paper, where no printing can take place. That's the part of the page that's held by the printer's paper-feeding mechanism, and its size and location vary from printer to printer.

Print in reverse order

When you have a printer that spits out its sheets of paper face up, notice that the sheets are always in reverse order. That is, Page 1 is on the bottom of the stack, and the last page is on the top. Rather than constantly reshuffle your pages, why not let the computer do the work?

Most programs give you the ability to print in reverse order. For example, in Microsoft Word, you click the Options or Properties button in the Print dialog box. In the next dialog box that appears, put a check mark by the item labeled Reverse Print Order or Back to Front. Click the OK button and then click the Print button to have your document print perfectly.

Printing in reverse order isn't a printer feature; it's part of the program you use. Some programs have that feature, and others don't.

Stop, printer! Stop!

The most frustrating printer experience you can have is wanting the dumb thing to stop printing. It happens. Often.

The easiest way to stop printing is to look on the printer's control panel for a Cancel button. Click that button, and all printing stops. Oh, a few more lines may print and a half-written page gets ejected from the printer, but that's it.

If you have an older printer (or just a cheap one) without a Cancel button, do this:

1. **Open the Printers window.**

2. **Open your printer's icon.**

   The printer's window is displayed, similar to what's shown in Figure 12-5.

Figure 12-5:
A printer's
window.

3. **Click to select the document you want to cancel.**

4. **Choose Document⇨Cancel from the menu.**

   Or, if you want to cancel all pending documents, choose Printer⇨Cancel All Documents.

5. **Wait.**

It may take a few moments for the last bit of text to print. But, seriously, if the printer continues to spew out pages at this point, just turn it off. Wait a few seconds, and then turn it back on again.

Chapter 13

Sounds Good

In This Chapter

▶ Understanding sound hardware

▶ Configuring speakers

▶ Setting up sound in Windows

▶ Changing the volume

▶ Using Windows to play sounds

▶ Playing sounds for certain events

▶ Recording sounds

Computers have always made noise. The early models couldn't help it; they used deafening teletype machines as input devices. Because the teletype featured a bell, many early computers also had bells, although they were simple speakers that droned a one-tone "bleep." Programmers then learned how to modulate the one-tone bleep into annoying multitone bleeps. Soon computers were singing like birds.

Yes, the computer can sing. It can act, too, but it can't dance; therefore, the PC is merely a "double threat." This chapter covers the audio abilities of the standard PC. That includes both its noise-making hardware as well as the hardware that can listen.

Audacious Audio

Your PC has powerful audio abilities, far beyond the feeble beeps and tinny music from computers of old. As with everything in the PC, it's a combination of hardware and software that gets these things done.

Noisy potential

All PCs include sound-generation hardware on the motherboard. This hardware has the ability to process and play digitally recorded sounds and CD music, and it has an on-board synthesizer for generating music. For most folks, that hardware is all that's needed to use the computer, play games, listen to music, and have some fun.

✔ More advanced sound hardware can be added to any PC via an expansion card. Such an upgrade is necessary only for diehard audiophiles, people who are composing their own music or using their PCs as the heart of their audio studios.

✔ If your PC lacks expansion slots or you have a laptop, you can upgrade your audio by adding an external, USB sound device, such as the Sound Blaster Audigy system.

✔ Standard PC sound is sampled at 16 bits. All you need to know is that 16 bits is a great rate, much better than 8 bits. Yes, 32 bits are available, but are necessary only for those interested in high-end audio work.

Speakers hither and thither

The PC has always come with an awful, internal speaker. It still does today, but in addition, your PC most likely came with a standard set of stereo (left-right) speakers. That's fine for basic sound, but the PC is capable of so much more.

The next step up from the basic speaker set is to add a *subwoofer*. It's a speaker box designed for low frequency sounds, which gives oomph to the bass in music or adds emphasis to the sounds in games.

Typically the subwoofer sits on the floor beneath your PC. It plugs directly into the PC's sound-out jack (see Chapter 3), and the stereo speakers plug into the subwoofer.

The final step up is to go with surround sound, similar to the sound setup for a home theater. In that configuration, you can have multiple speakers located around the computer, depending on the implementation of surround sound hardware you're using. Figure 13-1 illustrates all the possible locations for speakers in a surround sound setup, although no single configuration would use all the speakers listed. Instead, Table 13-1 lists the options.

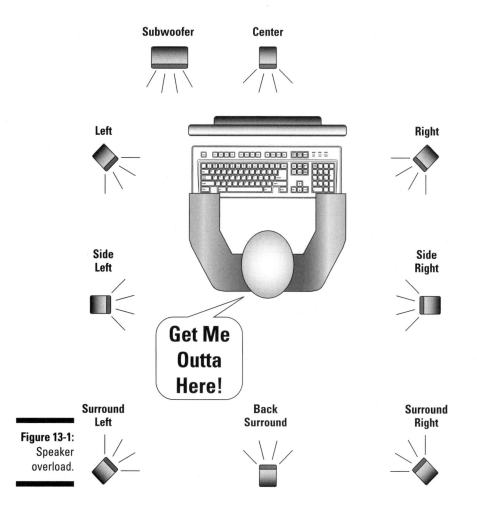

Figure 13-1:
Speaker
overload.

Table 13-1	Surround Sound Speaker Options
Surround Sound Version	*Speakers Used*
3.0	Left, Right, Back Surround
4.0	Left, Right, Surround Left, Surround Right
4.1	Left, Right, Surround Left, Surround Right, Subwoofer

(continued)

Table 13-1 *(continued)*

Surround Sound Version	Speakers Used
5.1	Left, Right, Center, Surround Left, Surround Right, Subwoofer
6.1	Left, Right, Center, Side Left, Side Right, Back Surround, Subwoofer
7.1	Left, Right, Center, Side Left, Side Right, Surround Left, Surround Right, Subwoofer

One step down from the traditional stereo speakers is to use headphones. Good headphones come with a volume control and maybe even a mute button on the same wire that connects the headphones to the PC. Better headphones come with a built-in microphone for online communications as well as game playing. Such headphones are often referred to as *headsets*. Headphones (or headsets) plug into the console's headphone jack.

- Left and right speakers are positioned on the left and right sides of the monitor as you're facing it.

- Run your speakers electrically rather than through batteries. If your speakers didn't come with an AC power adapter, you can usually buy one.

- I recommend getting speakers that have a volume control, either on the left or right speaker. Another bonus: a mute button on the speaker. Note that some high-end speaker systems have a control (wired or remote) that has the volume and mute buttons on it.

- The *x* part of a surround sound specification refers to the presence of a subwoofer: .0 means no subwoofer; .1 means one subwoofer; .2 means two subwoofers.

- Look for headphones that are comfy on your ears, with big puffy "cans."

- I don't recommend a nonstereo headset. It has only one earpiece, which is okay for online communications but lousy for game-playing.

- If you have an audio expansion card on your PC, be sure to plug the speakers into that card.

- Refer to my book *Troubleshooting Your PC For Dummies* (Wiley Publishing, Inc.) if you're having trouble hearing sounds from your PC.

Microphone options

Any cheesy microphone works on a PC. If sound quality is important to you and you're using your PC as a digital audio studio, you have to spend money on microphones and mixers and all that. But if that's not you, any old microphone does the trick.

- ✔ Two popular types of microphone are used on a PC: condenser and dynamic. *Condenser* mics can be plugged right into the PC's mic jack. *Dynamic* microphones require amplification and may work when plugged into the Line In jack, but may require a pre-amplifier for them to work best.

- ✔ If you plan to use voice over the Internet or dictation, get a headset.

Audio Control in Windows

Windows provides two locations for messing with your PC's sound system. The first is found in the Control Panel, where all things audio coalesce. The second location is in the Notification Area, where Windows has traditionally placed the volume control.

Controlling the sound hardware

Windows provides you with a Sound dialog box, in which you can make adjustments to your PC's audio software. To display the Sound dialog box from the Control Panel Home, choose Hardware and Sound and then choose Sound. From the Control Panel Classic view, open the Sound icon.

The Sound dialog box features three tabs for audio adjustment, fun, and folly:

- ✔ Playback, for controlling speakers and audio output

- ✔ Recording, for configuring microphones and such

- ✔ Sounds, for specifying which sounds play when Windows does certain things

Specific information about the Sound dialog box is covered in the sections that follow.

Configuring the speakers

To adjust the PC's speakers in Windows, follow these steps:

1. **Summon the Playback tab in the Sounds dialog box.**

   The shortcut: Right-click the Volume icon in the Notification Area and choose Playback Devices from the pop-up menu.

2. **Choose the playback device (if necessary).**

3. **Click the Configure button.**

   If the Configure button is unavailable (dimmed), there's nothing to configure; you're done.

4. **Work through the Speaker Setup Wizard to ensure that your speakers are set up properly and that everything is working.**

5. **Close the Sounds dialog box when you're done; click OK.**

Setting audio levels for a specific playback gizmo is done by following these steps but clicking the Properties button in Step 3. In the Properties dialog box, click the Levels tab to adjust output levels. This is especially handy for adjusting the volume on headphones that lack a separate volume control.

Configuring the microphone

To set up your PC's microphone, follow these steps:

1. **Open the Control Panel Home.**

   You must use the Control Panel Home here, not Classic view.

2. **Choose Ease of Access.**

3. **Choose Set Up a Microphone from beneath the Speech Recognition Options heading.**

4. **Work through the Microphone Setup Wizard to properly configure the microphone attached to your PC.**

You can configure the microphone's volume from the Sounds dialog box, on the Recording tab: Choose your microphone and click the Properties button. In the Properties dialog box, click the Levels tab to set the microphone's pick-up volume.

Switch between headphones and speakers

In some configurations you may notice that Windows forces you to choose between using external speakers and headphones. To make the choice, right-click the Volume icon in the Notification Area and choose Playback Devices from the pop-up menu. In the Sound dialog box, on the Playback tab, choose the device you want to use: speakers or headphone. Click the Set Default button to confirm your choice, and then click OK.

Adjusting the volume

To make the PC louder or quieter or just to shut it up, you can use the Volume icon in the Notification Area. Click that icon once to display the volume control slider, as shown in Figure 13-2. Use the mouse to slide the gizmo up for louder or down for quieter, or click the Mute button to turn the sound off.

Figure 13-2:
Volume
control.

✔ You can also adjust the volume on your PC's speakers, if they come with a volume control knob or remote control.

✔ Choosing Mixer from the volume control pop-up (Figure 13-2) displays a more complex volume setting window, where you can set the volume for various noise-producing gizmos and activities in Windows.

Windows Makes Noise

On the software side, Windows comes with plenty of sound tools and programs. Sounds can play during activities, and you can make your own
sounds. In fact, you can have lots of fun with Windows and sound. But keep in
mind that you're doing *important computer configuration,* not just having fun.

Playing sounds in Windows

Hearing any sound file in Windows is easy: Just double-click to open the file.
The sound plays in the Windows Media Player program.

To hear a musical CD, simply insert the CD into the PC's optical drive. Again,
Media Player appears to play the CD. (Or, you may have to choose Media
Player from a list presented in the AutoPlay dialog box.)

Use the controls in Media Player to start, stop, and repeat the audio files you
open. Media Player works just like a stereo or CD player, and the buttons are
labeled the same.

- ✔ Sound files prefer to play in the program that created them. To force a
  sound file to play in Windows Media Player, click to select the file, and
  then from the Play button's menu on the Windows Explorer toolbar,
  choose the Windows Media Player command.

- ✔ In some versions of Windows, the sounds may play using the Windows
  Media Center program rather than Windows Media Player.

- ✔ Refer to Chapter 18 for more information on Windows Media Player, as
  well as how to learn how to make the PC speak.

Assigning sounds to events

Windows can play sound files triggered by certain activities, events, actions,
or things that happen in your PC. The playground where that happens is in
the Sound dialog box, on the Sounds tab. Here's how it works:

1. **Open the Sound dialog box.**

   Refer to the directions in the section "Controlling the sound hardware,"
   earlier in this chapter.

TECHNICAL STUFF

Don't bother with this information on sound files

Sound recorded on a computer is merely raw data, digital information representing sounds in the real world. Like other data, sound is kept in a file. Windows stores such files in the Music folder found in your User Profile folder on the hard drive. Here are the most popular sound file types:

WAV: This basic *wave*, or audio, file simply contains a digital sound sampling. Most sounds you hear in Windows, or even sounds you record yourself, are WAV files, pronounced "wave" files.

WMA: The Windows Media Audio file format is a compressed form of audio file, occupying less disk space than a similar WAV file.

MP3: These audio files are compressed to take up less disk space. A typical MP3 file occupies

1MB of disk space for every minute of sound contained inside. MP3 files are the most popular form of audio file on the Internet.

MIDI: This synthesized music file format does not contain sound. Instead, the MIDI ("MID-ee") files contain instructions that play music by using the PC's music synthesizer. MIDI stands for Musical Instrument Digital Interface.

You can find other sound file formats, such as AU and AIFF and too many more to mention. The four in the preceding list are the most popular in Windows.

2. **Click the Sounds tab.**

    The dialog box sports a scrolling list of events, which are various things done by Windows or your applications. You can apply a specific sound to any of those events so that when such-and-such an event takes place, a specific sound is played.

    For example, the Critical Stop event — a bad one in Windows — is high-lighted in Figure 13-3. The sound associated with that event appears on the Sounds drop-down list as `Windows Critical Stop.wav`. That's the sound file that plays when Windows stops critically.

3. **Select an event to assign a sound to.**

    For example, select the New Mail Notification, which is the sound that plays when Outlook Express picks up new e-mail.

4. **Test the current sound, if any.**

    ▶ Test

    To test the sound, click the Test button.

5. **Assign a new sound.**

    Choose one of the preselected sounds on the Sounds list (where `Windows Critical Stop.wav` appears in Figure 13-3), or use the Browse button to fetch a sound file elsewhere on your PC's storage system. (Windows limits your choice only to WAV files, not other sound files types.)

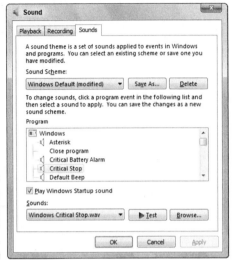

Figure 13-3:
Assigning
sounds to
events.

6. Repeat Steps 3 and 5 as you fritter the time away.

7. Click the OK button when you're done assigning sounds.

For the impatient, you can assign a whole slew of sounds all at once by choosing a theme from the Sound Scheme drop-down list. Likewise, you can save all your sound selections as a theme by using the Save As button.

✔ To remove a sound from an event, choose (None) from the top of the Sounds drop-down list.

✔ The best source for sounds is the Internet, where you can find Web page libraries full of sound samples. Go to Google (www.google.com/) and search for **Windows WAV file sounds** to find them.

✔ You can also use sounds you record yourself, assigning them to specific events in Windows. See the next section.

Recording your own sounds

For simple sound recording, you can use the Sound Recorder program that comes with Windows. Start it from the Start menu: Choose All Programs↪ Accessories↪Sound Recorder. The program sports a straightforward interface, as shown in Figure 13-4.

Figure 13-4:
The Sound
Recorder.

Recording works like this:

1. **Connect the microphone or audio device to the computer.**

   Refer to the section "Configuring the microphone," earlier in this chapter, to confirm that the PC's microphone is working.

2. **Start the Sound Recorder.**

3. **Click the Start Recording button.**

4. **Talk, "blah blah blah."**

   Or, start the phonograph, Victrola, or other sound-producing device.

5. **Click the Stop Recording button when you're done.**

6. **Use the Save As dialog box to save your audio recording to permanent storage.**

7. **Close the Sound Recorder window when you're done.**

Unlike in previous versions of Sound Recorder, you have no 1-minute time limit on your recording. Even so, Sound Recorder is a basic program good only for simple recording but not editing. If you need something better, I recommend Audacity, which is free and available on the Internet at `http://audacity.sourceforge.net`.

✔ Also unlike in previous versions of Sound Recorder, you cannot use the program to play sound files. Use Windows Media Player instead, as described earlier in this chapter.

✔ Save the files you record in your User Profile folder's Music folder. That's the general location where Windows expects to find music and audio files.

✔ The Sound Recorder saves your recordings in the Windows Media Audio File format, using the filename extension WMA. See the earlier sidebar "Don't bother with this information on sound files" for details.

✔ To record from a device other than a microphone, plug the device into the Line In or unamplified input jack. You can obtain the necessary patch cable at any Radio Shack.

✔ Refer to Chapter 18 for more information on PC dictation, which is a way of using a microphone and a computer in a more meaningful way than trying out your latest Ethel Merman-like rendition of "You've Got Mail!"

Chapter 14

Mighty Modems

. . . .

In This Chapter

▶ Understanding modems

▶ Gauging a modem's speed

▶ Adding a modem to your PC

▶ Configuring Windows to see the modem

▶ Setting up a dialup connection

▶ Connecting to a network

▶ Hanging up

. . . .

*B*ehold the strange and curious history of the modem. Today what we call a *dialup* modem was once just *the* modem. It went from being a peculiar peripheral to a vital necessity during the dawn of the Internet. Then it became a dialup modem, not to mention a *slow* modem, with the advent of faster, broadband modems.

You may still find a dialup modem nestled in your PC's bosom, but odds are greater that you use a broadband modem to communicate with the Internet and do all those so-necessary Internet things. Despite their speed, despite their official name, modems continue to be a vital part of any computer system. Welcome to the modem chapter.

What Does a Modem Do?

Modem is a combination of two technical and cumbersome words, *mo*dulator and *dem*odulator. It helps to think of a modem as a translator, converting the digital signals of a computer into audio signals that can be sent over a phone line. That's modulation. Likewise, the modem can digest audio signals and convert them back into digital information for the computer. That's demodulation.

Despite all the modulation-demodulation nonsense, a computer modem remains a simple device. In a way, it helps to think of the modem as merely a gizmo that lets your computer communicate with other computers. Whether that communications takes place over a phone line or a coaxial TV cable or through outer space, it's the modem's job to send and receive the details.

✔ High-speed modems don't modulate or demodulate any more. Those modems communicate entirely with digital signals.

✔ Of course, phone lines went all digital many years ago. A dialup modem sending digital information turns that information into audio signals, which the phone company turns back into digital information, which is then translated back into audio signals, which a receiving modem finally translates back into digital information for the computer. Yes, it's silly.

Types of Modem

In the old days, you could easily spy a modem, especially on TV or in the movies. Set designers prefer to use the old dialup acoustic coupler, into which you cradled the standard telephone receiver. A classic example can be found in the 1984 film *WarGames*. But while the acoustic coupler type of modem provides a great visual, in reality they were the worst type of modem you could use; they were slow and prone to noise leaks.

Welcome to the future!

Today, there are two popular types of computer modem:

✔ Dialup
✔ Broadband

The sections that follow provide the details on each type.

The dialup modem

Dialup modems are called such because they use standard telephone lines to transmit and receive information. That's the way modems worked for years, until the broadband modem debuted in the late 1990s.

A dialup modem can be either internal or external.

Internal dialup modems are typically part of the chipset on the motherboard, although many are also available as separate expansion cards. The advantage of an internal modem is that it doesn't take up any desk space, it uses the PC's internal power supply, and it's always on.

An external dialup modem exists as a boxy critter sitting on the desktop. It connects to the console via the serial port (traditional) or USB port. It also requires a separate power supply, which already means that a typical external modem sports two more cables than its internal counterpart. The advantages of an external modem are that you can see its many pretty lights and you can manually turn the modem off when it acts stubborn.

Identical to both types of modem is the phone cord, which connects the modem to a phone jack on the wall. Many modems also provide a second phone cord jack into which you can plug a standard telephone.

One advantage of a dialup modem is that you can use it anywhere you have telephone service. Simply plug the modem into the wall, and you can make phone calls with the computer just as you can make them yourself. No extra charges apply (well, other than long distance or other standard phone fees). Also, dialup is the least expensive way to get on the Internet.

The disadvantage of a dialup modem is that it's painfully slow when compared to other ways of accessing the Internet.

- ✔ Nearly all PCs sold come with dialup modems preinstalled.

- ✔ Most modems available today are also *fax modems*. So, whether you use a dialup modem to communicate with the Internet or not, you can still use it as a fax machine.

- ✔ The best way to use a dialup modem is with its own phone line. Just about every house or apartment can have a second line added without having to pay for extra wiring. If so, have your phone company hook up that line and use it for your modem. Why? Because —

- ✔ You can't use your phone while your modem is talking. In fact, if somebody picks up another extension on that line, it garbles the signal and may lose your connection — not to mention that the human hears a horrid screeching sound.

- ✔ Computer geeks may refer to a dialup modem as being *narrowband*, which is play on the term broadband (for faster modems).

Broadband modems

High-speed modems fall under the category of *broadband* modems. These modems connect to the Internet at top speeds. Their only downsides are that you must live in an area that provides broadband service and you pay more for access than you do with a dialup modem.

Three common broadband services are available: cable, DSL, and satellite. Each comes with its own type of modem.

Cable: This type of modem is the fastest you can buy. The only downside is that when more of your neighbors begin using their cable modems, the overall speed decreases. But at 2 a.m., your cable modem *smokes!*

DSL: This type of modem gives you fast access by taking advantage of unused frequencies in existing phone lines. The speed is limited by how far away your location is from the phone company's home office. Also, regular phones used on the same line as the DSL modem require special filters. But otherwise, next to cable, DSL gives you the fastest connection speeds.

Satellite: Combined with an outdoor antenna and a subscription to the satellite service, this is one of the fastest modem options available. Try to get a satellite modem that provides both sending and receiving abilities. Avoid satellite service that is "download only."

In all cases, you most likely connect the broadband modem to a router and use a computer network to connect the modem to your computer. Chapter 19 discusses how this is done. It's not a scary thing, but it does help provide fast Internet access to all your computers, unlike a dialup modem, which is almost always used by only one computer at a time.

✔ You can buy your own broadband modem or rent one from your Internet provider. I recommend buying the modem, especially when you know that you'll be in the same location and using the same service for at least a year.

✔ Broadband is synonymous with high-speed Internet access.

✔ DSL stands for Digital Subscriber Line. It has variations, such as ADSL and other *something*-DSL options. Your phone company knows more about this matter than I do. Basically, everyone calls it DSL, no matter what.

Modem speed

Modem speed is measured in *kilobits per second.* That's kilo*bits,* not kilo*bytes.* To give you an idea of how fast that is, 100 kilobits is about as much information as you see on a line of text in this book. If this book were appearing on your screen through your modem, one line per second, you would have a connection that flies by at 100 *kilobits per second,* or 100 Kbps.

The slowest modem you can buy now is a dialup model that whizzes out information at 56 Kbps. That modem can transmit approximately 14 pages of printed information every second.

What's a null modem?

A *null modem* isn't a modem at all. In fact, it's either a tiny adapter or a cable that works like a standard serial port (COM) cable, but with its wires reversed. Also called *twisted pair,* a null modem is designed to connect two computers for direct communications.

For example, if you're moving files from an older PC to a newer system and the older system lacks network access or a CD-R (both of which make transferring files easier), you can purchase a null modem cable at an office supply store along with file transfer software and use them to send files between the two systems.

The fastest modem you can buy (or rent) is a cable modem that whizzes along at 8,000 Kbps, also written as 8 Mbps (megabits per second). That's many, many pages of information per second, or enough speed to easily display a real-time video image with sound.

- ✔ A modem's speed rating is for comparison purposes only. Rarely do modems crank out information as fast as they're rated. It happens, but rarely. For example, a 56 Kbps dialup modem usually chugs along at about 48 Kbps. That's normal.

- ✔ Some cable companies may offer minimum speed guarantees — at a premium price.

- ✔ A DSL connection with the same sending and receiving speeds is *bidirectional.* If you have a 768 Kbps bidirectional DSL line, you're sending *and* receiving information at 768 Kbps.

- ✔ Values over 1,000 Kbps may be written as 1 Mbps, or 1 megabit per second. Sometimes, the M and K are written in lowercase: kbps and mbps.

- ✔ For dialup modems, the connection speed is displayed by Windows whenever the modem connects. You can also point the mouse at the tiny modem icon on the system tray to see your connection speed.

- ✔ You can gauge your broadband modem speed online by visiting a site such as www.dslreports.com.

Setting Up a Dialup Modem

Setting up a modem is so easy that most elected officials can do it in a matter of days. You can do it faster, of course, as an individual who is unused to making decisions in committee.

Adding an external dialup modem

External modems are easy to connect to the computer: Plug the modem into the console's serial (COM) or USB port. Plug in the power, and then connect the modem to the telephone jack on the wall. Turn on the power.

For a USB connection, Windows should instantly recognize the modem and set it up quickly. You're done. For any other type of external modem, you have to manually configure things in Windows. Here's how:

1. **From the Control Panel Home, choose Hardware and Sound and then Phone and Modem Options.**

   Or, from the Control Panel Classic view, open the Phone and Modem Options icon.

2. **If prompted, enter your location information.**

   This step is necessary the first time you set up a modem; Windows needs to know some basic dialing information.

3. **In the Phone and Modem Options dialog box, click the Modems tab.**

4. **Click the Add button.**

   A security warning appears; you cannot add a modem unless you have administrator access.

5. **Enter the administrator's password or click the Continue button.**

6. **Work through the Add Hardware Wizard to set up your modem.**

   I recommend that you not have Windows detect your modem.

7. **Click Finish to complete the wizard.**

After installing the modem, you still need to configure Windows to dial. See the section "Setting up a connection," later in this chapter.

Configuring an internal dialup modem

Internal modems are easier to configure than external modems, although adding such a modem requires that you go through the anxiety of opening the PC's console. If such a thing bothers you, simply beg someone else to do it for you.

Adding an internal modem all by yourself works by following these general steps:

1. **Shut down the PC.**

   See Chapter 4.

2. **Unplug the console.**

   You can never be too safe.

3. **Open the console.**

4. **Remove the back slot cover from the location where you plan on installing the modem.**

5. **Install the modem expansion card into an available expansion slot.**

6. **Properly secure the modem expansion card.**

7. **Close up the console.**

8. **Plug in the console.**

9. **Turn on the computer.**

Windows should recognize the new modem hardware as it starts, configuring everything else for you. You still need to tell Windows about which other computers you'll be connecting to. Refer to the later section "Setting up a connection."

Using the Dialup Modem

After the modem is set up, using it is easy: You create connection icons that you use to dial into the Internet or other computers. As long as you have the phone number to dial, it's really quite easy.

- ✔ Alas, Windows Vista doesn't come with any on-line communications programs. To connect to a BBS or other online or telnet-like service, you need *terminal* or *communications* software. I have nothing specific that I can recommend.

- ✔ Dialup modems are most often used on laptop computers for special situations. For more detailed information on using a dialup modem, including dialing rules and timeouts, see my book *Laptops For Dummies*, published by Wiley Publishing, Inc.

Setting up a connection

Using a dialup modem means that Windows must make the connection for you. Windows must take the modem "off the hook," check for a dial tone, and then dial the connection for you. Finally, it must ensure that the connection is made. It's all software, and it's all easy to set up. Follow these steps:

1. **Open the Control Panel.**

2. **From the Control Panel Home, click the link View Network Status and Tasks from beneath the Network and Internet heading; from the Control Panel Classic view, open the Network and Sharing Center icon.**

   The Network and Sharing Center window appears.

3. **From the list of Tasks (on the left), choose Set Up a Connection or Network.**

   The Set Up a Connection or Network Wizard appears.

4. **Choose the option Set Up a Dial-Up Connection.**

5. **Click the Next button.**

6. **Fill in all the information about the connection.**

   Enter the phone number and your username and password. Note that the username and password may not be the same login and password name you use for Windows.

   Be sure to give the connection a name.

7. **Click the Connect button.**

   Sit back and observe as Windows dials the connection.

After a successful connection, you see a new icon in the Notification Area. That's the "modem guys" (or so I call them). That icon is your assurance that the connection has been made, and also a subtle hint that your PC is now online. You can click on that icon to control the connection.

What you do next depends on the system you dialed. Also see "Hanging up the modem," at the end of this chapter.

Making the connection

After setting up a connection the first time, you can quickly and easily re-connect to the same system. To do so, pop up the Start button menu and choose the Connect To command. Use the Connect to a Network window to select a connection, and then click the Connect button to go online.

Also note that a dialup Internet connection is made automatically by starting any Internet program. For example, start Internet Explorer or Windows Mail and you may find Windows automatically dialing the modem to make the Internet connection.

Hanging up the modem

A dialup modem remains connected, or online, until the signal is broken, when there's no activity for a specific duration (a timeout) or when you direct Windows to hang up the modem.

To hang up the modem, locate the modem's icon in the Notification Area. Right–click the icon and choose the Disconnect command from the pop-up menu.

Chapter 15

Positive PC Power Management

●●●

In This Chapter

▶ Understanding power management

▶ Using power management in Windows

▶ Customizing a power management plan

▶ Saving your PC's battery or UPS

●●●

*O*verpopulation! Vanishing resources! Global warming! Pestilence! Toxic waste! Hooligans! Environmental catastrophes! Democrats and Republicans! Soylent Green! Pollution! Noxious bovine gas! Combine soldiers! Intoxicated Hollywood starlets! We're all doomed — doomed, I tell you!

Scare tactics aside, everyone should do their part in being good stewards of our dear planet Earth. Computer scientists know this well. Each PC is equipped with energy-saving abilities. They all fall under the broad category of *power management*, which is this chapter's topic.

What Is Power Management?

Power management is a general term used to describe the ability of computers and other appliances, such as television sets and teleportation pods, to become energy smart. That is, by using power management, a computer uses less electricity than it otherwise would. The idea is to save energy.

 In 1992, the US government created the Energy Star program, which encouraged manufacturers to design energy-efficient products. Many computer consoles and monitors of the mid-1990s sported the flashy Energy Star logo, indicating that they were designed with power saving in mind.

Because a computer is such a *smart* gizmo (for example, it can be programmed) designers took energy savings a step further and came up with even more ways to save energy in computers. Part of the motivation is heat, one of the PC's mortal enemies. Computers that use less power also generate less heat, and heat dissipation is a problem with faster microprocessors and memory chips.

Originally, the Advanced Power Management (APM) specification was implemented. It provided for a lower-power operating state for the computer's microprocessor and was used primarily in laptops to prolong battery life.

The current power management standard is the Advanced Configuration and Power Interface (ACPI). It specifies various ways the PC can reduce power consumption, including placing the microprocessor in low-power mode, disabling the monitor, halting the hard drives (which normally spin all the time), managing battery power in a laptop, as well as other more technical and trivial things.

> ✔ It's power management hardware that enables a computer to turn itself off.

> ✔ Power management also gives your PC the ability to sleep or hibernate. Refer to Chapter 4.

> ✔ One of the best ways to save power in your computer is to use an LCD monitor rather than a CRT. See Chapter 10.

> ✔ If you're really into saving the planet, be sure to properly dispose of old computer parts. Never just toss out a PC or monitor, especially the battery. Try to find a place that recycles old technology. (There be gold in them thar consoles!)

Power Management in Windows

The location in Windows for power-management control is the Power Options window, shown in Figure 15-1. To display that window, you must use the Control Panel: From the Control Panel Home, choose System and Maintenance, and then choose Power Options. From the Control Panel Classic view, open the Power Options icon to view the Power Options window.

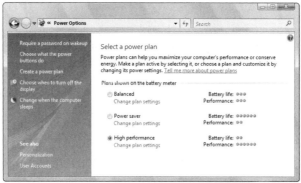

Figure 15-1:
The Power
Options
window.

The sections that follow describe PC power management using the Power Options window.

Choosing a power-management plan

The Power Options window features three preset plans for managing the power in your PC, as listed in Table 15-1. Each plan differs mainly in how two timeout values are set: for the display and for putting the computer into Sleep mode.

Table 15-1	Windows Vista Power Plans	
Plan Name	*Turn Off Display After*	*Put PC to Sleep After*
Balanced	1 hour	2 hours
Power Saver	20 minutes	1 hour
High Performance	1 hour	Never

To choose a plan, click a radio button next to the plan name. Close the Power Options window and you're done.

You can also customize any plan, or create your own plan, which is covered in the next section.

✔ Both power-saving options, turning off the display and putting the PC to sleep, are based on timeout values. The timeout takes place after a period of inactivity (no typing takes place at the keyboard and no mouse movement occurs). Whenever you then press a key or jiggle the mouse, the timeouts are reset.

✔ If the monitor timeout is less than the screen saver timeout, you never see your PC's screen saver in action. See Chapter 10.

✔ Power management doesn't turn the monitor off; it merely suspends the video signal to the monitor. An energy-smart monitor detects the lack of signal and then automatically enters a low-power state. This is often indicated by the monitor's power lamp, which dims, glows another color, or blinks while the monitor is in power-saving mode. (Also see Chapter 10 for more information on computer monitors.)

✔ See Chapter 4 for more information on Sleep mode.

Creating your own plan

Any power-management plan can be modified: Simply click the link below the plan labeled Change Plan Settings. But rather than do that, you should create your own, custom power plan, one ideally suited to your power-savings needs. Here's how:

1. **Open the Power Options window per the directions listed earlier in this chapter.**

2. **On the left side of the window, choose the link Create a Power Plan.**

3. **Choose an existing plan on which to base your plan: Balanced, Power Saver, or High Performance.**

   Descriptions of all three plan are offered in the preceding section.

4. **Enter your plan name in the Plan Name text box.**

5. **Click the Next button.**

6. **Choose a timeout value for the display.**

   Click the menu button and choose a timeout value.

7. **Choose a timeout value to put the computer to sleep.**

   Yes, the timeout value for sleeping the computer must be greater than the turn-off-display value.

   Choose Never to disable a power-saving feature.

   Refer to the next section for more information if you see two columns of timeout menu buttons rather than one.

8. **Click the Create button to create and implement your plan.**

The new, custom plan appears in the list of available power-saving plans, as shown in the Power Options dialog box. You can further modify the custom plan by choosing the link below it, Change Plan Settings.

Power-saving options for battery-powered PCs

If you have a laptop or are using a desktop PC with a UPS (Uninterruptible Power Supply) and the UPS is connected to the PC by a USB cable, the power-plan settings information you see in the Edit Plan Settings window sports *two* columns of options rather than one, as shown in Figure 15-2.

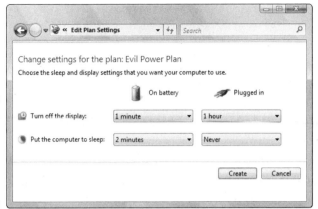

Figure 15-2:
Power-plan
settings
for battery-
powered
PCs.

The first column is labeled On Battery. The settings made there are active when a laptop is being powered by its batteries or when a desktop PC is powered by a UPS during a power outage.

The second column of settings is labeled Plugged In. Those settings are for when the computer is using power from the wall socket. That's the only power settings column that appears (untitled) when you have a PC that doesn't have a battery or battery-backed-up power source.

Obviously, you want more power savings when your PC is running on batteries. For a laptop, changing the display and sleep values to something quick makes sense, but not too short. For a PC running on a UPS, my advice is to sleep the computer as soon as possible: Set the timeout values to 1 or 2 minutes, as shown in Figure 15-2.

✔ When your desktop PC is running "on battery," the power is off and the only thing running the PC is the UPS. That doesn't mean that you can still work; it means that you should turn off the PC immediately. By setting the PC sleep time to something less than a few minutes, you help your computer survive the power outage.

✔ Also see Chapter 4 for more information on UPSs.

✔ For more information on using your laptop and managing its battery life, see my book *Laptops For Dummies* (Wiley Publishing, Inc.).

Part III
It's a Digital Life

In this part . . .

Despite the PC being more popular today than ever before, many folks still want to limit its abilities. They see computers as business machines, word processors, or kids' game-playing boxes. But the computer is O so much more, especially here at the dawn of the new millennium.

The PC is now more versatile than it ever was. In fact, it's quickly becoming the indispensable center of activity for your 21st century lifestyle. The PC won't merge with your telephone, but it will help you communicate. The PC won't become your television, but it will help you use the TV in new and useful ways. As the world becomes high tech, the PC once again proves its flexibility and necessity as the center of your digital life.

Chapter 16

Picture This

· ·

In This Chapter

▶ Getting images from your digital camera

▶ Scanning flat stuff

▶ Understanding resolution

▶ Working with various graphics file formats

▶ Converting graphics files

▶ Editing your pictures

▶ Looking at images

· ·

*T*hose of us who cannot draw or paint are extremely grateful for photography. Imagine the utter boredom you would go through as you stood for hours before the Eiffel Tower while Dad finished painting you and the family. But with a camera, *click!* — you're done. Not only that, with a *digital camera*, you can click, preview, and get an endless supply of do-overs if you're disappointed with the result. Ah, technology is grand.

Your PC may not take digital pictures, but it can certainly help you to manage them. The digital camera and your computer work hand in hand to provide a complete electronic photo studio. Inside the PC, you can view, print, e-mail, or edit pictures to your heart's content. In fact, I've found the Photoshop Diet to be an extremely effective, if not realistic, way to present a skinnier me. But I ramble. Welcome to the digital imaging chapter.

Getting Images into the PC

Sure, you can create your own images on the computer. Windows comes with a Paint program. Even those of us lacking the talent to draw a stick man by a lollipop tree can use Paint to doodle the time away. But more often than not, the images you have on your computer come from the real world. The two most common gizmos for getting real-world images into the computer are a digital camera and a scanner. How to get those images out of those devices and into the PC has been a mystery for the ages — until now!

✔ Scanners and digital cameras use the same technology. The main difference is that a digital camera is portable and uses a lens to focus the image.

✔ Digital cameras and scanners come with special software. I recommend using that software, which is often better than the simple tools available with Windows.

The digital camera

As far as your PC is concerned, the most important thing you can do with your digital camera is to get the images from the camera into the PC. You have two choices:

The cable catastrophe: The most awkward option for getting images from a digital camera is to connect the camera to your PC by using a USB cable. The images must then be "beamed" into the PC from the camera, or the camera may appear as a "disk drive" in the Computer window. Either way, this process isn't the most efficient way to snag the images.

The memory card method: The best way of liberating images from your digital camera is to remove its memory card and plug the card into the PC. Upon plugging in the memory card, you're greeted by an AutoPlay dialog box, as shown in Figure 16-1, or perhaps some picture management program, such as Windows Photo Gallery or Windows Media Center, automatically appears. If so, you're ready to go.

Figure 16-1: Importing images from a memory card.

When you see the AutoPlay dialog box, you need to choose a program to use for managing the images. You most likely see the options shown in Figure 16-1, including perhaps any custom software you've installed. I recommend that you use one of the following import options:

Import Pictures using Windows. All images are read from the memory card and transferred to the PC's hard drive. The images are organized and can be viewed by using the Windows Photo Gallery program.

Import Pictures and Videos to My Computer: By running a special import wizard, this option gives you the most control over which images are copied to the PC. It's available only on versions of Windows Vista that come with the Microsoft Digital Image Starter Edition.

Open Folder to View Files: A Windows Explorer window opens, allowing you to view files stored on the memory card. You can then manually copy the image files from the memory card to your PC's hard drive.

No matter which of these options you choose, the final result is that the images are stored on the PC's hard drive — the best place for long-term storage of anything. After the images are on the hard drive, you can view them, edit them, print them, e-mail them, store them to a CD, or otherwise manage and mangle them.

✔ Additional options may be available in the AutoPlay dialog box, including custom software you've installed on your PC. If you use that custom software, ensure that it copies the images from the memory card to the PC's hard drive.

✔ Store images in the Pictures folder found in your main User Account folder. See Chapter 25 for information on the Pictures folder. Refer to Chapter 26 on how to copy files.

✔ Most digital cameras store their images on the memory card in a folder named DCIM, for *d*igital *c*amera *im*ages. Open that folder and you'll find additional folders in which the digital images are stored.

✔ The images sucked in from the digital camera are stored on your PC's hard drive as *files*. See the section "Graphics file types," later in this chapter.

✔ You don't really need to use the PC to print digital images. Many photo printers can read memory cards from digital cameras and print the images directly. See Chapter 12 for more information on printers.

✔ Another non-PC option is to drop off the digital camera's memory card at a photo place. The photo place will print the pictures for you "in about an hour" and probably give you a CD of the images to sweeten the deal.

✔ Refer to Chapter 9 for more information on memory card storage.

The scanner

Scanners are nifty little devices that work like photocopiers. Rather than make a copy, the scanner takes the original and creates a graphics image that's then stored in your computer. So, in a way, the scanner itself is the device that gets the images into your computer; no extra transfer work is necessary.

Figure 16-2 illustrates the typical computer scanner, not because you may be unfamiliar with what it looks like, but more because I really like that illustration. Most scanners are thin (like the model in the picture), use the USB interface, and have handy function buttons that let you immediately scan, copy, fax, e-mail, or read text from whatever item is placed on the scanner glass.

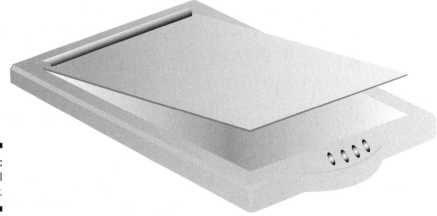

Figure 16-2:
A typical
scanner.

Basically, scanner operation works like this:

1. **Place the material to be scanned into the scanner, just as though you were using a photocopier.**

2. **Turn the scanner on, if necessary.**

3. **Press the scan button on the scanner, which is the button to acquire a digital image; or, if the scanner lacks a button, run the scanner software in Windows that acquires a digital image.**

   You might make additional adjustments here, for example, when scanning transparencies or slides.

4. **Preview the scan.**

5. **Select the scan area.**

   Use a zoom or magnification tool to ensure that you select the proper portion of the scanner glass.

6. **Set other options.**

   For example, set the type of scan: color, grayscale, or document. You can also set resolution, although the scanner software probably makes the proper adjustment for you. (If not, 200 dpi is good.)

7. **Scan the image.**

8. **Save the image to disk.**

   See the section "Graphics file formats," later in this chapter, on graphics file formats, although choosing the JPEG, or JPG, file format is a good one.

Why bother understanding resolution?

When you deal with digital images, the topic of *resolution* rears its ugly head. Resolution deals with dots, specifically the number of *dots per inch*, or *dpi*. Each dot represents the smallest part of an image, a teeny splotch of color.

Resolution comes into play in two areas: when an image is created and when an image is reproduced.

You set resolution when you take a digital picture or scan an image. The resolution determines how much detail, or visual information, the image contains. Simply put, an image with 400 dpi resolution contains twice the information of the same image with 200 dpi; 400 is double 200. But whether that resolution is important really depends on the output device, or where the image ends up.

For example, a PC monitor has a resolution of 96 dpi. If you scan a 4x6 photograph at 100 dpi and then display that image on the PC's monitor, it appears at nearly exactly its original size and detail. If you scan the same photograph at 200 dpi, however, it appears twice as large when displayed on the monitor. That's because the image's 200 dpi is more than twice the 96 dpi of the monitor.

A printer's resolution can often be 300 dpi or higher. So an image taken at 100 dpi prints at one-third its original size when the printer uses 300 dpi output resolution. If you resize the image to print larger, the result is jagged and boxy; you cannot create pixels where none exists.

To get the best results, you must set an image's original resolution based on its eventual output. When sending an e-mail image, one that will only be displayed on a monitor, 100 dpi is a fine resolution. When taking a photograph you plan on printing, you need to do some thinking. Given that the printer's resolution is 300 dpi, you have to scan a 4x5 image at 300 dpi to get good output at 4x5 inches. But to print the image to 8x10, you have to scan the image at 600 dpi for it to enlarge well.

When working with photographs, you must consider the entire image area. So, to get a decent 4x5 printed image, you have to calculate 4x300 vertical dpi by 5x300 horizontal dpi. That works out to 1200 by 1500 dpi, or 1,800,000 dots. There are one million dots in a *megapixel;* therefore, a camera setting of 2 megapixels is okay for printing a standard 4x5 image on a 300 dpi printer. A higher resolution setting, of course, yields better results.

An alternative to saving the image to disk is to open the image in a photo- or image-editing application, where the image can be further refined or edited. See the section "Editing images," later in this chapter, for thoughts and suggestions.

✔ Yes, scanning an image is slow and tedious, but it's one of the best ways to get your existing photographs or slides copied into the PC's digital world.

✔ You can scan only film negatives or transparencies (slides) when the scanner is equipped with a negative/transparency adapter.

✔ Scanners come with software. You usually get three packages. The first is a utility that lets you use the scanner to scan in an image. The second is typically some type of photo-editing program, such as Adobe Photoshop Elements. The third is an OCR program, which is used to translate written documents into editable text.

✔ OCR stands for *optical character recognition*. It's the only way to read text from a scanned item and be able to edit that text. (When you scan text as an image, you cannot edit the text.)

✔ When you have a lot of images to scan, such as a lifetime of vacation slides, consider sending the slides out to a scanning service. No, this isn't cheap, but consider what your time is worth and how much you really need to digitize your pictures.

✔ Those buttons on the scanner can be handy. For instance, I use the Copy button all the time to make quick copies (my office doesn't have a photocopier). The only reservation I have with the buttons is that the tiny icons by the buttons are confusing; if need be, use a Sharpie and write down the button's function in English.

Working with Graphics Files

Information is stored on your PC's permanent storage devices in the form of *files*. The whole subject of files is a necessary one if you plan on enjoying an amiable, long-term relationship with your PC. I highly recommend that you consider reading Chapter 24 to bone up on the subject. For now, the topic is graphics files, or the information chunks in which the computer stores images and pretty pictures.

Graphics file formats

A graphical image saved to disk doesn't just become a "graphics file." No, the digital information can be saved in a variety of graphics file formats. This was done not only to annoy you but also because of the evolution of PC graphics, not to mention the needs of various graphics programs and gizmos, like digital cameras.

Here are the popular PC graphics file formats:

JPG: The Joint Photographic Experts Group file format is currently the most popular format for storing digital images. JPG, or JPEG, uses compression to ensure that images don't consume too much disk space or take too long to send on the Internet. Sadly, the image quality isn't as good when the image is compressed. Also the JPG compression is *lossy,* which means that each time a JPG image is compressed, some information is lost in the translation.

PNG: The Portable Network Graphics format, also known as *ping,* was designed to replace GIF (see the end of the following list) as a better way to store images on the Internet. PNG images are also compressed, and the compression is better than JPG, which makes PNG an ideal standard, although JPG is still the top dog.

TIFF: The Tagged Image File Format graphics standard is ideal for storing graphics images long term as well as for exchanging graphics images between photo- or image-editing applications. TIFF images tend to be rather large, which makes them impractical for the Internet or e-mail. But the great detail offered by TIFF images makes them ideal for use in professional applications, for publishing or archiving.

Some other common graphics file formats include:

BMP: The Windows Bitmap file format is used primarily in Windows, although not as commonly as in years gone by. The image files are large and therefore impractical for use on the Internet or in e-mail. Avoid using BMP for anything other than simple doodle files you create in Paint. TIFF is a better file format choice for images used in applications or for storing uncompressed images long term.

CRW: The Camera Raw format is an uncompressed, unmodified image taken at high resolutions in certain high-end digital cameras. It's preferred for professional photographs and people who need the purest, rawest images possible. Unless you're doing professional work, you can avoid this format.

GIF: The Graphics Interchange Format is an older, simple format for storing simple color images. It was (and still is) popular on the Internet because the file size is small, but the files don't contain enough information to make them worthy of modern digital imaging.

There are other graphics file formats as well, but most of them deal with drawing or vector graphics. For digital imaging, the file formats in these lists are the most commonly used.

✔ A graphics file of a specific format uses the graphics file format as its filename extension. For example, IMAGE.JPG is a graphics file, named IMAGE, of the JPG type.

✔ The image file format is set when you create and save an image to disk. Use the File⇨Save As command and choose the image type from the File Type part of the Save As dialog box. (See Chapter 24.) You may also see a File⇨Export command to save images as a specific file type.

✔ Refer to Chapter 25 for information on the Pictures folder, where Windows Vista insists that you save your graphics files.

✔ Also see "Changing graphics file types," later in this — why, It's right here!

Changing graphics file types

Occasionally, the need arises to convert a graphics image from one type to another. For example, you may have been silly and saved your digital camera images as TIFF files. Although that file format has its purposes, and TIFF images are by no means shoddy, they're just *too freakin' huge* to send as e-mail attachments. Instead, you're better off converting the TIFF image to JPG. Here's how I do that:

1. **Open the folder window containing the image file icon.**

   See Chapter 25 for information on folders.

2. **Select the image icon.**

3. **On the toolbar, click the menu button by either the Open or Preview toolbar button.**

   The menu button is just to the right of the toolbar button, adorned with a down-pointing triangle.

4. **Choose the Paint program from the menu.**

   The graphics image opens in the Paint program.

5. **Choose File⇨Save As.**

   The Save As dialog box appears. (See Chapter 24 for more information on the Save As dialog box.)

6. **From the Save As Type menu button, choose JPEG (*.jpg, *.jpeg, *.jfif).**

   Or, to save the image in another file format, choose that format from the Save As Type menu button.

7. **Click the Save button.**

   The file is saved under the new format.

8. **Close the Paint program: choose File⇨Exit.**

If you have a more sophisticated graphics program, like Photoshop Elements, you can use it, rather than Paint, to make the conversion. Or, you can use any of the popular graphics conversion programs available, none of which I can name off the top of my head.

Editing images

You can do some very simple things to images after you get them inside your PC. You can employ the Power Of The Computer to refine and perfect any photograph or image. The actual tools and specific commands vary from program to program. But on a simple level, here are the tools you can use:

Crop: To crop an image is to reduce its size, just like an angry teenage girl would use a pair of scissors to remove her former boyfriend from a picture, although without the angst or meandering lengthy phone calls. See Figure 16-3.

Figure 16-3:
An image is cropped.

Resize/scale: Because the image is stored in the computer, you can change its size, smaller or larger (see Figure 16-4). Making an image smaller is easy; digital images reduce well. But enlarging an image requires that its resolution be high enough to handle the bigger size.

Figure 16-4:
An image is
resized.

Note that there's a difference between resizing an image and using a Zoom or magnifier tool. The Zoom tool merely makes the image appear larger or smaller on the monitor. Resizing or scaling an image changes its size, specifically its dpi (resolution).

Adjust contrast/brightness: You can adjust an image's tone by using a contrast/brightness tool. Contrast can modify the differences between the dark and light parts of an image, and brightness makes the overall image darker or lighter (see Figure 16-5).

Low ← Brightness → High

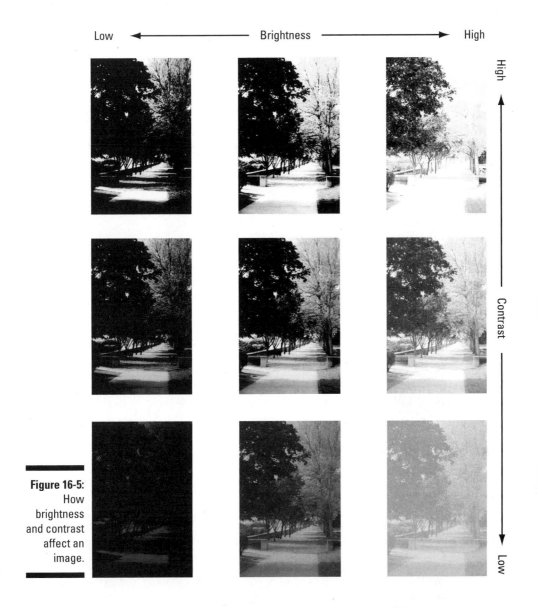

Figure 16-5:
How
brightness
and contrast
affect an
image.

In addition to contrast and brightness, many photo editing programs sport color and tone adjustments. For example, you can fix the fading blues or reds of older photographs you scan in by using a tool for fixing color tone.

Flip/rotate: Even the most basic photo editing program sports flip and rotate tools. As their names suggest, flip and rotate allow you to change the image's orientation. See Figure 16-6.

Original image   Flip vertical   Original image   Rotate 90°

Figure 16-6:
An image is
flipped,
rotated,
folded,
spindled,
and
mutilated.

Flip horizontal   Flip horizontal   Rotate 180°   Rotate 270°
                   and vertical

In addition to these basic tools, photo editing programs come with a host of image editing, fixing, and repairing tools — plus perhaps some tools that can stretch or exaggerate facial features or add cartoon bubbles to an image. Oh, you can have so much fun with your pictures on a PC.

Viewing images in Windows

Windows Vista is the best version of Windows for viewing files. In fact, you don't even need a program: Simply change the icon size in any folder window and you see a tiny preview, or *thumbnail,* of images stored in your PC.

To view any specific image, obey these steps:

1. **Select the image's icon.**
2. **Click the Preview button on the toolbar.**

A program then displays the image; the specific program that's used depends on which software you have installed in Windows. You can choose a specific preview program by using the menu button just to the right of the Preview button.

✔ To view all files in a folder, click the Slide Show button on the toolbar. That runs the Slideshow program and displays the images one after the other.

✔ You can also select a specific folder to use as a screen saver. The image files in that folder appear on the display when the screen saver is activated. See Chapter 10 for more information.

✔ Images shown using the Extra Large Icons, Large Icons, Medium Icons, or Tiles options from the toolbar's View button menu appear as thumbnails.

Chapter 17

PC TV

In This Chapter

▶ Watching TV on your PC

▶ Using Windows Media Center

▶ Checking the program guide

▶ Recording programs

▶ Creating a video DVD

▶ Managing your TV recordings

▶ Using a web camera

▶ Understanding video file types

▶ Editing video

*O*h, I remember the days not so long ago when a television set was a necessary part of a personal computer system. Many of the old, original hobbyist microcomputers, such as the Commodore 64, used a standard color TV as a monitor. Eventually computers became "serious" and demanded their own, exclusive, expensive monitors. So who would have guessed, some 25 years after the PC revolution, that computers and televisions would meet again? But this time it's the TV that needs a PC, not the other way around.

This chapter covers an interesting part of your digital life, where your PC deftly and masterfully consumes the television set. Not only can you use the PC for viewing and creating digital video, but your PC can also become the locus of your home's visual entertainment system. It's what they call the *media PC*, the subject of this chapter.

How to Turn a PC into a TV

As with all computer activities, to do television on your PC, you need a combination of hardware and software. The software comes with certain editions of Windows Vista, and it's called the Windows Media Center. You use Windows Media Center to view and record television, as well as do other media things (music and pictures).

For the hardware, you need to equip your PC with a TV tuner. It's a gizmo that pumps the television signal into the computer. The TV tuner comes as an external device, or it can dwell on an expansion card installed inside the console.

The TV tuner accepts its input from a standard coaxial video cable. External tuners connect to the PC by using the USB port. Some TV tuners may have extra jacks for plugging in a TV or accessing FM radio. The feature list of these gizmos, as well as their prices, varies widely.

- ✔ There's a difference between Windows Media Player and Windows Media Center. Windows Media Player is an audio and music program. Windows Media Center does what Windows Media Player does, but also works with TV, FM radio, pictures, and digital video.

- ✔ The TV tuner requires a television signal, which is provided by whichever cable or satellite TV service you subscribe to. Using the TV tuner with your PC doesn't add to the cost of your cable or satellite subscription, and there's no need to alert your provider or alarm them in any way about your using a TV tuner with your computer.

- ✔ Yes, forget about those expensive digital video recorders (DVR) and similar TV-recording gizmos. When you buy a TV tuner, you're getting the best that those devices have to offer, plus you pay only once to have a service that others pay for monthly.

- ✔ Some TV tuners are HDTV capable. Consider getting one if you have HDTV or digital cable in your area.

- ✔ Don't confuse a TV tuner with a video capture card. A *video capture card* reads a video signal from some video gizmo, such as a video camera or VCR, and records, or *captures,* the signal, storing it digitally inside the computer. A TV tuner is used for watching and recording cable or satellite TV on your PC.

Connecting a TV tuner

Installing the TV tuner is a snap, although I still recommend that you consult with the documentation that came with whichever TV tuner you're using. Generally speaking, you simply plug the TV tuner into the same coaxial cable you plug into the TV. If you have an external TV tuner, plug it into a power supply as well as into the PC console.

Perform any needed software setup per the directions that came with the TV tuner. Sometimes, the software must be installed before the hardware, sometimes afterward, sometimes it doesn't matter.

After doing additional setup, or running a configuration program (per the documentation that came with the TV tuner), you're ready to configure Windows Media Center, as described in the next section.

Configuring Windows Media Center

After connecting your PC to a TV tuner and connecting that TV tuner to your cable or satellite TV, you're ready for the software side of configuration. You do this by running the Windows Media Center for the first time.

Windows Media Center asks you a few questions about your TV tuner and your television setup, such as which cable company you're using and your location. It does this so that information about the cable TV schedule can be downloaded into the PC. The Media Center uses the TV schedule not only as a program guide but also to assist in the recording of programs off the air.

After the Media Center is configured, you can begin watching TV on your PC.

Something's on Television!

Feeling the urge to watch television on your computer is satisfied by simply running the Windows Media Center program: From the Start button menu, choose All Programs⇨Windows Media Center.

The Media Center sports a simple interface, which scrolls up and down for major media categories and then left to right for subcategories (see Figure 17-1). The whole thing is designed to be easily viewed on a TV set and manipulated using a television remote.

On the whole, the Media Center is painless to figure out. For the purposes of "TV on your PC," the sections that follow concentrate on the TV + Movies part of the menu and on recording television, which is one of Media Center's strengths.

✔ The Media Center is designed to look good on a television, which has a lower resolution than a standard computer monitor.

✔ You can maximize the Media Center window to view television full screen on your PC monitor; click the Maximize button in the window's upper right corner. Or, you can view TV in a window.

✔ Some special wireless keyboards work directly with the Media Center. Again, they're designed for use with a home media center setup, where the computer is tied into a television monitor and the keyboard sits on a coffee table across the room. At least that's the way it looks in the magazine ads.

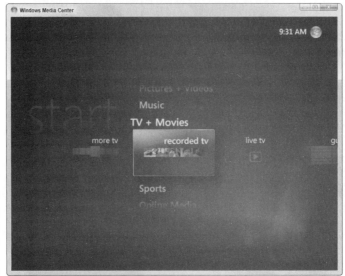

Figure 17-1:
Windows
Media
Center.

Seeing what's on

The Live TV subcategory under TV + Movies lets you watch television on your computer just like on TV. Here are some tips and suggestions to boost the power of your TV watching:

- ✔ Change the channel by typing a number on the keyboard. There's no need to press Enter; just type the number.

- ✔ Right-click the screen to see a special pop-up menu listing various options for whatever you're doing.

- ✔ Right-click and choose Program Info to get more information about what you're watching.

- ✔ If you miss the start of the show and want to see it again, right-click the screen and choose Program Info, and then on the next menu, choose Other Showings.

- ✔ Moving the mouse redisplays the recording and play controls, as shown in Figure 17-2.

- ✔ To pause live TV, move the mouse to display the recording and play controls and click the Pause button. Click the Play button to resume, or the Fast Forward button to catch up with real time.

- ✔ Some channels feature "restricted content." The broadcaster doesn't allow you to view (or record) the information on that channel. This is not a parental-control issue but rather a copyright issue with the broadcaster.

Menu   Maximize

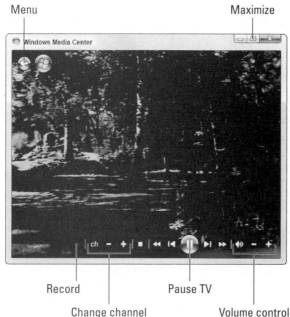

Figure 17-2:
Watching
live TV.

Record   Pause TV

Change channel   Volume control

Seeing what's on next

The Media Center downloads information about your cable or satellite TV service and creates its own guide. To see the guide, choose Guide under TV + Movies. You can scroll through the entire channel lineup, move up and down, and even check times in the future by scrolling the list to the right.

- ✔ To check a specific channel's lineup, click on the channel to select it. You can then peruse the programming for that channel up to one week in advance.

- ✔ Click a program name to see a more detailed description. You'll find, along with the advanced description, a button to record the program, a button to record the entire series, plus a button to check other showings of the program.

Recording on the fly

You can easily record anything you see on TV in the Windows Media Center. Simply click the Record button (refer to Figure 17-2) while you're watching live TV.

To stop recording, click the Record button again. When you stop, you're taken to the Recorded TV part of the Movies + TV menu. Just choose Live TV from the menu to continue watching the show. See the later section "Watching Recorded TV" for more information about recorded TV.

Scheduling a recording

There are many ways to record a program in the Media Center. In addition to recording on the fly (in the preceding section), you can do any of the following:

Record a show found in the guide. Use the guide as covered in the earlier section "Seeing what's on next." Click to select a show you want to record, and then click the Record button. The program listed in the guide then sports a red Record dot, which is your clue that a program has been scheduled for recording.

Record a future broadcast of the current show. The mantra "nothing is on TV" is true mostly because a lot of television consists of shows broadcast over and over. Therefore, if you miss recording a program, you can check for another showing and schedule it to be recorded. To record a full copy of the show you're watching now, follow these steps:

1. **Right-click the Media Center window.**
2. **Choose Program Info.**

   A second menu appears.
3. **Choose Other Showings.**
4. **Scroll through the list to find the future showing you want.**
5. **Click the future showing.**
6. **Choose Record from the menu.**

Record a series. To record all programs in a series, such as your favorite show every Saturday night, follow these steps:

1. **Choose from the guide.**
2. **Click Record Series.**

Every instance of that show is then flagged for future recording. Note that recording all instances of a show consumes a hefty amount of disk space. See the later section "Purging recorded TV" before it's too late!

✔ There's no need to set an "end time" when scheduling a show to record in the Media Center. Thanks to the guide you downloaded from the Internet, Media Center knows when a program starts and ends. The recording starts one minute before the program starts, and it ends about three minutes after the program finishes — automatically.

✔ Recorded TV is, logically, kept in the Recorded TV subcategory under TV + Movies. See the next section.

Watching recorded TV

The Media Center stores the TV shows you record, as well as information on upcoming recordings, in the Recorded TV subcategory under Movies + TV. Already recorded programs are listed, left to right: Point the mouse at a recording to highlight it and see more information; click a recording to see a menu, from which you can choose Play to view the recording.

To view upcoming or scheduled recordings, click the View Scheduled item at the top of the Recorded TV area. The schedule appears as a list that you can sort by date, title, series, or history.

One outstanding benefit of watching recorded TV is that you can skip the commercials. Use the Next Chapter button to skip ahead to the next break.

Burning a DVD from recorded TV

You can create a video DVD of the shows and programs you record. It's really cinchy; follow these steps:

1. **Insert a DVD-R or DVD+R disc into your PC's DVD drive.**

   Yes, it must be a recordable DVD drive.

   I prefer DVD-R disks because they're more compatible with DVD players.

2. **Close the AutoPlay dialog box if it appears.**

   Click the X button in the AutoPlay dialog box's upper right corner.

3. **Record a show by following the directions offered earlier in this chapter.**

4. **In the Media Center, choose Movies + TV and then Recorded TV.**

5. **Click to select the show you want to burn to disc.**

6. **From the menu that's displayed, choose Burn CD/DVD.**

7. **Click the Yes button if you see a prompt warning about media playback being stopped.**

8. **If you're prompted that a lower quality must be chosen to fit the show on the media, click Yes or OK to proceed.**

9. **Choose Video DVD to create a disc that can be played like any other video. Choose Data DVD for a disc that can be viewed only by a computer.**

10. **Click the Next button.**

11. **(Optional) Name the disk.**

    The program's recorded name is preselected for you.

12. **Click the Next button.**

13. **Click the Burn DVD button.**

14. **Click Yes to confirm.**

15. **Wait while the disc is created.**

    (Optional) Click the OK button to go off and do other things with your PC while the disc is being created. Note that some discs take an awfully long time to burn.

16. **Remove the disc from the PC.**

    Burned discs are automatically ejected.

17. **Click the Burn button to create a duplicate disc, or click Done and you're finished.**

I recommend labeling the disc. I use a Sharpie and write the program name, the time, and the date I made the disc. Then I put the disc into a special disc envelope for long-term keeping.

After burning the disc, consider removing the program from the Recorded TV library. That way, you have more hard disk space on your PC for other information.

✔ The program may not fit on a disc. If so, the Media Center tells you so. In that case, you cannot make a DVD, but you can still view the recorded show on your PC.

✔ You can find disc envelopes at any office supply store.

✔ The DVD you create is for your own purposes only. You cannot make additional copies for friends, nor can you sell the discs you create.

✔ Also see Chapter 28 for information on creating data DVDs.

Purging recorded TV

Yes, video on your PC is one of those things that gobbles up disk space faster than a teenager consumes cell phone minutes. But the Media Center isn't foolish about using disk space. Most programs you record stick around as long as you have room for them. So, the more you record, the less you keep.

The best way to keep a program you've recorded is to make a DVD, as described in the preceding section. Otherwise, you can manually purge older shows to make more room for future shows. The following activities assume that you're using the Media Center and have the Recorded TV area visible:

✔ **Remove a recorded show.** To remove a show that you recorded already, click to select that show. From the menu that appears, choose Delete. Click the Yes button to confirm.

✔ **Remove a future recording.** To remove a show you've scheduled to record in the future, choose the View Scheduled item from the top of the Recorded TV window. Click to select the show. From the menu that appears, choose Do Not Record. The show is removed from the schedule list.

✔ **Remove a series.** To remove an individual episode from a series, follow the steps in the preceding paragraph. Otherwise, choose View Scheduled and then click to select any episode of the series. From the menu that appears, choose Series Info. Finally, click the Cancel Series button and then Yes to confirm.

Unlike what NBC did to *Star Trek* in 1969, when you cancel a series you merely direct Windows Media Center to not record the series; the series still airs on television.

If you don't delete a recording, then Media Center keeps the recording until your PC gets low on hard disk space. At that time, older shows are removed first to make room for newer recordings.

Moving Pictures

In addition to watching TV, you can use your computer to help you create or view your own videos. It's called *digital video,* and it's *another* way you can extend your PC's operation into the real world.

Digital video involves using a video camera to record videos — moving images. The video camera, or digital video, isn't the same thing as a digital camera, which usually captures only still images. (Some digital cameras can record brief videos). The information in the following sections is about digital video only; for information on digital cameras, see Chapter 16.

It's live, and it's living on top of your monitor!

The simplest digital camera you can get for your PC is the desktop video camera, also referred to as a *web camera.* Most of these cameras are fist-sized, although often smaller, and they commonly attach to the top of the monitor. A USB cable makes the connection with the PC.

You can check the connection by using the Control Panel. From the Control Panel Home, choose Hardware and Sound and then Scanners and Cameras. From the Control Panel Classic view, open the Scanners and Cameras icon.

What you can do with the web camera depends on the software available. Most of the common tasks include participating in video chat (or the professional term *video conference*), uploading images to the Web as a *webcam*, or simply capturing images to e-mail or save for later use.

> ✔ Web cameras come with a host of sample programs that let you test the gamut of their capabilities.

> ✔ I have a webcam outside of my office, although it needs a software update. Hopefully, it will be up and running when this book goes to press. Check out my webcam by visiting www.wambooli.com/fun/live/.

Video file types

As with anything stored on a computer, moving images are saved to disk as files. And, like other media files (pictures and sound), you have a whole host of file formats to choose from, all depending on which program saved the video file, which type of compression is being used, and other boring details. Generally speaking, the following types of video files are popular in the computer world:

AVI: The Audio Video Interleave file uses an older video and audio format designed by Microsoft a long, long time ago. You may still find AVI files on the Internet, although they're quickly vanishing from the scene.

MOV: The MOV file, used by Apple's QuickTime player, can store not only videos but also audio information. MOV is quite popular on the Internet, although you need to obtain a free copy of QuickTime to view or hear MOV files on your PC: http://www.apple.com/quicktime.

MPEG: The Motion Pictures Experts Group is a general compression format for both video and audio. Occasionally, you may see video files with the MPG or MPEG extension, although commonly the MPEG compression is used by other formats, such as WVM and MOV.

WMV: The Windows Media Video format is the most popular video format used in Windows and pretty common on the Internet as well.

About that "codec" thing

When you deal with media on a computer, such as audio or video stored in a file, you often encounter the word *codec*. Like *modem*, codec is a combination of two words — *compressor-dec*ompressor. A codec decompresses compressed information stored in a media file so that you can be entertained or enlightened.

A variety of codecs are used to encode and decode media information. The problem with the variety is that your PC doesn't come with all the codecs needed for every type of media file. So, when you go to view a certain media file, you see a message saying that a codec is unavailable or prompting you to visit some Web page to download a codec. And that's where you can get into trouble.

My best advice is to be very cautious about installing codecs. Often, the bad guys disguise a malevolent program as a codec required to view some media file, typically pornography. Installing that false codec is detrimental to your PC.

I'm not saying that all codecs are evil. Many are good and required in order to view certain media files. But ensure that you obtain codecs only from reliable sources, such as brand-name Web sites or from Microsoft directly.

Other formats exist, of course, but the ones just listed are the most common.

- ✔ Most video files use the file format acronym as their filename extension. See Chapter 24 for more information on filename extensions.

- ✔ Video files are *huge!* They're not only the most complex type of files, they gobble up lotsa disk space.

- ✔ If you plan on doing a lot of work in video, I highly recommend that you use a hefty, high-capacity (300+ GB) external drive to store your video files, projects, and snippets. You can also configure most video programs to use the external drive as a video scratch pad in many of the intermediate to advanced video-editing programs.

Video editing

Fear not, my video-happy friend. Windows gives you something to do with all those video snippets you sneak from the Internet, pull from your video camera, capture from TV, or grope from your webcam. Gather yourself a rich library of snippets because Windows comes with the easy-to-use video editing program Windows Movie Maker, shown in Figure 17-3.

Windows Movie Maker uses video images saved on your PC's hard drive and allows you to assemble them, along with various professional-level transitions and edits, into your own video movie. After you hone everything, you can even burn your own DVD to send off to friends and relatives or perhaps some Hollywood agent looking for new talent.

Using Windows Movie Maker is a topic for an entire book, but you should know that such a tool exists, is quite powerful, and isn't available with all versions of Windows Vista.

Chapter 18

The Digital Ear

In This Chapter

▶ Working with Windows Media Player

▶ Ripping music from CDs

▶ Building playlists

▶ Using a portable music player

▶ Burning a music CD

▶ Listening to Windows talk

▶ Making the PC listen to you

Computers have had the ability to make noise ever since some bean counter okayed the engineer's desire to stick a cheap speaker into the console. By manipulating the speaker, programmers could make primitive sounds — even digitized voices or audio playback. And the sound was *terrible*. Yet it was only a few years until computers could be upgraded with quality digital sound, synthesizers, and a whole host of audio goodness.

Today the PC is a natural for playing sounds and making music. Ever since the CD-ROM drive became standard equipment back in the mid-1990s, computers have had the ability to play music CDs. Couple that with the advancement of digital jukebox software and you have a computer that sings, talks, and listens. Now if they can only get the thing to dance. . . .

Your PC Is Now Your Stereo

Yes, the PC has been making your home stereo jealous for over a decade. In fact, buying a PC and a portable music player pretty much makes the home stereo obsolete. But don't tell that to Crazy Omar's Discount Stereo, at least not yet.

As with everything, music is played on your PC by a combination of hardware and software. The hardware is the DVD drive, which can also play music CDs. The software is *Windows Media Player,* which lets you collect, play, and share your music.

Running Windows Media Player

Start Windows Media Player by choosing it from the All Programs menu: Click the Start button and choose All Programs and then Windows Media Player. You might also find the Windows Media Player's icon on the Quick Launch bar.

Windows Media Player sports a simple and easy-to-use interface, as shown in Figure 18-1. Media are organized on the left. You can find your music listed under Library and get even more specific by choosing a category, such as Album or Songs.

To play a tune or listen to an album, click to select what you want to listen to and then click the big ol' Play button in the lower center of the Windows Media Player window.

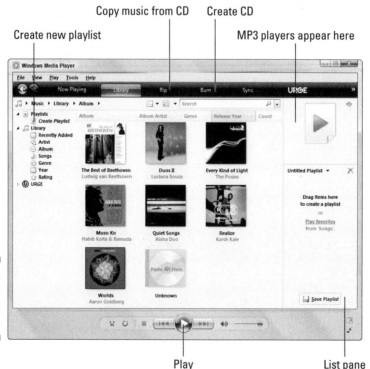

Figure 18-1:
Windows
Media
Player.

The remaining sections in this chapter cover various common things you can do in Windows Media Player.

> ✔ Windows Media Player isn't the only digital jukebox available for Windows. Other choices include the Musicmatch Jukebox (www.musicmatch.com) and Apple's iTunes (www.apple.com). Note that Windows Media Player is the jukebox that Windows prefers.

> ✔ You can change the look of Windows Media Player by choosing a new *skin,* or visual interface, from the View menu. Figure 18-1 shows Windows Media Player as it appears in a standard window without any particular skin applied.

Collecting tunes

The most common way to get music into Windows Media Player is to *rip* that music from a CD you own. Heed these directions:

1. **Insert a music CD into your CD-ROM drive.**

2a. **Windows Media Player automatically starts and begins copying music from the CD.**

    Or:

2b. **You see the AutoPlay dialog box, in which case you choose the option Rip Music from CD Using Windows Media Player.**

    Or:

2c. **Start Windows Media Player and choose Rip from the toolbar.**

    In a few moments, you see a list of tracks on the CD. If your PC is connected to the Internet, you might see information about the disc and the tracks appear as if by magic! Then Windows Media Player copies the music from the CD to the library.

    The speed at which music is copied from the CD depends on the speed of the CD/DVD drive. Refer to Chapter 9 for more information on CD drive speed.

3. **Eject the disc after the songs have been copied: Choose Play⇨Eject from the menu or press Ctrl+J.**

    Put the disc away.

After the songs are copied, they appear in the library along with other music and albums. Click the Library button on the toolbar to peruse the list.

Creating a playlist

Windows Media Player allows you to organize your music into *playlists*. For example, you can create your own party mix, driving music, or top hits. I listen to inspirational "brain music" when I write. It's all made by creating a playlist. Heed these directions:

1. **Click the Library button on the toolbar.**

2. **From the left side of the window, beneath Playlists, select Create Playlist.**

   Refer to Figure 18-1 for the exact location.

3. **Type a name for the playlist, something short and descriptive.**

   The name is echoed on the right side of the window, in the list pane area, where you create the playlist (refer to Figure 18-1).

4. **Locate a song in the library to add to the playlist.**

   Click Songs from the list on the left side of the window to see the list of all songs stored in the library.

5. **Drag the song from the library to the list pane on the right side of the window.**

6. **Repeat Steps 4 and 5 to build your playlist.**

7. **Click the Save Playlist button at the bottom of the list pane.**

8. **Click the X button to clear the playlist and stop editing.**

   You cannot listen to the playlist until it's cleared.

Completed playlists are shown under the Playlists heading in your music library. To listen to the songs collected in your playlist, select the playlist from the left side of the window and select the first song in the list. Click the Play button at the bottom of the window.

✔ To reedit a playlist, click to select it and then click the Edit in List Pane button at the bottom of the window.

✔ When a playlist appears in the list pane, it's being "edited." That's when you can add or remove songs or rename the playlist. To remove a song, right-click it and choose Remove from List from the pop-up menu. To rename the playlist, click the playlist's name button and choose Rename Playlist from the menu.

✔ The songs in a playlist play in the order they appear. To rearrange the songs, simply drag them up or down by using the mouse.

Taking your music with you

The notion of using a computer as a jukebox didn't take off until two things happened. First, on the software side, the simple CD-playing programs on the PC had to evolve into programs that could rip music from the CD and store it long term in the computer. Second, and most important, portable music-playing devices had to evolve.

Portable music players, often called *MP3 players,* existed for some time before they really caught on. The early models were bulky, didn't have long battery lives, and could store only a handful of tunes. With the dawn of Apple's iPod, MP3 players not only became sexy but also interfaced well with computer-based jukebox software.

Windows Media Player works with a variety of portable music devices. The operation generally goes like this:

1. **Attach the portable MP3 player to your PC.**

   Normally, you use a USB cable.

2. **Open Windows Media Player, if necessary.**

   The AutoPlay dialog box may prompt you to open Windows Media Player when you initially attach the device, or you can manually start Windows Media Player.

   The portable gizmo appears in the upper right portion of the Windows Media Player window (refer to Figure 18-1).

3. **Drag to the list pane the music you want to copy to the portable thingy.**

   This step works just like creating a playlist. In fact, you can drag playlists to the gizmo in the same manner.

4. **Click the Start Sync button to copy music to the portable device.**

   Watch as the songs are copied.

5. **Disconnect the device.**

   You're ready for the open road!

Your portable MP3 thingy no doubt came with special software for managing music. Although these steps get you through basic music synchronizing using Windows Media Player, you might still need to use the MP3 player's extra software to help manage your music, remove tunes, or organize how the music is played.

✔ Ensure that your portable music doodad is properly charged. Check the batteries before you do any extensive syncing.

✔ *iPod* isn't a generic name applied to all MP3 players. Your PC can use an iPod, but note that the iPod, not Windows Media Player, is designed specifically to use the iTunes software.

Making your own music CDs

Creating a music CD in Windows Media Player is a snap. Pursue this procedure:

1. **Start Windows Media Player if you haven't already done so.**

2. **Insert a CD-R into the drive.**

   Use a CD-R disc. Although you can record music to a CD-RW, that type of disc isn't as compatible with various CD players on the market, not to mention that CD-RW discs are more expensive than CD-Rs.

Audio file types

As with other media on a computer, audio information is stored in a file. As storing audio files has progressed, various file formats have evolved. The file formats most commonly used now to store audio on a PC are listed here:

AIFF: The Audio Interchange File Format is an old format, although it's still used on the Macintosh computer for storing sound files. Odds are good that you won't encounter these audio files unless you find your PC communing with a Mac.

Au: The Au file format (yes, that's a little U) was developed by Sun Microsystems and is commonly used on Unix and Linux systems for audio files. Although you can find a smattering of Au files on the Internet, Windows cannot play those files unless you download an audio player that supports the Au format.

MP3: The MPEG-1 Audio Layer 3 format, dubbed MP3, is one of the most common audio file formats. MP3 files are compressed, storing about one minute's worth of sound in one megabyte of data. Most music stored on the Internet is available in the MP3 format.

OGG: The Ogg file format is an *open* standard, which means that it's not owned by anyone and can be used without paying a fee. You'll most commonly find Ogg sound files on the Internet, especially on Wikipedia. Ogg isn't an acronym for anything in particular.

WAV: The Waveform audio format is the previous standard file format for Windows (before WMA). WAV files aren't compressed and are therefore larger than MP3 files.

WMA: The Windows Media Audio file is a compressed audio format designed to replace the WAV file format in Windows.

Audio files stored on your PC often use the file format acronym as their filename extension. Refer to Chapter 24 for more information on filenames and extensions.

---

3. **Dismiss the AutoPlay dialog box, if it appears.**

4. **Click the Burn button on the toolbar.**

   The CD-R appears in the upper right corner of the window.

5. **Drag individual songs or playlists to the list pane.**

   The songs you place in the list pane are written, or *burned*, to the CD — and in the order you have placed them.

   Keep an eye on the "MB remaining" thermometer just above the list pane. That indicator lets you know how full the disc will be; you don't want to add more music than the disc can hold.

6. **Click the Start Burn button.**

   Watch as the items are burned to the CD. The time required depends on the CD-R's burning speed (see Chapter 9) as well as the number of songs you're burning to disc.

7. **Remove the disc, label it, and store it in a safe place.**

   The disc is automatically ejected when the burning is complete; you're done.

You can play the disc in any CD or DVD player or in any computer.

✔ Some older CD players may not be able to read a CD-R music disc.

✔ Also see Chapter 28 for information on burning data CDs.

✔ Unlike with a data CD-R created in the Live File system, you cannot add more music to a CD-R after it has been burned once. (Again, see Chapter 28.)

✔ Not all sound files can be copied to an audio CD. MIDI files, for example, must be converted into an audio file format to be recorded to a CD. Special software is required in order to make this conversion. Also, some audio files may be recorded in a low-quality format that makes them incompatible with CD audio. Again, the files must be converted by using special software.

The PC Can Talk and Listen

Don't get your hopes up. The days of talking casually to the computer are still *far* in the future. In fact, I doubt that we'll ever just bark orders at a PC; if *Star Trek* were to be redone today, I'm certain that Mr. Spock would have a computer keyboard and mouse at his workstation (along with a minimized game of Spider Solitaire). But I digress.

Yes, your PC can talk and listen. The following sections mull over the current state of speech on a PC running Windows Vista.

Babbling Windows

Your PC is more than capable of speaking. The sound card can be programmed to emulate the human voice, and software is available to dictate things you type or to read entire documents. Sadly, that software doesn't come with Windows.

What you do find in Windows is a program named Narrator, as shown in Figure 18-2. Narrator is a tool designed to help visually impaired folk use the Windows interface. It doesn't read text. In fact, it spends most of its time parroting whichever keys you press on the keyboard. That sounds nice, but after a while it just gets very irritating.

Figure 18-2:
Narrator is
of no help.

To run Narrator, from the Start menu choose All Programs⇨Accessories⇨ Ease of Access⇨Narrator. The program starts, and begins by immediately telling you about the options available in its window. If you can tolerate that, fine. Otherwise, click the Exit button and be done with it.

A better tool in Windows for the visually impaired is the Magnifier, which is also found in the All Programs⇨Accessories⇨Ease of Access folder on the Start menu.

Dictating to the PC

Blabbing to your PC isn't perfect, but it has come a long way from the days when you had to spend hours (up to 20) to train the computer to understand your voice. Man, that was tiring, not to mention the cotton mouth you'd get from talking for such long stretches! Things are better today.

To get started with speech recognition in Windows Vista, you need a micro-phone or, preferably, a headset. The next stop is the Control Panel: From the Control Panel Home, choose Ease of Access and then Speech Recognition Options. From the Control Panel Classic view, open the Speech Recognition Options icon. Either way you get there, you see the Speech Recognition Options window, illustrated in Figure 18-3.

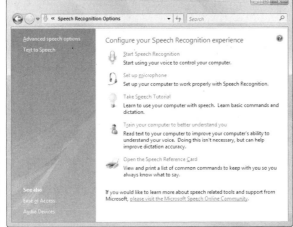

Figure 18-3:
The Speech
Recognition
Options
window.

Generally speaking, you work through the options from the top, with the exception of the first two items. Do this:

1. **Set up microphone.**

2. **Start Speech Recognition.**

3. **Take speech tutorial.**

4. **Train your computer to better understand you.**

Step 3 is pretty interesting and takes only about an hour. But you have to go through the training in Step 4 to make the PC *really* understand you. That takes time, but the investment pays off because you can dictate to the com-puter rather than type.

When speech recognition is turned on, the Speech Recognition microphone window appears on the desktop, as shown in Figure 18-4. If you don't see the window, double-click the Speech Recognition icon in the Notification Area. Right-clicking the Speech Recognition icon displays a handy and helpful pop-up menu of options.

Figure 18-4:
The Speech
Recognition
microphone
window.

✔ People who get the most from dictation software spend lots of time training the computer to understand them.

✔ Another popular dictation package is Dragon Naturally Speaking, at www.nuance.com/.

Part IV
Networking and Internet-Working

The 5th Wave   By Rich Tennant

"You know, Jekyll, this is a single log-on ID system. There's no need for multiple identities anymore."

In this part . . .

Computer networking has long been sacred turf upon which only the most elite of nerds could tread. Nay, no common computer user was allowed to meddle with the network or even gaze upon its workings. The division between computer user and network priest was cosmic and jealously guarded. Thank goodness those days are over.

Networking isn't the big scary booga-booga thing it was in years past. Just about anyone can hook up a simple network at home or in a small office, allowing two or more computers to share a printer or a high-speed Internet connection. Having a network is a good thing because it sates the desire for computer communications and the sharing of resources. This part of the book helps you conquer the mysteries of computer networking — including that Internet thing.

Chapter 19

N Is for Networking

In This Chapter

▶ Understanding networking

▶ Connecting a network

▶ Using the Network and Sharing Center window

▶ Giving your computer a network name

▶ Creating a peer-to-peer network

▶ Setting up a router

*I*n the computer networking restaurant, many decisions must be made. For example, would you like wired or wireless seating? Perhaps you'd like to share a printer? Or maybe share files with another computer? And, naturally, you'll want to share that modem and access the Internet? Of course! It can all be done happily and efficiently and without a false French accent! This chapter shows you the basics.

The Big Networking Picture

Computer networking is all about sharing with others — just like kindergarten. But rather than share colors or toys, you use a computer network to share *resources* and communicate information. For a computer, it's a natural.

But what is a resource?

A *resource* is something a computer uses to get work done, such as memory or processor power. For networking purposes, three resources are commonly shared among computers connected to a network:

▶ Disk storage

▶ Printers

▶ Modems (Internet access)

When a resource is made available for others to use on the network, that resource is said to be *shared*. So Serge can share his color printer or Antoinette can share extra hard drive space, making them available for use by anyone connected to the network.

Internally, the network itself, like everything else in the computer, is a combination of hardware and software. The hardware physically connects the computers and allows communications to take place. On a PC, the hardware can be wired or wireless.

The software controls the hardware, by giving the operating system access to the network and giving *you* access to those resources on other computers. On a PC, Windows supplies all the networking software you need.

Here are some important network terms to familiarize yourself with:

802.11: Neither a Dewey decimal number nor Abe Lincoln's hat size on Mount Rushmore, the number 802.11 refers to the current wireless networking standard. The 11 is followed by a letter: a, b, g, or n, which describes how old the standard is (n is the newest and fastest) and how compatible two wireless networking gizmos can be.

Ethernet: The term *Ethernet* refers to the standards and protocols used by Windows for networking. Ethernet is the most popular personal networking standard, and it's a standard for communications on the Internet as well (which is why networking is closely tied to the Internet). The specifics of Ethernet aren't really important to understanding the whole networking ball of wax. Just be sure that you say it properly: "EETH-er-net."

LAN: When you connect a group of computers to form a network, it's a local area network, or LAN. You pronounce LAN like *land* without the *d* at the end, like how Aunt Minnie pronounced "land sakes!"

Peer-to-peer network: A network that simply connects computers is known as a *peer-to-peer network*. In that scheme, no single computer is in charge; each computer is "on the network," just like any other computer. Peer-to-peer contrasts with another scheme, *client-server*. In that setup, there's one main computer, the *server* (or a computer that merely runs special server software). Servers aren't typically found on peer-to-peer networks, and this book doesn't cover using servers or installing server software.

Networking Hardware

Networking doesn't happen without hardware. First comes the networking adapter, required in order to interface the PC with the network. Wire-based networks need wire, obviously. And all networks, wired or wireless need a central location, or *hub,* where all the wires are connected or wireless signals go to complete the network.

Figure 19-1 illustrates a typical network layout. At the center of the network is a combination wireless base station and router. The router is connected to a broadband modem that's connected to the Internet. The router is also wired into one PC and a printer. Two additional PCs access the base station by using wireless Internet.

The network setup illustrated in Figure 19-1 is typical but not standard. The network you create may look similar, be all wireless, be all wired, or have more or fewer components. This is all good news because the network can be configured to your needs. It's very flexible.

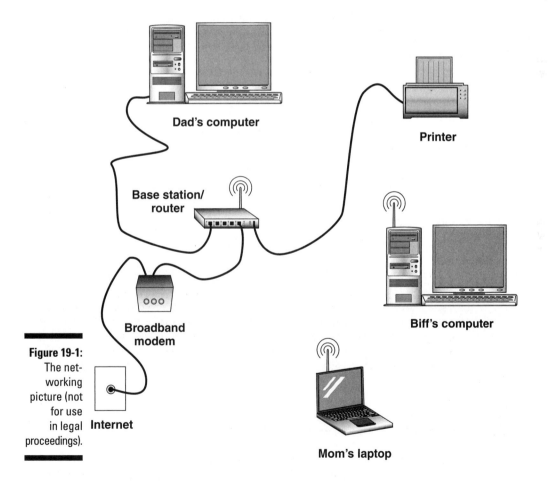

Figure 19-1:
The net-
working
picture (not
for use
in legal
proceedings).

Saint NIC

Your PC requires proper Ethernet networking hardware to connect to the network. The specific hardware is a *network information card,* or *NIC.* It may also be known as an Ethernet card or a network adapter. The circuitry is most often part of the chipset on the motherboard.

There are two types of NICs: The traditional one, which uses the RJ-45 adapter (refer to Chapter 2, for identification), and a *wireless* NIC, which may or may not be visible as a tiny antenna sticking out the back of your PC. A wireless NIC can also be added by using a special USB adapter.

- ✔ If your PC doesn't have a NIC, adding one is easy. You can find a variety at any computer or office supply store.

- ✔ If you choose to go wireless, ensure that all the wireless gizmos in your network adhere to the same wireless networking standard. For example, if you settle on the 802.11g standard, get all 802.11g wireless network adapters as well as an 802.11g router, as described later in this chapter.

- ✔ The standard wired NIC is measured by its speed in Mbps, or megabits per second: 10 Mbps is too slow, 100 Mbps is faster, and 1000 Mbps (1 *gigabit*) is the fastest and bestest.

- ✔ I recommend getting a wireless adapter with an external antenna. For some reason, the antenna makes picking up the wireless signal all the easier — especially if the antenna is *directional* (can be moved).

- ✔ A laptop equipped with built-in wireless networking rarely has an external antenna; the antenna is there — it's just inside the laptop's case.

- ✔ Yes, you can have both wireless and standard NICs inside your PC.

Network hoses

Unless you go totally wireless, you need wires to connect the computers, thus creating the network. The wire you use is a cable known as Cat 5, or Category 5, networking cable. One end of the cable plugs into your computer, into the NIC, and the other plugs into a central location, or hub (covered in the next section).

- ✔ Cat 5 cable comes in a variety of lengths and in several bright and cheerful colors.

- ✔ You can also use Cat 5 networking cable with your telephone system.

✔ You can get creative in wiring your home or office with networking cable. I crawled under my house to wire it all up, and I used the attic and outside walls. You can also buy raceways and connectors and boxes if you don't want to tear up your walls. (Unless you're into such things, though, I recommend having an electrician do it for you.)

✔ It's possible — and rather convenient — to run networking cable through your home's heating ducts. If you choose to do it this way, be sure that you buy special high-temperature cable, rugged enough to stand being inside a heating duct. You use *plenum cable,* and it ain't cheap.

✔ Yes, heating ducts are filthy.

✔ Another way to network computers is by using the IEEE 1394, or *FireWire,* port. It's possible to connect two PCs, such as a desktop and laptop, by using the IEEE port and then configuring Windows to use the port for networking. This is not, however, a solution for connecting many PCs or for sharing a printer or a broadband modem.

The hub

At the center of your network is a hub. It's the location where all the network wires connect and communicate. The hub can be one of several specific pieces of hardware:

Hub: The simplest way to connect a network is by using a hub. It's a simple, inexpensive piece of hardware that merely connects the network.

Switch: Better than a hub, the switch not only connects the network, it helps manage the signals.

Router: The best way to connect your network is by using a router. It's quite sophisticated and has the brains to not only manage hundreds of networked computers but also deal with Internet traffic.

Which should you get? Easy: If you have only two computers and speed isn't an issue, get a hub. If you want better performance, get a switch. If the network is connected to the Internet, a router is a must.

✔ Many wireless routers also support wired networks, as illustrated earlier, in Figure 19-1. The router may also have USB ports for adding a printer or networked hard drive. That's a plus.

✔ I recommend getting a router with built-in firewall protection. Considering that nearly every router (wired and wireless) comes with built-in firewall protection these days, it's not really a big deal. But do check!

✔ The wireless networking signal goes only so far, so placement of a wireless hub is important. You may hear of some wireless networking signals being good for "several hundred feet." But that must be on the moon. Here on Earth, simple obstacles, such as walls and windows, dramatically affect a wireless signal. For your home or small office, consider keeping the wireless hub in the same room as the computer (or computers). If you have computers in multiple rooms, get multiple wireless hubs, one for each room.

The Software Side of Networking

Windows Vista is quite adept at handling the software setup of your PC's networking abilities. In fact, there's really very little to do any more, unlike in days of old, where setting up a network required many steps, several computer restarts, and massive amounts of frustration. Those days are gone for good!

Getting to Network Central

The main location for nearly all networking things in Windows is the Network and Sharing Center window, shown in Figure 19-2. To display that window from the Control Panel Home, select View Network Status and Tasks from beneath the Network and Internet heading. From the Control Panel Classic View, open the Network and Sharing Center icon.

What is Bluetooth?

Bluetooth is the name of a wireless gizmo standard, which can be confused with wireless networking, although the only similarity between the two is the wireless part.

The Bluetooth standard allows for various gizmos or PC peripherals to wirelessly communicate with each other over short distances. For example, you can buy a Bluetooth expansion card and allow your PC to talk wirelessly with compatible Bluetooth peripherals, such as a keyboard, a mouse, a printer, or even a monitor. Theoretically, you could use a Bluetooth MP3 music player with your PC and then take it into your Bluetooth-enabled car and hear the music in the car using Bluetooth-enabled headphones.

Although Bluetooth has been around a while, it's not really popular on the PC. Someday, it may be an interface worth knowing about and using, but for now it's just one of many wireless solutions for adding peripherals to your PC.

All Bluetooth devices sport the Bluetooth symbol, which I would illustrate in this book if the Bluetooth people weren't so uptight about their trademarks.

Figure 19-2:
The
Network
and Sharing
Center
window.

The top part of the Network and Sharing Center window shows visually how your PC is connected to a network and, optionally, the Internet.

The Network area of the window contains details about your network connection. Click the View Status link on the right for the tedious technical details.

The bottom part of the window deals with sharing network resources, which is covered in Chapter 20.

Finally, on the left side of the window, you find some useful links to common networking tasks as well as locations for networking fun and action in Windows.

Connecting to a network

You must direct Windows to find and connect to a specific network before you can use any of the network's resources. Follow these general steps:

1. **Open the Network and Sharing Center.**

2. **From the tasks on the left side of the window, select Connect to a Network.**

3. **If no networks are found, you're done; the network has already been set up automatically. Otherwise, continue.**

4. **Choose a network from the list.**

   Some wireless networks hide their names as a security precaution. If so, you see it listed as Unnamed Network in the Connect to a Network window.

5. **Click the Connect button.**

6. **If prompted, enter the network's password.**

   When there's no password, you see a warning displayed, alerting you about the unsecured network. Don't be alarmed; unsecured wireless networks are common in public places, like cafes. Click the Connect Anyway button to proceed.

7. **Choose whether the network is public or private.**

   A *private* network is one that you use in your home or office — one that you have control over. A *public* network is one you connect to on the road, in a cybercafe or hotel lobby.

8. **Save the connection information.**

   By saving the connection information, you make reconnecting to the network easier in the future.

9. **Click the Close button.**

   A UAC warning may appear, which is normal at this point. Click the Continue button to complete the network connection setup.

After successfully connecting to the network, you should see a new icon in the Notification Area. I call the icon the "networking buddies" because it looks like two computers being very friendly. You can click the icon to see a pop-up bubble describing the network connection.

- ✔ There's no procedure for disconnecting from a network; simply turn your PC off or, for a wireless connection, close the laptop's lid or just move elsewhere.

- ✔ As a shortcut to Steps 1 and 2 in the preceding set of steps — especially for wireless networking laptop users — choose Connect To from the Start button menu.

- ✔ The public/private question (in Step 6) is about security. When you tell Windows that you're connecting to a public network, extra security precautions are set in place.

- ✔ A wireless network is said to be an *ad hoc* network (if a wireless router isn't used). This term implies that the network connections come and go, unlike in a peer-to-peer network that has more continuous connections.

Setting your computer's network name

All computers on the network are known by names. You can specify this name, which gives your computer more of a personality than the common name Microsoft Home or Windows PC or even NCC1701. To change your PC's network name, mind these directions:

1. **Open the System window.**

   From the Control Panel Home, choose System and Maintenance and then System; from the Control Panel Classic view, open the System icon.

   Networking settings are summarized at the bottom of the System window.

2. **Choose the Change Settings link found in the Computer Name, Domain, and Workgroup Settings area of the System window.**

3. **Enter the administrator password or click the Continue button when prompted with a UAC warning.**

   The System window appears.

4. **In the System window, on the Name tab, click the Change button.**

   The Computer Name/Domain Changes dialog box appears.

5. **Type the computer's new name into the Computer Name text box.**

6. **Click OK.**

7. **Click OK to close the System window, and then close the System window.**

   If you're prompted to restart Windows after making this change, do so now.

The computer name you choose shows up when browsing computers connected to the network. See Chapter 20 for more information.

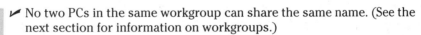

- ✔ No two PCs in the same workgroup can share the same name. (See the next section for information on workgroups.)
- ✔ After you assign your computer a name, don't change it. That can screw up connections made by other computers on the network.

Joining a workgroup

The simple type of network shown earlier, in Figure 19-1, is a peer-to-peer network, but it's also known as a workgroup. The term *workgroup* simply refers to a group of computers that all share a similar location or organization in a network. You can save time by having all your computers belong to the same workgroup. To do that, pursue these steps:

1. **Follow Steps 1 through 4 in the preceding section.**

   You need to open the Computer Name/Domain Changes dialog box.

2. **Choose Workgroup, if it's not already selected.**

3. **Type the name of your network's workgroup.**

   It might already say Microsoft Home or simply Workgroup. I recommend changing the name to something unique, for security reasons. For example, all the computers in my office belong to the CAT workgroup.

4. **Click OK to close the Computer Name/Domain Changes dialog box.**

5. **Click OK to close the System window.**

6. **Close the System window.**

   If you're prompted to restart Windows after making this change, do so now.

There's no need to go nuts here. Putting all your PCs into one workgroup is fine; don't bother creating separate workgroups when fewer than 10 or so computers are on the network.

Where workgroups really come into play is when you browse the network by using the Network window, which is covered in Chapter 20.

Configuring the router

One final thing to configure to make your network complete is the router. Unlike a hub or switch, a router is a very technical gizmo that oftentimes requires some attention before you plug it in and let 'er rip. Fortunately, the configuration you need in order to do is really rather light.

After you connect the router to the network, or simply turn on a wireless router, you connect to the router by using your PC's Web browser, such as Internet Explorer. The documentation that came with the router gives you the router's Web page address. Usually, it's numerical, such as

```
http://192.168.0.1/
```

Getting the MAC address

Each networking adapter in your PC sports a number called the Media Access Control, or MAC, address. This number is unique; no two network adapters share the same MAC address. Therefore, you can use your PC's MAC address as a form of security to limit access to your wireless network.

To obtain your PC's MAC address, follow these steps:

1. Open the Network and Sharing Center window.

2. Click the View Status link by your network connection.

3. In the Connection Status dialog box, click the Details button.

The Network Connections Details box lists the MAC address as the physical address. It shows up as six pairs of values separated by hyphens. Values include the numbers 0 through 9 and the letters *A* through *F.* Make a note of the address, in case you need it for access to a wireless router or to win a PC trivia contest.

After accessing the router, and (optionally) entering its password, you see a Web page displayed. The Web page is really the router's configuration program. Follow the directions that came with the router for its basic configuration. In addition to those directions, here are my suggestions:

- ✔ Enable the router's firewall. There's no need to adjust the firewall; most routers set things up just as you need them. However:

- ✔ When you use a hardware firewall, such as the one that comes with most good routers, there's no need to use a software firewall, such as the one that comes with Windows Vista. The two firewalls are redundant and don't offer any extra protection; one hardware firewall is enough. See Chapter 23.

- ✔ Set a *Service Set Identifier,* or *SSID,* for your wireless network. This is the name by which the wireless network is known.

- ✔ You may have the option of making the SSID name visible or invisible. If security is an issue, make the name invisible. That way, the base station doesn't broadcast the name, and only computers that know the name can connect to the wireless network.

- ✔ Set the encryption for the network, known as the WEP, or Wired Equivalent Privacy. Make sure that you note the password! It's a long string of numbers and letters, and you must enter it exactly to access the network.

✔ You may hear or read that the password is optional. My opinion: It's not. Don't compromise your network by omitting the password. In fact, Windows may not even connect to a wireless network that lacks a password.

✔ (Optional) Configure the base station to allow connections only from known computers. You specify this setting by listing the MAC address of the wireless Ethernet adapter in each PC. See the nearby sidebar, "Getting the MAC address," for information on getting the MAC address.

✔ Tell the wireless router to provide IP addresses dynamically for all computers on the network. This is also known as DHCP.

✔ The most important pieces of information you need from a wireless router are the SSID and the long, cryptic password, which you need in order to access the network. I recommend that you write those things down and keep them in a safe place.

Chapter 20

I've Been Working on the Network

In This Chapter

▶ Exploring your PC's network

▶ Viewing a map of networked PCs

▶ Setting up Windows to share folders and printers

▶ Sharing a folder

▶ Mapping a network disk drive

▶ Unsharing a folder

▶ Sharing your PC's printer

▶ Unsharing the printer

I wonder if computers get lonely. Are they just so busy that the notion of isolation never flies across a microprocessor? If so, imagine the shock when you connect a PC to a network! Would your computer be thrilled upon seeing other PCs? Or, maybe the thought that there's such a thing as a network printer or a lone network hard drive fills the PC with thoughts of inadequacy? Perhaps the noise from all the communications that come with a network and broadband Internet connection would cause your PC to revert to DOS as an operating system?

Don't worry: Your computer isn't about to go primitive on you. Getting a computer network up and running is one thing, covered in Chapter 19. There's immense satisfaction from getting computers connected and sharing printers, disk drives, and a modem. But that's not the entire picture. The rest of the story is about the communications you can make between network computers. That's the story for this chapter.

Windows Does the Network

 The main networking window thing in Windows is named, surprisingly, Network. It can be accessed by opening an icon on the desktop or from a menu item on the Start button menu or from the Address bar in any folder window. No matter how you get there, you see the Network window, a sample of which is shown in Figure 20-1.

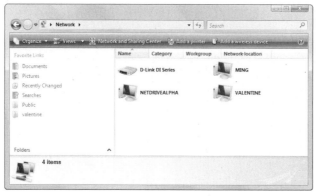

Figure 20-1:
The
Network
window.

The Network window lists all the various networking gizmos attached to your computer's network. Specifically, you should see other computers using the same *workgroup* as your PC. (If not, and other PCs are connected to your network, refer to Chapter 19, the section about joining a workgroup.) You might also see some network printers, a network hard drive (if you have one), and perhaps the network's router, shown as D-Link DI Series in Figure 20-1.

✔ If you don't see any icons and you *know* that you have a proper workgroup set up, you may not have activated network discovery. See the section "Turning On Network Discovery," later in this chapter.

 ✔ Windows scans the network for available computers and then populates the Network window with what it discovers.

✔ You can refresh the Network window by pressing the F5 key, which shows any new computers that have joined the network.

 ✔ The Network window was formerly named My Network Places in Windows XP. In even older versions of Windows, the folder was named Network Neighborhood.

Browsing the network

The Network window is the main location from which you can browse your network, to examine other computers on the network and discover which resources they're sharing.

For example, on my network, I can double-click a computer icon in the Network window (refer to Figure 20-1) to display whatever resources that computer is sharing. In Figure 20-2, you can see that the NETDRIVEALPHA computer is sharing two folders and a printer.

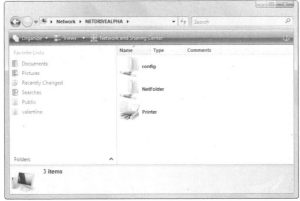

Figure 20-2:
Folders and a printer shared on the network.

- Browsing through the network works just like browsing through folders on your own computer. See Chapter 25.

- Folders displayed in a network computer's window are *shared* folders, available for access by others on the network.

- Some shared folders require password access or that you have an account set up on the computer that's sharing the folders.

- Both shared folders and shared printers appear as icons with "network plumbing" beneath them.

- Opening a shared folder allows you to view and access files inside that folder — just like in Windows — but the files actually exist on another computer on the network.

- You can assign a drive letter to any shared folder, to make that folder part of your own PC's disk system. See the section "Mapping a network folder as a disk drive letter," later in this chapter.

- Printers available for use on the network also show up in the Printers window, as well as in any Print dialog box. See Chapter 12.

Turning on network discovery

Before you can direct your PC to go out slumming it on the network, you must ensure that network discovery has been activated for Windows Vista. Here's what to do:

1. **Open the Network and Sharing Center window.**

   To get there, you can click the Network and Sharing Center toolbar button in the Network window or refer to Chapter 19 for directions.

2. **If necessary, click the Show More arrow to reveal the Network Discovery area of the window.**

3. **Choose Turn On Network Discovery, if it isn't on already.**

4. **Click the Apply button.**

5. **Enter the administrator password or click the Continue button to proceed.**

6. **(Optional) Close the Network and Sharing Center window.**

You set other networking options in the Network and Sharing Center window elsewhere in this chapter, so you might consider leaving that window open for now.

Viewing the network map

An interesting feature of Windows Vista is that it enables you to view a graphical map of your network. To do so, open the Network and Sharing Center window and click the View Full Map link near the upper right corner.

The graphical network map, similar to the one shown in Figure 20-3, illustrates well those Windows Vista PCs attached to the network. Older Windows computers, as well as some network-independent devices (hard drives and printers), may not show up on the map, but appear at the bottom, similar to MING and NETDRIVEALPHA in Figure 20-3.

Network Sharing, Shared, and Unshared

To take full advantage of your computer network, know that you can do more than just share an Internet connection. You can also access information on other computers by sharing folders, plus you can share printers. The following sections mull over the possibilities.

Figure 20-3:
The network
map (more
or less).

- Refer to Chapter 19 for more information on setting up a network.
- Also see Chapter 19 for directions on visiting the Network and Sharing Center window; and refer to Chapter 5 for information on getting to other, specific places in Windows.
- See Chapter 25 for information on folders if the concept is new to you.

Configuring Windows to share stuff

To enable sharing between your PC and others on the network, you need to make certain settings in the Network and Sharing Center window. Specifically, the six settings near the bottom of that window control networking and sharing, as listed in Table 20-1.

Table 20-1	Settings That Control Sharing on the Network
Setting	*Effect of Enabling*
Network discovery	Allows your PC to see other computers on the network and allows other computers to see your PC
File sharing	Allows others on the network to access shared folders and files on your PC
Public folder sharing	Controls access to the public folder on your PC
Printer sharing	Allows other network users to use any printers attached to your PC

(continued)

Table 20-1 *(continued)*

Setting	Effect of Enabling
Password protected sharing	Controls who has access to shared files and printers on your PC
Media sharing	Allows other network users to access your PC's music and media files by using Windows Media Center across the network

To turn an option on or off or make other necessary settings, click the Show More button by a setting's title. Clicking the Show More button displays more information about the setting and displays the options that control the setting. After changing a setting, click the Allow button, and then confirm that choice by entering the administrator password or clicking the Continue button. Here are my recommendations:

- ✔ *Network discovery* should be turned on as described earlier in this chapter, in the section "Turning on network discovery."

- ✔ *File sharing* must be turned on when you want to share folders (and their files) on your computer with others on the network. Choose the option Turn On File Sharing after opening the File Sharing area.

- ✔ *Public folder sharing* controls access to the public-level folders in Windows. Normally, the Public folder is used to share files between multiple users on a single PC. But you can allow anyone on the network to make changes. My recommendation is to choose the option Turn On Sharing So Anyone with Network Access Can Open, Change, and Create Files. That option permits full access. (Use the first option to prevent others from deleting or changing your files.)

- ✔ *Printer sharing* can be turned on when your PC is connected to a printer you want to share on the network.

- ✔ *Password protected sharing* limits access to your PC and its files to only those who have a password-protected account on your PC. This option is a bother for home networks and where security isn't an issue. I turn it off in my office but recommend turning it on in just about any but the most secure situations.

- ✔ *Media sharing* needs to be turned on only when you plan to use Windows Media Center to play or access media files on another PC in the network.

Sharing one of your folders

If you want others on the network to have access to a folder on your computer, you *share* the folder. This makes the folder — and its contents (all files and subfolders) — available to all other computers on the network. Here's how to share a folder:

1. **Ensure that Network Discovery and File Sharing are enabled on your PC.**

   Refer to the previous section.

2. **Right-click the folder you want to share.**

3. **Choose Properties from the pop-up menu.**

   The folder's Properties dialog box appears.

4. **Click the Sharing tab.**

5. **Click the Advanced Sharing button.**

6. **When prompted with the UAC warning, enter the administrator password or click the Continue button.**

   The Advanced Sharing dialog box appears.

7. **Click to put a check mark by the option labeled Share This Folder.**

8. **Optionally, change the share name.**

   The *share name* is the same as the folder's name, but remember that it can be vague; I have many folders named work on my computer. A more descriptive name for the network is better, something like 2008 Summer Vacation or Shield Project.

9. **Click OK.**

   The folder is now shared.

10. **Click the Close button to dismiss the folder's Properties dialog box.**

 Shared folder icons appear with the graphical "sharing friends" flag beneath them, as shown in the margin. Other PCs can now access the folder, which appears on their PCs using the name you chose in the Advanced Sharing dialog box (refer to Step 8).

✔ Don't share an entire disk drive. This is a security risk; Windows warns you when you try to do so.

✔ You may be tempted by the Share button on the toolbar or the Share command on an icon's shortcut menu. That type of sharing is *local* only: It affects only multiple users on a single PC. To share a file on the network, you must follow the steps as outlined in this section.

Accessing a network folder

You access a folder elsewhere on the network just as you would access any folder on your PC's disk system. The difference is that you need to browse to the folder from the Network window.

After opening the Network window, as discussed earlier in this chapter, you can then open any computer to see which folders it's sharing. Open a folder icon to reveal its contents.

Mapping a network folder as a disk drive letter

If you find accessing a folder on another computer (as described in the preceding subsection) tedious, you can opt instead to *map* that folder to a disk drive letter. This choice provides easy, quick, and consistent access to the folder's contents, just as though the folder were another form of permanent storage inside your PC.

To map a folder, follow these steps:

1. **Browse to the network folder you want to map.**

   Open the Network window and then the icon for the computer sharing the folder you want to map.

2. **Right-click the folder's icon.**

3. **Choose Map Network Drive from the shortcut menu.**

   The Map Network Drive dialog box appears.

4. **Choose a drive letter for the network folder.**

   You can give the network drive any unused drive letter.

   The drive letter you assign is personal to your computer. It doesn't affect any other computer on the network.

5. **Ask yourself, "Do I always want to use the network drive?"**

   If so, put a check mark by the item labeled Reconnect at Logon. That way, Windows always maps in the folder to that specific drive letter every time you start your computer. Otherwise, the mapping is forgotten when you log out.

6. **Click the Finish button.**

   Windows opens that folder and shows you its contents.

Mapped folders appear in the Computer window, along with other storage devices connected to your PC. Specifically, mapped folders appear under the category Network Location. Accessing that network folder is as easy, and the same as, using the drive letter on your own PC; you can even choose the folder from any Save As or Open dialog box.

Unsharing a folder

To remove the magical sharing properties from a folder, repeat Steps 2 through 10 in the section "Sharing one of your folders," earlier in this chapter. This time, however, remove the check mark to share the folder in Step 7.

Disconnecting a mapped network drive

To remove a mapped network drive, open the Computer and right-click the mapped drive. Choose the Disconnect command from the pop-up menu. The drive is unmapped.

Sharing a printer

Sharing a printer connected to your PC works just like sharing a folder, although you must ensure that you've activated Printer Sharing in the Network and Sharing Center window, as discussed earlier in this chapter. Beyond that, follow these steps:

1. **Open the Printers window.**

   To quickly view the Printers window, click in any folder window's address bar and type the word **printers**. Press Enter.

2. **Right-click the printer you want to share.**

3. **Choose Sharing from the pop-up menu.**

   The printer's Properties dialog box appears, with the Sharing tab selected.

4. **Click the Change Sharing Options button.**

5. **If you see a UAC warning, enter the administrator password or click the Continue button.**

6. **Place a check mark by Share This Printer.**

7. **(Optional) Give the printer a name.**

   For example, name it Color Laser to let everyone know that you're finally sharing your darn precious color laser printer.

8. **Click the OK button.**

   You can optionally close the Printers window.

As with sharing a folder, a shared printer's icon appears with the sharing-buddies flag beneath it.

What about network printers?

Network printers, or printers with their own networking cards, don't need to be connected directly to any PC. To access the network printer, however, you must have software installed on each computer by using the installation program that came on a CD with the printer. Unlike printers directly connected to a given PC, network printers don't have the brains to announce their presence and share their drivers.

Using a network printer

Because Windows automatically spies and then loads network printers, all you have to do to use one is select it from the drop-down list in a Print dialog box. Refer to Chapter 12 for more information on printing.

Unsharing a printer

Unsharing a printer is as simple as sharing one: Repeat the steps in the subsection "Sharing a printer," a little earlier in this chapter, but in Step 6 click to remove the check mark.

Chapter 21

Cowboy Dan's Internet Roundup

· ·

In This Chapter

▶ Understanding what the Internet is

▶ Obtaining an ISP

▶ Setting up Windows for the Internet

▶ Connecting to the Internet

▶ Using the Web

▶ Enjoying e-mail

· ·

*H*owdy, boys and girls!

Howdy, Cowboy Dan!

Guess what time it is? It's time to do the Internet!

Ah, yes. The silence from the peanut gallery is shrill. That's because they're asleep. You see, perhaps 10 or 15 years ago, it was necessary to provide a careful introduction to the Internet. There was a need to explain what it was and how to get it to work — especially in Windows! (If you can believe that.) Today, however, there's little need to explain to anyone how to use the Internet. In fact, a more complicated argument is to explain to someone how to avoid using the Internet.

You probably already know a bit about the Internet — even if you've never used a computer. So, rather than bore you and all the boys and girls in the peanut gallery, Cowboy Dan presents this chapter, the Internet Roundup. Consider it my quick Internet introduction plus tips for the Web weary and e-mail exhausted.

What Is the Internet?

The *Internet* is composed of hundreds of thousands of computers all over the world. The computers send information. They receive information. And, most important, they store information. That's the Internet.

Quiz Time.

Given what you know about the Internet, which of the following statements is true:

1. The Internet is a piece of software or program you buy.
2. The Internet is a single computer.
3. Bill Gates, Google, and A&T own the Internet.

Answers are at the end of this chapter.

How to Access the Internet

Getting on the Internet is no ordeal. Windows is geared to use the Internet. In fact, Windows prefers that you have a broadband Internet connection and that your PC is *always* connected to the Internet. But before sating the PC's online lusts, there are a few things to attend to, as covered in the sections that follow.

Choosing an ISP

You need five things to access the Internet:

- A computer
- A modem
- Internet software
- Money
- An Internet service provider, or ISP

The first three items you should already have. The fourth item, money, is needed to pay for the fifth item, which is the outfit that provides you with Internet access.

Your ISP can be your telephone company or cable company, both of which compete to provide you with broadband DSL or cable service.

For satellite Internet access, you have to check the yellow pages, which is also what you do for plain old dialup Internet access. ISPs are listed under *Internet* in any yellow pages book or phone directory.

The ISP provides you with the Internet access. (Remember: No one owns the Internet, not even your ISP.) It may configure your broadband modem for you or provide information on how to set things up yourself. In addition, it should also give you the following items:

- ✔ For a dialup modem, the phone number to call
- ✔ For a broadband modem, the modem's IP address, the DNS address, and possibly a gateway address
- ✔ Your ISP's domain name — the `blorf.com` or `yaddi.org` part
- ✔ Your Internet login ID and password
- ✔ Your Internet e-mail name, address, and password (if it's different from your login ID and password)
- ✔ The name of your ISP's e-mail server, which involves the acronyms POP3 or SMTP
- ✔ A personal Web page or "Web space" for you to place a Web page, plus the address of that page (optional, but good to have)
- ✔ A phone number to call for help (very important)

Be sure to check these items when you choose an ISP.

Finally, the ISP will bill you for Internet access. The prices can be cheap, sometimes less than $10 per month for dialup access. You pay more for faster connections, with some high-speed broadband connections costing upward of $50 per month. Be sure to compare prices when choosing an ISP.

- ✔ The S in ISP stands for *service*. You pay them a fee, and they provide you with Internet access *and* service. That means technical support: someone you can phone for help, classes, software — you name it. The more support, the better the ISP.
- ✔ In some situations, you may not need any of the five items on my Internet access list. For example, if you work for a large company, it may already give you Internet access through the network at your office. Ditto for universities and some government installations. And, you can always find free Internet access at a community library near you.

Configuring Windows for the Internet

Windows is automatically configured to use the Internet. Merely by connecting a broadband modem to your PC or to the PC's network, you suddenly and instantly have Internet access. Windows sees it. You're all set.

Things work differently when you have dialup access. In that case, you must create a network connection for the modem to use. Directions for this task should come from your ISP. It gives you a phone number to dial, plus perhaps other options to set, such as configuring your e-mail program or setting a home page in Internet Explorer.

Connecting to the Internet

There's no need to fuss over connecting to the Internet when you have a cable, DSL, or satellite modem: A broadband connection is always on. Internet programs start up quickly and access the Internet just as fast.

Dialup connections are active only when you use the Internet. When you run an Internet program, or when any software attempts to access the Internet, the PC directs the modem to dial into your ISP. After making the connection, you're "on" the Internet and can use Internet software.

✔ To test the Internet connection, run the Internet Explorer program. By running Internet Explorer, or any program that accesses the Internet, your computer attempts to make an Internet connection. When the connection works, you see a Web page displayed in Internet Explorer. Otherwise you see an error message. If so, contact your ISP for assistance.

✔ As long as you have an Internet connection, you can run any program that accesses information on the Internet.

✔ Yes, you can run more than one Internet program at a time. I typically have three or four of them running. (Because the Internet is slow, I can read one window while waiting for something to appear in another window.)

✔ You can also stay on the Internet while using an application program, like Word or Excel. Just don't forget that you're online.

✔ You should hang up, or *disconnect,* from the dialup connection when you're done using the Internet. Refer to Chapter 14 for more information on disconnecting the modem in Windows.

✔ For several reasons, you may always have to manually enter your password when you connect to the Internet. The first reason is that you're using a laptop, which doesn't save your Internet password, for security reasons. The second is that you didn't properly log in to Windows with a password-protected account. The third is that, for some reason, Windows forgets your password and forces you to reenter it (perhaps for security reasons).

✔ For other Internet connection problems, woes, and worries, refer to my book *Troubleshooting Your PC For Dummies* (Wiley Publishing, Inc.), available only in bookstores with good-looking employees worldwide.

✔ To cancel a dialup connection, click the Cancel button when you see it dialing.

✔ Why is your computer connecting to the Internet? Most likely, it's because some program or Windows itself is requesting information. Canceling that request isn't a problem, nor does it mess things up. Programs can wait until *you* want to connect to the Internet to conduct their business. Dammit! You're in charge!

It's a World Wide Web We Weave

The World Wide Web — or "the Web" — is directly responsible for making the Internet as popular as it is today. The Web introduced pretty graphics and formatted text to the Internet, which propelled it from its ugly all-text past into an appealing popular present.

Browsing tips

You probably don't have any trouble browsing the Web, so a review of the basics would again bore the peanut gallery. Rather than rehash what you already know, here are my Web browsing tips and tricks. Note that many of these are specific to Internet Explorer (IE), the Web browser that's included with Windows Vista.

✔ If you prefer to see a real, live menu bar in Internet Explorer 7.0, press the F10 key on the keyboard. To keep that menu bar on all the time, choose View⇨Toolbars⇨Menu Bar from the menu.

✔ In the lower right corner of the IE window you find a Zoom menu. Use it to help make Web pages with small text more visible.

✔ You can easily recall previously typed Web page addresses from the address bar: Click the down-arrow button to the left of the address bar.

✔ To remove all previously typed Web page addresses, click the Tools button on the toolbar and choose Delete Browsing History. In the dialog box that appears, click the Delete History button.

✔ The easiest way to set a home page is to visit the Web page you want as your home page. Once there, click the menu button by the Home icon on the toolbar. Choose Add or Change Home Page from the menu. In the dialog box that appears, choose Use This Webpage As Your Only Home Page, and click the Yes button.

✔ If a Web page doesn't load, try again! The Web can be busy, and often when it is, you get an error message.

✔ When you get a `404` error, you probably didn't type the Web page address properly. Try again.

✔ You can type a Web page address without the `http://` part, but if you don't get to where you want to go, try again with the `http://` part.

✔ If the URL starts with `ftp://` or `gopher://`, you're required to type those commands.

✔ Not all Web page links are text. Quite a few links are graphical. The only way to know for certain is to point the mouse pointer at what you believe may be a link. If the pointer changes to a pointing hand, you know that it's a link you can click to see something else.

✔ There's a tiny menu button to the right of IE's Forward button. Use that menu button to recall recent Web pages you visited.

✔ When you accidentally click a link and change your mind, click the Stop button. The Internet then stops sending you information. (You may need to click the Back button to return to where you were.)

✔ IE's Refresh button serves a useful purpose in the world of ever-changing information. Refresh merely tells the Internet to update the Web page you're viewing.

✔ Clicking the Refresh button is one quick way to fix the "missing picture" problem.

✔ Press Ctrl+D to add any Web page you're viewing to your Favorites. Don't be shy about it! It's better to add it now and delete it later than to regret not adding it in the first place.

Printing Web pages

To print any Web page, click the Printer button on the toolbar. That's pretty much it.

Sadly, some Web pages don't print right. Some are too wide. Some are white text on a black background, which doesn't print well. My advice is to use the Print Preview command, found on the Print toolbar button's menu, to look at what will print before you print it. If you still have trouble, consider one of these solutions:

✔ Consider saving the Web page to disk; choose Save As from the Page toolbar button's menu. Ensure that you choose from the Save As Type drop-down list the option labeled Web Page, Complete. Then you can open the Web page file in Microsoft Word or Excel or any Web page editing program and edit or print it from there.

✔ Use the Page Setup command, found on the Print toolbar button's menu, to select landscape orientation for printing wider-than-normal Web pages.

✔ Use the Properties button in the Print dialog box to adjust the printer; press Ctrl+P to see the Print dialog box. The Properties settings depend on the printer itself, but I have seen printers that can reduce the output to 75 or 50 percent, which ensures that the entire Web page prints on a single sheet of paper. Other options may let you print in shades of gray *(grayscale)* or black and white.

Searching tips

The Web is full of information, and some of it is even accurate! Of course, the issue is getting to the information you want. The following are my Web-page searching tips.

✔ My main search engine these days is Google, at `www.google.com`. I admire it for its simplicity and thoroughness.

✔ Google, like many search engines, ignores the smaller words in the English language. Words like *is*, *to*, *the*, *for*, *are*, and others are not included in the search. Therefore:

✔ Use only key words when searching. For example, to look for *The Declaration of Independence*, typing **declaration independence** is good enough.

✔ Word order matters. If you want to find out what that red bug with six legs is called, try all combinations: *bug red six legs*, *red bug six legs*, or even *six legs red bug.*

✔ When words *must* be found together, enclose them in double quotes, such as **"Gilligan's Island" theme MIDI** or **"Toro riding lawnmower" repair**. A quoted search finds only Web pages that list the words *Toro riding lawnmower* together in that order.

✔ If the results — the matching or found Web pages — are too numerous, click the link (near the bottom of the page) that says `Search within results`. That way, you can further refine your search. For example, if you found several hundred pages on Walt Disney World but are specifically looking for a map of the Animal Kingdom, you can search for **"Animal Kingdom map"** within the results you found for Walt Disney World.

E-Mail Call!

Nothing perks up your Internet day like getting fresh e-mail. *Ahhhh, people care enough about me to write! I'm loved!*

Windows Vista comes with the new e-mail program Windows Mail, which is essentially an upgraded and better version of the old Outlook Express. The following are general e-mail tips and suggestions for using Windows Mail, as well as e-mail in general.

- Don't put spaces in an e-mail address. If you think that it's a space, it's probably an underline or a period.

- You must enter the full e-mail address: `zorgon@wambooli.com`. Note the single exception: If you have e-mail nicknames set up, you can type the nickname rather than the full e-mail address in the To field.

- You can type more than one address in the To field. If so, separate each one with a semicolon or comma, as in

  `president@whitehouse.gov, first.lady@whitehouse.gov`

- Type the message's subject. What is the message about? It helps if the subject is somehow related to the message (because the recipients see the subject in their inboxes, just like you do). Avoid the habit of using brief, meaningless subjects.

- When you're done composing your e-epistle, check your spelling by clicking the Spelling button.

- When you don't want to send the message, close the New Message window. You're asked whether you want to save the message. Click Yes to save it in the Drafts folder. If you click No, the message is destroyed.

- When you type the wrong e-mail address, the message *bounces* back to you. It isn't a bad thing; just try again with the proper address.

- Please don't type in ALL CAPS. To most people, all caps reads like YOU'RE SHOUTING AT THEM!

- Be careful what you write. E-mail messages are often casually written, and they can easily be misinterpreted. Remember to keep them light.

- Don't expect a quick reply from e-mail, especially from folks in the computer industry (which is ironic).

- To send a message you have shoved off to the Drafts folder, open the Drafts folder. Then double-click the message to open it. The original New Message window is then redisplayed. From there, you can edit the message and click the Send button to finally send it off.

- When you have trouble seeing the text in an e-mail message, choose View⇨Text Size from the menu and choose a larger or smaller size from the submenu.

- Also see Chapter 22, which covers e-mail file attachments.

TIP

Putting Bcc to work

The sneaky Bcc field is used to *blind-carbon-copy* a message, which involves sending a copy of a message to someone and having that person's name *not* appear in any copy of the e-mail. That way, you can clue people in to a message without having its true recipients know the names of everyone else who received the message.

To access the Bcc field, choose View⇨All Headers from the New Message window's menu. The people in the Bcc field receive a copy of the e-mail message, just like everyone else; however, the people in the To or Cc fields don't see the Bcc field names listed.

A great way to use Bcc is when you send a message to several people. For example, when sending out That Latest Joke, just put everyone's name in the Bcc field and put your own name in the To field. That way, everyone gets the joke (or not, as the case may be), and they don't see the huge stack-o-names at the start of the e-mail message.

Quiz Answers

Here are the answers to the quiz at the start of this chapter.

1. False. Although you use software to access the Internet and you need software to send or retrieve information from the Internet, the Internet itself isn't a software program.

2. False. The Internet consists of all the computers connected to the Internet. Whenever your computer is "on" the Internet, it's part of the Internet.

3. False. No lone person can own the Internet, just as no lone person can own the oceans.

Chapter 22

Flinging Files Freely

In This Chapter

▶ Grabbing text or graphics from the Web

▶ Finding files and programs on the Internet

▶ Downloading programs

▶ Installing downloaded software

▶ Receiving a file with your e-mail

▶ Sending a file with your e-mail

*N*etworking, which includes the Internet, was borne of the need for those early steam-powered computers of the past century to communicate. No, they didn't play *World of Warcraft* back in the 1960s. In fact, the communication that existed was mostly in the form of sending chunks of data back and forth between two computers. In fancy computer lingo, those chunks of data are *files*. Even now, sending files between two computers is a common and necessary thing, and it's much easier than it has been in years past.

✔ Copying a file to your computer is known as *downloading*. When someone sends you a file over the Internet, you *download* it. (Think of the other computer as being on top of a hill; it may not be, but it helps to think of it that way.)

✔ Sending a file to another computer is known as *uploading*.

✔ Complaining to your best friend over a beer is known as *unloading*.

Snagging Stuff from a Web Page

Anything you see on a Web page is already on your computer. The text has been sent to your PC for display in your Web browser. Ditto for the images. But the Web browser keeps that information in a special location that's not easy to get to. So, when you want to keep a picture from a Web page or copy some text, extra work is required. It's nothing difficult; the following sections explain how it works.

Saving an image from a Web page

To save an image from a Web page to your PC's hard drive, right-click the image and choose Save Picture As from the pop-up menu. Use the Save As dialog box to find a happy home for the picture on your hard drive.

  ✔ Windows prefers to store images in the Pictures folder, found in your main account, or User Profile folder. See Chapter 25 for more information on folders.

  ✔ Nearly all images on the Web are copyrighted. Although you're free to save a copy to your hard drive, you're not free to duplicate, sell, or distribute the image without the consent of the copyright holder.

  ✔ To set the image as your desktop wallpaper, choose Set As Background from the pop-up menu after right-clicking the image.

Saving text from a Web page to disk

In addition to graphics, Web pages are composed of text. You can copy that text and save it to disk just as you would copy text from one application and paste it into another. Here's how:

1. **Select the text you want to copy.**

   Drag the mouse over the text, which highlights it on the screen. The text is now selected.

2. **Press Ctrl+C to copy the text.**

3. **Start any word processor.**

   You can start Notepad, WordPad, or your word processor, such as Microsoft Word.

4. **Paste the text into your word processor.**

   Ctrl+V or Edit➪Paste.

5. **Print. Save. Whatever.**

   Use the proper menu commands to save or print or edit the text you copied from the Web page.

The text you copy from a Web page carries with it certain formatting information. That formatting is retained only when you paste the text into a program that understands Web page, or HTML, formatting.

Software from the Internet

The Internet is a great repository of software, various programs available for free or nearly free, which you can download to your computer for use, tryout, or just because. You can also find updates for software you already own, or you can find support software, or *drivers,* for your hardware. Obtaining such software is a common activity on the Internet.

The key, of course, is to find the software. For software you own, visiting the developer or manufacturer's Web page should be your first choice. Avoid visiting those "free driver" Web pages, because they're mostly advertisements and often contain spyware or download viruses — not legitimate hardware drivers — to your PC.

For general software, I can recommend the SourceForge.net Web page: www. sourceforge.net You can also use Google or any Web search engine to help you locate programs.

- ✔ A *repository* is a location where things are stored.
- ✔ A *suppository* is medicine you take internally, but not through any hole on your face.

Downloading software from the Internet

It's easy to get a file from the Internet. The more you do it, the better you get — though it's always best to be careful! Do not randomly download files, and especially avoid downloading a file you did not request. Otherwise, here's how it's done:

1. **Click the link or graphical image that begins the download.**

   Sometimes, clicking the link starts the download immediately, and sometimes you're taken to another page. Be patient; eventually you get the file.

2. **If the Information Bar warning appears, click the Close button.**

3. **Click the Information bar.**

4. **From the pop-up menu that appears, choose the Download File command.**

   A File Download dialog box appears.

5. **Click the Save button.**

   I recommend clicking Save because it allows you to reinstall the program more easily if something goes wrong. Choose Open only if you're directed to do so.

6. **Click the Save button in the Save As dialog box.**

   Generally speaking, the filename and location are fine. The Internet uses the same filename as the original file, which is generally a description of what you're downloading, plus maybe a version number. The file's location is the Downloads folder, which is perfect.

7. **Sit and watch as the file is copied from the Internet to your computer.**

   Figure 22-1 illustrates the download progress, albeit in a static manner.

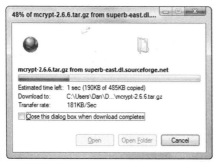

Figure 22-1:
A file
is down-
loading.

8. **To immediately install the program, click the Open button.**

9. **Obey the directions on the screen to finish the installation.**

   The directions are specific to whatever it is you're installing.

After installing the program, you can run it or do anything you would normally do with any software installed on your computer. See Chapter 27 for more information on installing software.

✔ Downloading a program and installing it works just like installing software you bought from the store. The only difference is that rather than use a CD or DVD, you use a file you download from the Internet to install.

✔ For more information on the program, look for a README file among the files that are installed or downloaded .

✔ Downloading the file is free. If the file is shareware, however, you're expected to pay for it if you use it.

✔ Even though the file was downloaded, if you don't want it, you have to uninstall it as you would uninstall any program (refer to Chapter 27).

How long does it take to download a file?

Honestly, the progress meter you see when a file is being downloaded is for entertainment value only; no one really knows how long it takes to download a file. If the Internet is busy, it may take longer than estimated — even for a fast modem. Consider the time that's displayed as only a rough estimate.

✔ Sometimes you're given a choice of servers or *mirrors* from which to download the file. If possible, try to choose a server or mirror close to your location, which speeds up the download process.

✔ It's okay to delete a file from the Downloads folder after the file's program has been installed. I don't do it, however, because I like to keep everything, in case I need to reinstall it again.

✔ Another folder, found in the Windows folder, is named Downloaded Program Files. This folder is used for updates to Internet Explorer, and its contents aren't for you to play with.

Installing from a Zip file

When you download software, I recommend downloading the self-installing version. If the Web site lists the filename, notice that self-installing programs end in EXE. Beyond that, you can download the compressed version of a file. Those files end in ZIP, and they're known in Windows as *compressed folders*.

Downloading a compressed folder works just like downloading any file from the Internet; refer to Steps 1 through 7 from the preceding section. Then continue here:

8. **Click the Open Folder button.**

    The Downloads folder appears. The compressed folder you just downloaded is selected, ready for action.

9. **Open the compressed folder you just downloaded; press the Enter key.**

10. **Click the Extract All Files toolbar button.**

11. **Click the Extract button in the Extract Compressed (Zipped) Folders window.**

    Windows creates a folder with the same name as the compressed folder and copies all files from the compressed folder into the new folder. That new folder then opens, appearing on the screen.

12. **Run the Setup or Install program or whatever is required to continue installing the software.**

When you're done, you can remove the folder you created in Step 11, although I recommend keeping the original compressed folder in case you need to reinstall the program later.

You've Got an E-Mail Attachment!

The ability to send and receive files along with your e-mail is possibly one of the things that makes e-mail so incredibly popular. Not only can you send pictures back and forth, but e-mailing documents has also nearly put the post office out of business. In fact, it has been 17 years since I last sent in a printed manuscript of a book. Just about all file transfers done between individuals now is done by e-mail attachments.

All e-mail programs have the ability to send and receive attachments. The following sections are specific to the Windows Mail program that comes with Windows Vista. Your e-mail program may be different, but the advice I offer applies to anyone using any e-mail program.

Grabbing an attachment with Windows Mail

An attachment to an e-mail message shows up in the Windows Mail inbox with a teensy paperclip icon. That icon is your clue that the message contains an attachment.

To save the attachment, follow these steps:

1. **Choose File⇨Save Attachments.**

   The Save Attachments dialog box appears.

2. **(Optional) Use the Browse button to find a proper folder for the attachment.**

   For example, I browse to my Video folder to save all those movies people send me.

3. **Click the Save button.**

   The file is saved.

To view or access the file, you need to switch away from Windows Mail and open the folder into which you saved the attachment. At that point, accessing the file works just like accessing any other file on your computer.

- ✔ Don't open attachments you weren't expecting, especially program files — even if they're from people you know. Just delete the message. Or, if you're using antivirus software (which I highly recommend), the antivirus program may alert you to the nasty program's presence even before you open the e-mail.

- ✔ At some point, you may receive a file that your PC cannot digest — a file of an unknown format. If so, Windows displays a "Windows cannot open this file" type of dialog box. My advice? Click the Cancel button. Respond to the e-mail and tell the person that you can't open the file and need to have it re-sent in another format.

Sending an attachment in Windows Mail

To attach a file to an outgoing message, follow these beloved steps:

1. **Compose the message as you normally would: Enter the name, subject, and message content.**

   Some people wait to write the message content *after* they attach the file. That way, they don't forget to send the attachment.

2. **Click the Attach File to Message button (the paperclip icon, as shown in the margin) on the toolbar.**

3. **Use the Open dialog box to locate the file you want to attach.**

4. **Select the file in the Open dialog box.**

5. **Click the Open button.**

6. **(Optional) To add another attachment, repeat Steps 2 through 5.**

7. **Click the Send button to send the message.**

Sending a message with a file attached takes longer than sending a regular, text-only message.

- ✔ You should ensure that the recipient of a message can read the type of file you're sending. For example, sending a Word file to a WordPerfect user may not meet with the results you want.

- ✔ Note that some folks cannot receive large files. Sometimes, the limit is 5MB, but I have seen it as low as 1MB. The alternative? Burn a CD-R and send the files through the regular mail. (Refer to Chapter 28 for information on burning CD-Rs.)

Things you don't need to know about FTP

FTP is one of those ubiquitous three-letter acronyms (TLAs) that litter computer jargon like empty Pabst cans at a NASCAR race. It stands for File Transfer Protocol, and it's also a verb that generically means "to send files hither and thither on the Internet." For example, when you grab a file from the Web, as described in this chapter, your PC is really using FTP to get the file.

You can also use specific FTP programs if all you want is to get files. Just as there are Web *servers* on the Internet — computers that dish up Web pages — there are *FTP servers,* or computers that just list a host of files. You can use your Web browser to access an FTP server, or you can use specific FTP software, such as FileZilla, from `http://filezilla.sourceforge.net`.

Theoretically, using FTP is just like working with files in Windows. The difference is that rather than copy files between one disk drive and another, you copy them from one computer to another over the Internet. Also, some FTP servers require a password for access, and that seems to bewilder some folks.

The only real reason to mess with FTP any more is when you plan to create your own Web page. In that case, you need an FTP program, or to use FTP as part of your Web page creation program, to get the Web page from your computer onto the Internet. That's a whole other book, so I think I'll stop writing about FTP right here.

✔ Send JPEG or PNG pictures. Any other picture format is usually too large and makes the recipient wait a long time to receive the message.

✔ You can send more than one file at a time — just keep attaching files.

✔ Or, rather than send several small files, consider putting them all in a compressed folder and just sending the single compressed folder instead.

✔ Don't send file shortcuts; send only originals. If you send a shortcut, the people receiving the file don't get the original. Instead, they get the 296-byte shortcut, which doesn't do them any good.

✔ Try not to move or delete any files you attach to e-mail messages until *after* you send the message. I know that it sounds dumb, but too often, as I wait for my e-mail to be sent out (while I'm not busy), I start cleaning files. Oops!

Chapter 23

Internet and PC Security

In This Chapter

▶ Understanding what computer nasties are

▶ Fighting pop-up windows

▶ Dealing with fake Web pages

▶ Using a firewall

▶ Keeping Windows up-to-date

▶ Stopping spyware

▶ Coping with the UAC warnings

*T*he Internet may be a thriving community and full of information, but it's not exactly the safest place to be. Because just about anyone can get on the Internet, and because the Internet is an open system, lots of bad guys are prowling out there. They make nasty programs and can do nasty things to your computer if you're not careful.

Fortunately, Windows Vista is just chock-full of helpful tools and programs that assist in keeping your PC safe. This chapter covers the gamut, although I also recommend taking a peek at my book *Troubleshooting Your PC For Dummies* (Wiley Publishing, Inc.) for more information on fixin' computer woes.

Bad Guys and Superheroes

Yes, your PC can often play host to a throng of bad guys and their superhero counterparts. The bad guys have names you've probably heard:

✔ Phishing

✔ Pop-up

✔ Spyware

- ✔ Trojan
- ✔ Virus
- ✔ Worm

These are all names of nasty or annoying things that can make the Internet less fun to use. Fortunately, Windows offers you many ways to defend yourself against these nasty programs. Specifically, you can look to three programs:

 Internet Explorer: The latest version of Internet Explorer (7.0, as this book goes to press) comes with a rich set of features for keeping your PC safe. These include ample warnings when software tries to install itself into your PC from the Internet.

 Windows Defender: A new treat with Windows Vista is Windows Defender, which is a collection of programs and utilities designed not only to fight the bad programs but also help you remove them.

 Windows Firewall: A firewall is a necessary part of using the Internet, sad to say. Windows Firewall has grown up since its original version and now helps to close the windows and bar the doors that the bad guys once used to infect PCs.

The following sections provide more information on using these tools to help keep your PC safe and its owner happy.

- ✔ All nasty programs fall into the *malware* category, which is a combination of the words *mal*icious and soft*ware*.

- ✔ You can avoid many nasty programs by simply using common sense. In fact, the most successful computer viruses have propagated simply because of human nature. It's that *human engineering* that the bad guys count on, or your ability to be tricked into doing something you wouldn't do otherwise, such as opening a questionable e-mail attachment or clicking a Web page link because you're fooled into thinking that "your PC is at risk!"

- ✔ To help you keep your kids safe on the Internet, I recommend that you peruse the Parental Controls feature in Windows Vista. A good source of information about the Parental Controls can be found in my book *Find Gold in Windows Vista* (Wiley Publishing, Inc.).

- ✔ Your ISP can be of great help when it comes to dealing with nasty programs on the Internet. Don't forget to use their assistance, especially when you first try fixing things on your own and it doesn't help.

Know the bad guys

As with everything about computers, malicious software, or *malware,* is named in either an overly technical or often silly manner. The name is cute, but it doesn't really help in understanding what it is that the bad program does. So, here's your handy guide to the bad guys that enjoy preying upon your PC:

Phishing: Pronounced "fishing," this term applies to a Web page or e-mail that's designed to fool you into thinking it's something else, such as your bank's Web page. The idea is to *fish* for information, such as account numbers and passwords. The Web page or e-mail tricks you into providing that information because it looks legitimate. It isn't.

Pop-up: A pop-up isn't really a nasty program, but it can be annoying — especially when you're assaulted with several pop-ups all at once. How any legitimate marketing person would believe that multiple, annoying pop-up windows would entice anyone to buy something is beyond me, but it happens and you can stop it.

Spyware: A rather broad category, *spyware* refers to any program or technique that monitors,

or spies on, what you do on the Internet. The reasoning is advertising: By knowing where you go and what you do on the Internet, information obtained about you can be sold to advertisers who then target ads your way.

Trojan: A program is labeled a *Trojan* (horse) when it claims to do one thing but really does another. For example, a common Trojan is a special screen saver that saves the screen but also uses your PC on the Internet to relay pornographic images.

Virus: A *virus* is a nasty program that resides in your PC without your knowledge and infects the computer. The program may be triggered at any time, where it may take over the computer, redirect Internet traffic, use your computer to flood out spam messages, or do any of a number of nasty and inconvenient things.

Worm: A *worm* is simply a virus that replicates itself, by sending out copies to other folks on your e-mail list, for example.

Internet Explorer Tools

Internet Explorer (IE) version 7.0 comes with a host of new features as well as extra bulletproofing to help keep you safe on the Internet. The feature list is vast, but for brevity I'm limiting my discussion in the following sections to the two most annoying issues that IE 7.0 addresses: pop-up windows and phishing.

You can start Internet Explorer in 17 different ways. The most popular way is to locate the IE icon on the desktop or on the Start button menu. Opening the icon runs IE. The following two sections assume that IE is open and ready for action on your computer screen.

Blocking pop-ups

Banishing the annoying pop-up window is a natural in IE. To confirm that pop-ups are being blocked, follow these steps:

1. **Click the Tools button on the toolbar.**

   The Tools menu appears (pops up, actually).

2. **Choose Pop-up Blocker.**

   The Pop-up Blocker submenu is displayed.

3. **Choose Turn On Pop-up Blocker, if necessary, and then click the Yes button to confirm.**

   Otherwise, if the menu command is Turn Off Pop-up Blocker, you're already set.

When set in action, the pop-up blocker suppresses almost any pop-up display window. That means you miss out on all those ads! Boo-hoo!

When IE blocks a pop-up window, you see a warning banner displayed just above the part of the window where you view the Web page. The banner reads "Pop-up blocked. To see this pop-up or additional options, click here." Clicking the banner displays a menu of options.

✔ Blocking pop-up windows may disable some Web page features, such as a pop-up video window, a menu, or another informative display. In those cases, it's obviously okay to allow pop-ups for that window or Web page: Click the warning banner and choose Temporarily Allow Pop-ups from the menu.

✔ IE's pop-up blocker doesn't work to block certain animated pop-up windows. For example, Flash animations can display pop-up windows regardless of the pop-up blocker's settings. (Yes, it seems like every time you gain some ground on the bad guys, they think of some new way to assault you.)

Phighting phishing

The *phishing* scam is quite popular, mostly because it effectively fools innocent people into doing something they would never in their right mind do otherwise. (See the earlier sidebar "Know the bad guys" for more information on phishing.) Happily, you can worry a bit less (but not completely) about phishing scams when IE is configured to assist you in finding them.

To check IE's phishing filter settings, mind these directions:

1. **Click the Tools button on the toolbar.**

2. **Choose Phishing Filter to display that submenu.**

3. **Confirm that the second command reads Turn Off Automatic Website Checking.**

   If so, you're done; otherwise, continue:

4. **Choose Turn On Automatic Website Checking.**

   A special security dialog box, Microsoft Phishing Filter, appears.

5. **Click OK.**

   The phishing filter is now activated.

The phishing filter alerts you to any Web page link that, well, appears to be fishy. The link may claim that it goes to one Web page when in fact it goes to another. Or, the link may go to a Web site known for doing naughty things with people's personal information. Either way, you're warned.

If you suspect a Web page of not being the real deal, click the Tools toolbar button and choose Phishing Filter➪Check This Website from the menu. After clicking the OK button, IE does a specific and thorough check of the Web site to confirm whether you're being duped.

Don't lower your guard just because IE features a phishing filter. Remember: It's human engineering that the bad guys count on to make their scams work. No financial institution sends vital information over e-mail. None of them does! When in doubt, phone your banker and confirm the message. Often times, you discover that the message is bogus. Even if it shouldn't be, it's better to be safe than to be violated by a crook.

The Windows Security Center

The headquarters for all security things in Windows is a place called the Windows Security Center, illustrated in Figure 23-1. The Security Center window provides a quick summary of just about every important aspect of your PC's security settings, plus it offers links to other vital locations and security programs in Windows.

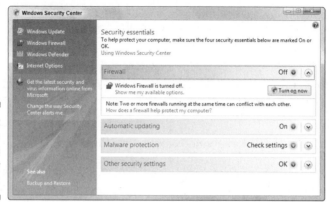

Figure 23-1:
The
Windows
Security
Center.

To start the Windows Security Center, first open the Control Panel. From the Control Panel Home, beneath the Security heading, choose the link labeled Check This Computer's Security Status. From the Control Panel Classic view, open the Windows Security Center icon.

Anything that requires immediate attention is highlighted in red in the Windows Security Center window. Lesser warnings are shown in yellow. Green information is deemed okay.

To view more information, click the Show More arrow in any particular area, although often when things are important, the area is opened for you, as with the Firewall area, shown in Figure 23-1.

- Generally speaking, follow the advice in the window.

- In Figure 23-1, Windows Firewall is disabled. This is because my PC sits behind a firewall with a hardware router. A duplicate firewall would be redundant in that situation.

- Also in Figure 23-1, the Malware Protection area is colored yellow. This is because my PC doesn't have antivirus software installed.

Windows Firewall

The term *firewall* comes from the construction industry, where a building's firewall is used to slow the advance of a fire. The firewall is created from special slow-burning material, rated in *hours*. For example, a three-hour firewall theoretically takes three hours to burn through — and that helps protect a building from burning down before the fire department shows up.

On a computer with an Internet connection, a *firewall* is designed to restrict Internet access, primarily to keep out unwanted guests. The firewall effectively plugs holes through which bad guys could get in and mess with your PC.

Windows Vista comes with a firewall named, coincidentally, Windows Firewall. You can start Windows Firewall from the Windows Security Center window (from a link on the left), or you can locate Windows Firewall in the Control Panel.

As far as you're concerned, Windows Firewall has only two settings: On and Off. Unless your PC is sitting behind a hardware firewall in a router (see Chapter 19), you want Windows Firewall set to the On position. Otherwise, if your PC sits behind a firewall, or you prefer to use other firewall software, you can safely turn off Windows Firewall.

✔ I recommend testing your PC's firewall. Many programs available on the Internet probe your PC's firewall and look for weaknesses. One such program is ShieldsUP, from Gibson Research:

```
http://grc.com/
```

✔ The firewall tests both incoming and outgoing information. In fact, unexpected outgoing information is typically a sign that your PC is infected with a virus or spyware.

✔ When the firewall detects unwanted access, you see a pop-up window alerting you to the intrusion. At that point, you can choose to allow or deny access, although if it's unexpected, you should click the Deny button. In fact, clicking the Deny button doesn't harm any software; if you improperly block a legitimate program, though, you see a lot of Deny messages.

✔ The Internet wasn't designed with security in mind. Back in the original days, scientists were open about their systems and didn't feel the need to protect their computers from other Internet users. Therefore, the *ports*, or avenues of communications between computers on the Internet, were left wide open and unprotected. That tradition continues today, which is why extra software — a firewall — is needed.

Updating Windows

I highly recommend that you keep your PC's operating system updated. This requires regular communications between your computer and the Microsoft mothership. No need to fret; the scheduling happens automatically (typically on Tuesday, for some reason). If any new updates, or *patches,* are needed, they're automatically installed on your computer. You need to do nothing.

Well, you do need to ensure that you configured your PC to accept automatic updates by using the Windows Update service. Here's how:

1. **Open the Windows Update window.**

   You can easily get there from the Windows Security Center, as described earlier in this chapter. You can also open the Windows Update window from the Control Panel.

   The Windows Update window lists updates that are installed, plus any pending updates, as shown in Figure 23-2.

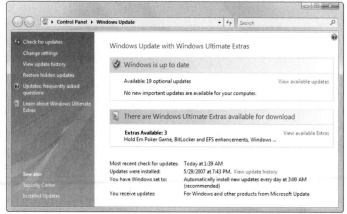

Figure 23-2:
The
Windows
Update
window.

2. **On the left side of the window, click Change Settings.**

3. **Ensure that the top option is selected, Install Updated Automatically (Recommended).**

   For laptop computers, I recommend the second option, Download Updates But Let Me Choose Whether to Install Them. That option is more convenient, especially when you're running your laptop from battery power.

4. **Click the OK button.**

5. **Enter the administrator password or click the Continue button to confirm the change.**

By automatically updating Windows, you're assured that you have the latest security patch from Microsoft. Because Windows is a *huge* target for the bad guys, that's just a good idea.

✔ In the past, I recommended against updating Windows. But after a few years Microsoft has finally figured out how to do it correctly. Assuming that you have Windows Vista, I highly recommend that you keep it updated with Windows Update.

✔ When you're connected to the Internet via a broadband connection, you receive updates all the time. When updates are waiting, a pop-up bubble from the Notification Area alerts you to their presence. You may also see a tiny shield icon on the Start menu power button.

✔ The Windows Update program may occasionally restart your computer. This is most noticeable when you leave your PC on 24 hours a day; you may approach your computer in the morning and discover that it has been reset. No problem — that's just the result of an automatic update.

Defending Windows

Windows Defender isn't really a single program as much as it's multiple tools you can use to help protect your computer from hostile takeover. Specifically, Windows Defender helps protect your PC against spyware and other nasty programs that attempt to monitor, or even control, your computer's activities.

What about antivirus software?

The Windows Security window has a space available for antivirus software. The space is found in the Malware Protection area. The problem is that Windows itself offers nothing to fill that space; You must find and use a third-party antivirus program to complete your PC's protection against nasty programs, especially those that infect your PC through e-mail attachments.

The top two antivirus programs are Norton AntiVirus and McAfee VirusScan. I personally recommend Kaspersky Anti-Virus: www.kaspersky.com. It seems to be more effective at fighting viruses because it's not as popular or as widely used as Norton or McAfee (and thus is not subject to as many attacks).

Incidentally, the reason that viruses spread is simple human engineering. Most folks know not to open strange or unexpected e-mail attachments. Yet viruses continue to be spread by such techniques. Perhaps the best antivirus tool you have is your own brain: Being thoughtful and not careless prevents viruses from being installed in the first place, making antivirus programs necessary but not vital.

To Start Windows Defender, you must visit the Control Panel, or you can click the Windows Defender link from the Windows Security Center window (refer to Figure 23-1).

The Windows Defender main window is rather boring — well, unless you have a problem. Otherwise, it just lists a quick summary saying that your PC is running normally. Whew. For the real action, click the Tools button on the toolbar to see something like Figure 23-3. The various settings and tools that are listed can help you not only track down awful programs but also eliminate them.

Figure 23-3: Windows Defender tools.

For example, clicking the Software Explorer link displays information about various programs started or running in your PC. Removing malicious programs is a snap, thanks to that information. (Refer to my book *Troubleshooting Your PC For Dummies*, published by Wiley, for additional information on using Windows Defender.)

Dealing with annoying User Account Control warnings

The biggest part of Windows Vista security is the ubiquitous User Account Control (UAC) warning dialog boxes, shown in Figures 23-4 and 23-5. These things seem to pop up all the time, but in fact they're very predictable.

Figure 23-4:
The
Standard
account's
UAC.

Figure 23-5:
The admin-
istrator's
UAC.

The only time you should see a UAC dialog box is when you do something to change the PC system. For example, installing new software or new hardware activates a UAC warning. Accessing the Device Manager or any sensitive part of Windows summons a UAC. Even changing the system time causes the UAC to pop up. The action you take is simple: If the UAC is expected, either enter the administrator's password or click the Continue button.

 How can you tell when a UAC is expected? Simple: Any button, link, or command that requires administrator approval is labeled with the Shield icon, as shown in the margin. If you access whichever feature is labeled with the Shield icon, you should expect a UAC to appear.

When you do not expect a UAC to appear is when you should be worried. For example, when you're on the Internet and you see a UAC warning about installing some software or changing your home page, click Cancel!

✔ Vista has two types of UACs. The first requires you to enter the adminis-trator password to continue. You see that UAC when you're logged in to Windows using a Standard account. When you're logged in as an administrator, you see the second type of UAC, which is a simple Continue or Cancel type of dialog box.

- ✔ Refer to a good Windows Vista book, such as *Find Gold in Windows Vista,* for more information on Administrator and Standard accounts.

- ✔ UACs also have varying levels of warning. The topmost level is the red UAC, which indicates a potentially serious change to the computer. Then comes orange UACs, followed by yellow and blue UACs. The color appears at the top of the dialog box, although it's fairly obvious from the dialog box's text whether the situation is serious.

Part V
The Soft Side of Computing

The 5th Wave   By Rich Tennant

"Oh look, this must be one of those PCs that are assembled by prison inmates. It came bundled with a homemade shank in the mousepad."

In this part . . .

There are some common and refreshing universal truths about computers. First, it's very common to be angry with your computer. Second, computers can terrify you when they screw up, but nothing beats that reassuring delight when suddenly the PC starts operating normally again. And third, lulled into believing the hype that computers are easy to use, too few people bother to learn about the software side of computing, which is covered by the chapters in this part of the book.

Chapter 24

Files: The Key to Understanding Software

In This Chapter

▶ Understanding the whole file thing

▶ Describing a file

▶ Naming files

▶ Viewing filename extensions

▶ Understanding icons

▶ Saving files to disk

*E*very day, millions of people sit down at a computer and go about their work. They do e-mail. They process words. They browse the Internet. They play games. Some work may be done. Because computers have become easier to use over the past few years, it's relatively easy for anyone to sit down at a computer and do *something*. Even so, the computer remains a mysterious and often frustrating device for most people.

The problem with computers is that the software is so easy to use that no one bothers taking that extra bonus step of *understanding* how things work. Despite your ability to get work done, you really need to know a few software basics to get the most from your computer. I'm serious! It all starts with the knowledge unfolded in this chapter, the nucleus of all software: the *file*.

Do You Know What a File Is?

I would guess that 80 percent of everyone who uses a PC doesn't have the slightest idea what a file is. Yes, there's a File menu. You save files to disk and you open files on disk. But, only when you truly understand what a file is can you begin to really appreciate your computer and start to take control of the beast.

Presenting the file

A *file* is a chunk of information stored in a computer. The word *file* is used because, in an office setting, information is traditionally stored on paper, and those papers are grouped into file folders, stored in a file cabinet. The same analogy applies to computer files, though I don't think that the comparison has been successful.

When you think of a file, don't even think of a paper file. Instead, the file is a container. The container can be any size, small or large. Unlike a printed sheet of paper, a file can contain a variety of stuff. The container keeps that stuff together and separate from other containers, which also contain stuff separate from other containers.

 ✔ A file is really nothing more than a container, a place to hold a chunk of information stored in a computer.

 ✔ I think *file* is a bad choice for describing something stored in a computer. Had I been one of the computing pioneers, I would have called it a *container* or *holder* or even made up a word using flowery Greek or Latin. The problem with *file* is that it's ambiguous and doesn't adequately describe the nature of the "container o' stuff" inside a computer. Also, as with many computer terms, *file* is used as both a noun and a verb.

What's in a file?

On the atomic level, all the information in a file is *binary,* or just a series of ones and zeroes, like this:

```
1100010011011110111001011010010110111001100111100001
```

Boring! Computers can do miraculous things with ones and zeroes, however, so — categorically speaking — there are really three types of files:

 ✔ Document
 ✔ Program
 ✔ Data file

These types describe the contents of the file, or how the ones and zeroes are interpreted by the software you use.

A *document* includes any file you've created. It can be a true text document, such as a to-do list, a chapter of a novel, or a note to Jimmy's teacher explaining that his skin condition isn't contagious. Documents can also be sound files, graphical images, or any other type of information the computer can create, store, or seize from the Internet.

Program files contain instructions for the computer's microprocessor; they tell the computer what to do. Note that programs are also files. Even the operating system, which is a program, is also a file. In fact, the operating system consists of many files.

Data files include all other files on disk that aren't exactly programs or documents. These include support files for programs, temporary files, and other random stuff that must be saved inside the computer.

Everything stored inside the computer is a file. There are files you create, program files you buy, program files that are part of the operating system, and data files that make up just about everything else. Everything is a file!

Describing a file

Just as people are different, so are files. People are described by how they look and act and by their given names. People also have birthdays and live in certain places. The same is almost entirely true for files, though files don't usually get moody or care whether other files think that they're fat.

All files stored inside the computer have various *attributes,* or specific ways of describing the files and keeping each file unique and separate from the other files. Five of these attributes help you not only identify what the file is but also keep each file unique:

- ✔ Name
- ✔ Size
- ✔ Date and time
- ✔ Type
- ✔ Icon

All files have a name, or *filename.* The name describes the file's contents or gives you a clue to what the file will be used for. The name is given to the file when it's created. This is true for all files.

Files have a physical size. They occupy storage space inside memory, and they also occupy storage space on disk. Some files are tiny, some can be quite large.

When a file is created, the operating system slaps it just like a doctor slaps a human baby. But a file doesn't breathe, and it lacks a butt, so what's slapped on it is a *date-and-time stamp.* This stamp helps keep your files organized and allows you to sort through your files based on their creation dates and times. A second date-and-time stamp is applied to a file whenever it's updated, changed, or modified. (The original creation date and time remain the same.)

Finally, each file has a type, which is closely related to the file's icon you see in Windows. The file type depends on the file's contents, and each program that creates a document assigns that file a specific type and related icon. This is a big topic, so it's covered later in this chapter, starting with the section "File Types and Icons."

✔ The size of a file is measured in bytes, just like memory. Refer to Chapter 8 for more information on bytes.

✔ A file can consist of zero bytes, in which case the file exists but lacks any contents.

✔ The largest a file can be is 4GB. Rarely, however, do files get that big.

✔ The date-and-time stamp is one reason that the PC has an internal clock. It also explains why it's important to keep the PC's clock up to date. Refer to Chapter 6 for more information on setting the clock.

✔ Additional attributes are used to describe files — for example, whether a file is a system file or hidden, read-only, compressed, archived, encrypted, or a bunch of other trivial things. The operating system keeps track of all that stuff.

Files dwell in folders

Another description of a file, missing from the list in the preceding section, is that files are all stored on disk in containers called *folders*. Again with the file cabinet metaphor! Will they ever learn?

The folder helps keep files organized, which allows you to separate files into groups for similar uses. Using folders is one key way to keep from going insane when you use the computer — just as using a closet or cupboard is a way of keeping stuff around the house organized.

Folders are a big part of organizing and using files, so they're covered by themselves, in Chapter 25. That chapter also covers the Windows Explorer program, mentioned in this chapter.

Slap a Name on That File

All files need to have names, and it's good that the computer affords you the opportunity to name your files. If things were up to the computer, files would be named like car license plates, but without the optional wildlife or historical themes.

Because the computer lets you, the human, name the files, you can get as wise and creative as you were when you named the dog or your motorcycle or that comet you discovered that's on a collision course with Earth and will wipe out all life. Have fun! Be playful! This section reviews the basics for naming files.

Choosing the best name

Be clever when you name a file! Naming stuff is one thing humans are good at. I'm referring to older humans, of course. If 2-year-olds were in charge of naming things, all animals would be named Dog.

You name a file when you're saving it to disk, which happens in the Save As dialog box (see the section "The Save As dialog box," later in this chapter). When naming a file, be brief and descriptive. Try using only letters, numbers, and spaces in the name. For example:

```
Argh
Chapter 11
Hidden Political Agenda
2006 Vacation to Wichita
Places in Town to Dump Toxic Waste
```

Each of these examples is a good filename, which properly explains the file's contents.

✔ Upper- or lowercase doesn't matter. Although capitalizing Pocatello is proper, for example, Windows recognizes that filename the same as pocatello, Pocatello, POCATELLO, or any combination of upper- and lowercase letters.

✔ Although case doesn't matter in a filename, it *does* matter when you're typing a Web page address.

✔ The file's name reminds you of what's in the file, of what it's all about — just like naming your dog Not On The Neighbor's Lawn tells everyone what the dog is all about.

✔ You can rename a file at any time after it has been created. See Chapter 26 for information on the Rename command.

✔ All the rules for naming files in this and the following subsections also apply to naming folders, though folders are covered in Chapter 25.

Official file-naming rules

Here's the law when it comes to naming files in Windows. All this stuff is optional reading; as long as you stick with the simple rules in the preceding subsection, this stuff is merely trivia.

Characters: Files can be named using any combination of letters and numbers, plus a smattering of symbols.

Length: Technically, you can give a file a name that's over 200 characters long. Don't. Long filenames may be *very* descriptive, but Windows displays them funny or not at all in many situations. Better to keep things short than to abuse long-filename privileges.

Forbidden characters: Windows gets angry if you use any of these characters to name a file:

```
* / : < > ? \ | "
```

These symbols hold special meaning to Windows. Nothing bad happens if you attempt to use these characters. Windows just refuses to save the file — or a warning dialog box growls at you.

Use periods sparingly: Although you can use any number of periods in a filename, you cannot name a file with all periods. I know that it's strange, and I'm probably the only one on the planet to have tried it, but it doesn't work.

Spaces: Filenames can contain spaces. Try not to start a filename with a space, though, because it's difficult to see. It's common in computerland to use the underscore (or underline) character rather than a space.

Numbers are okay: Feel free to start a filename by using a number. You can even use symbols, though not the forbidden characters just listed. I mention this because there are rumors out there about not starting a filename with a number. Poppycock.

File Types and Icons

Who knows what evil lurks inside a file? Well, honestly, no one does! A file by itself knows nothing of its contents. In fact, the best the operating system can do is to *guess* about a file's contents. Most of the time, it makes a good guess. The system that's used to determine the stuff of a file's guts, however, isn't that solid.

The key is something called the filename extension. That extension is used by Windows to help identify not only the file's contents (its type), but also which program created the file and which icon is displayed on the screen. This section mulls all this over.

The supersecret filename extension

The filename *extension* is a secret bit of text that's added to a filename when the file is first created. The filename extension is applied by the program used to create the file. It tells the operating system three things:

✔ The type of file that's created — document, graphics, or sound, for example

✔ The program that created the file

✔ Which icon to use to represent the file

It's the extension that offers a clue to what's inside a file, and the operating system relies heavily on that extension.

Filename extension details

The filename extension is the last part of a filename, usually hidden from view. It starts with a period, which is then followed by one to four characters. For most files, the extension is three characters long.

For example, the .doc filename extension is used by Microsoft Word to identify Word documents. The extension is pronounced "dot dock," with the dot or period followed by DOC, which is short for document.

Web page files use the .HTM or .HTML filename extension.

Graphics files have a number of filename extensions, depending on the graphics file type: JPG, GIF, TIFF, and PNG, for example.

Note that it's common to write the extension without the leading period, though in a filename the period and extension are there. For example:

```
Chapter 20.DOC
```

The name of this chapter's document file on disk is Chapter 20.DOC. You may see only Chapter 20 on the screen, but the DOC part is there.

✔ There are gazillions of common filename extensions.

✔ Most program files in Windows use the EXE extension, where EXE stands for *exe*cutable file.

✔ A full list of filename extensions is maintained on the Internet, at this Web page:

    www.filext.com

✔ A filename extension is created by the program used to create the file. The extension is added automatically, and it's necessary in Windows. As the computer operator, it helps if you know about extensions, but beyond that, don't mess with them.

How to see or hide a filename extension

You can tell Windows whether you want the filename extension displayed when you view a list of files. Most beginners prefer to hide the extension; old-time PC users like to see the extension. Either way, showing or hiding the extension is done in the same place. Abide by these steps:

1. **Display the Computer window.**

   You can see the Computer window by opening the Computer icon on the desktop or by choosing the Computer command from the Start button menu.

2. **Click the Organize button on the toolbar.**

3. **Choose the Folder and Search Options command.**

   The Folder Options dialog box appears.

4. **Click the View tab.**

5. **Locate the item on the list that says Hide Extensions for Known File Types.**

6. **Put a check mark there to hide the extensions, or remove the check mark so that Windows displays the extensions.**

   Or, if the item is already set the way you like, you're just dandy.

7. **Click OK to close the Folder Options dialog box.**

8. **Close the Computer window.**

If you elect to show the extension, refer to the next subsection for important information on renaming extensions.

Don't rename the extension

If you have configured Windows to display filename extensions (refer to the preceding subsection), be careful when you assign a file a new name by using the Rename command: You must not rename the extension!

The filename extension is just an extra appendage on a filename. It's utterly possible to rename the extension — or delete it. But, when you do so, you deny Windows the opportunity to know what's really in the file. It really messes things up!

Fortunately, Windows warns you when it comes time to rename a file and you either forget to keep the same filename extension or type a new one. When that happens, use the Rename command again, and carefully edit the name so that you keep the file's original extension.

See Chapter 26 for more information on renaming files.

Icons

Windows is a graphical operating system, and, as such, it uses *icons,* or tiny pictures, to represent files. The picture supposedly relates directly to the type of file as well as to the program that created the file. After reading the previous sections, you should recognize that both those attributes are directly related to the filename extension.

Figure 24-1 shows a file as Windows displays it; a graphical icon representing a Word document appears, along with the full filename, including the .DOCX extension.

Figure 24-1:
A file with
an icon,
a name,
and an
extension.

Chapter 1.docx

Each filename extension, or file type, sports a unique icon in Windows, as you discover while you use Windows.

Creating Files

Files are created by using programs — software. Specifically, the software that creates stuff is an *application*. For example, you use the word processing application Microsoft Word to create text documents, brochures, novels, plays, and left-wing manifestos.

The good news is that it's easy to create things with a computer and the proper software. The bad news is that the computer happily and repeatedly loses anything you create — until you save that something to disk.

Saving to disk is important! Nothing is truly created until you save!

It doesn't matter how long you worked to create the thing — the document, image, or whatever: Until you use the Save command, that information exists only in the wispy gossamer of the computer's fickle imagination (also known as RAM). Pull the plug and — *POOF!* — that stuff is gone for good.

To avoid disaster, you must save your stuff to disk. Your tool for doing so is the Save command.

The Save command

Windows has two Save commands: Save and Save As. Both exist on the File menu.

The first time you save your stuff to disk, the Save As command is used (even if you choose File➪Save). Save As directs Windows to give the file a name and save it on a specific disk drive and in a specific folder. The Save As command *creates* the file.

After your stuff is saved to disk with Save As and the new file is created, you use the plain Save command to update the file. So, after initially saving, you work a little bit, and then you use the Save command, File➪Save, to update the file on disk. It works this way until you're done, when you save one last time before quitting the program.

✔ In Microsoft Office 2007, the Save and Save As commands are found on the Office button menu.

 ✔ The Save command can also be accessed from the Save button on a toolbar or by pressing Ctrl+S on the keyboard.

✔ You can also use the Save As command specifically to save a file with a new name or in a new location.

 ✔ After a file has been saved, the file's name appears on the title bar (at the top of the window).

The Save As dialog box

The first time you save your stuff to disk, a Save As dialog box appears. The purpose of this dialog box is, obviously, to save your precious work to disk, or permanent storage. That way, you always have a copy of your stuff handy for future use.

The Save As dialog box is also the place where you assign your stuff a file-name and set the file in a specific folder on a specific disk drive. (Folders are covered in Chapter 25.)

Figure 24-2 shows the typical Save As dialog box. It contains a lot of controls specifically designed to baffle the new computer user. What you need to find specifically is the text box, near the bottom, labeled File Name. That's where you type the name of the file you're saving.

Figure 24-2:
The typical
Save As
dialog box.

Here's how the Save As dialog box works on the simplest level:

1. **Type a name for your file.**

   Refer to the file-naming rules earlier in this chapter. Be clever. Be descriptive. Be brief.

2. **Click the Save button.**

   The file is safely stored on your hard disk.

Trust me: The file is saved to disk. There's no need to confirm this. Had there been an error, Windows would promptly inform you.

If clicking the Save button doesn't work, you probably used a forbidden character in the filename or used the name of a file that has already been saved. The more polite programs tell you specifically the booboo you made. Ruder programs just don't let you click the Save button.

Additional controls in the Save As dialog box allow you to select a specific disk drive and folder for your stuff. I recommend that you read Chapter 25, on folders, before you attempt to do that.

✔ The Save As dialog box appears only the first time you save your stuff to disk; from that point on, the Save command merely resaves a file to disk.

✔ Not every Save As dialog box looks like the one shown earlier, in Figure 24-2. In fact, that image is simply the quick view. By clicking the Browse Folders button in the dialog box's lower left corner, you can see more information displayed, which makes the Save As dialog box appear more like a Windows Explorer window.

✔ Use the address bar to save the file in a specific folder. Clicking the triangles separating folder names on the address bar displays a menu of other folders you can use to save the file.

✔ If you directed Windows not to display the filename extension, you don't see the extension used in the Save As dialog box. On the other hand, if the extensions are visible, you see them as shown in Figure 24-2, where it says (in tiny letters) .rtf after the filename.

✔ The Save As Type drop-down list directs the program to save the file as a specific file type. This tool can be used to override the program's normal file type and save your stuff in a specific type. For example, you can use this option to save a Word document in the plain text (TXT) file type. Mess with the option only when you know that you want to save the file as a different type.

Chapter 25

Organizing Your Compu-Junk

In This Chapter

▶ Knowing what a folder is

▶ Discovering the root folder

▶ Finding your account folder

▶ Understanding forbidden folders

▶ Using the Windows Explorer program

▶ Creating new folders

▶ Working in the Open dialog box

Stuff happens, and on your PC you soon discover that it happens quite a bit! If you do any work at all with your computer, you soon discover yourself buried hip deep in files. Files everywhere! Files you created, files you snagged from the Internet, and files that seem to grow like warts on a witch. What to do, what to do?

The solution to the file flood is a wee bit of organization. It comes from the concept known as a *folder,* which is the first step in organizing your stuff. Even programs and Windows itself use folders for organizing things, which makes the folder the equivalent of the California Closet or extra-bonus garage shelving — what everyone with a lot of stuff needs. This chapter explains how it's all done.

The Folder Story

Folders exist to organize your files, which continues the office metaphor that computers use — the one I totally dismiss in Chapter 24. *Folders* are merely containers for files. Folders keep files of similar types together, or they allow you to organize files by project, theme, or however you want to use them to keep your stuff sane.

Yes! Sanity is the key! Without folders, files would litter the hard drive like pieces of a casino after a Las Vegas demolition. The typical PC hard drive now stores between 10,000 and 50,000 files. Imagine finding just one file! Heck, it would take you a week to scroll through the list. I won't even go into the madness of duplicate filenames and how sluggish the computer would behave any time you saved or opened anything on the hard drive. Yech!

No, folders are the key to organizing files on your computer's hard drive, and on other permanent storage media. Windows uses folders. You should use them, too.

- ✔ A folder is a storage place for files.

- ✔ Refer to Chapter 24 for information on files. It's very important! Understanding files is the key to using software on your computer.

- ✔ All files stored on your computer's permanent storage devices are kept in folders. The folders keep files together — like barbed wire keeps prisoners, vicious animals, and kindergartners from wandering off.

- ✔ Folders appear in Windows using the folder icon, as shown in the margin. When the folder is empty, it appears as shown in the margin. A folder with contents appears full, sometimes even previewing the contents in the folder icon itself.

- ✔ To open the folder, double-click it with the mouse. Folders open into a window that displays the folder's contents.

- ✔ Folders hold files. They can also hold other folders. Folders within folders! Just like those Russian matryoshka dolls.

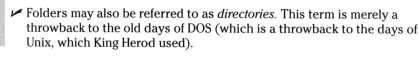

- ✔ Folders may also be referred to as *directories.* This term is merely a throwback to the old days of DOS (which is a throwback to the days of Unix, which King Herod used).

Famous Folders throughout History

Whether you like it or not, all your computer's storage media are organized into folders. Storage media exist to store files, and files *must be* stored in folders. Beyond that, some specific and aptly named folders are available on your PC when you run the Windows operating system. This section mulls over the lot of them.

The root folder

Every storage media — from the mighty hard drive to the teensiest wafer-thin memory card — has at least one folder. That one folder — the main folder on the disk — is the *root folder*. As on a tree, all other folders on your hard drive branch out from that main, root folder.

The root folder doesn't have a specific icon. Instead, it uses the icon for the media that the root folder is on. So, the root folder on drive C has the same icon as drive C. You can see those icons in the Computer window.

- ✔ The root folder is simply the main, or only, folder on any storage media.
- ✔ The root folder is like the lobby of some grand building: It's merely a place you pass through to get to somewhere else. Where else? Why, other folders, of course!
- ✔ The root folder may also be called the *root directory*.

Subfolders and parent folders

Folders can contain both files and other folders. When one folder exists inside another, it is said to be a *subfolder*. This term has nothing to do with underwater naval vessels or hoagie-like sandwiches.

Say you have a folder named Vacation and that folder exists inside a folder named 2008. The folder Vacation is said to be a subfolder of the folder 2008. Conversely, the folder 2008 is said to be the *parent* folder of the Vacation folder.

A subfolder can also be called a *child* folder, but that's just a tad cheeky now, isn't it?

- ✔ No limit exists on the number of subfolders you can create. You can have a folder inside a folder inside a folder, and so on. If you name the folders well, it all makes sense. Otherwise, it's just like a badly organized filing cabinet, without the smell of booze.
- ✔ You can create folders any time you like. See the section "Let There Be Folders," later in this chapter, for the details.
- ✔ As the topmost folder on any storage media, the root folder has no parent folder, though in the Windows hierarchy of things, the "parent folder" of any storage media is the Computer window, and the Computer window's parent folder is the desktop.

The User Profile folder

Humans don't use the root folder; the root folder is for the computer only. And although you can store files on the desktop, the Windows Help file recommends that you do not. Don't fret: Windows has the perfect place for your stuff. It's the User Profile folder.

The *User Profile* folder is the main folder for storing your stuff on the computer. Yes, I agree that it's a horrible, clunky name. But again Bill Gates didn't phone me to ask my opinion, so we're all stuck with the term *User Profile* folder. I believe mankind will survive this travesty.

Your user account name is used to name the User Profile folder. So, the easiest way to get to that folder is to choose your account name from the left side of the Start button menu. Or, you may see on the desktop an icon representing your account name. Choosing the Account menu item or opening the desktop icon displays the User Account Folder window, shown in Figure 25-1.

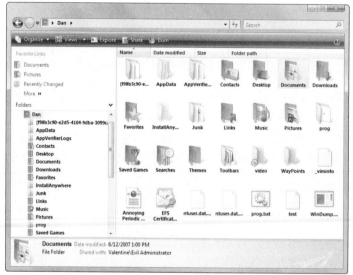

Figure 25-1:
The User
Account
Folder
window.

Inside the User Account Folder window, you find about a dozen folders precreated for you, each of which helps you organize the contents of your computer. Table 25-1 lists the folders commonly found.

Table 25-1	Subfolders Found in the User Profile Folder
Folder Name	*Contains*
Contacts	A database of people's names used by Windows Mail and other contact- or personal-information programs
Desktop	A local copy of shortcuts and other files placed on the desktop
Documents	Text documents and similar files
Downloads	Files downloaded from the Internet

Folder Name	Contains
Favorites	Bookmarks set and used by Internet Explorer
Links	Shortcuts to popular files and folders, which are displayed in the Windows Explorer window
Music	Audio and music files, used by Windows Media Player and other musical programs
Pictures	Digital images, photographs, drawings, and artwork
Saved Games	Information retained by games so that you can remember your spot or high score from a previously played game
Searches	A set of predefined or saved file searches (see Chapter 26)
Videos	Films, movies, and animations

You find that certain programs use these specific folders, so you should keep them. For example, graphics applications prefer to save images in the Pictures folder. Of course, there's nothing wrong with your taking extra steps and creating sub-subfolders to organize the dozen or so that Windows already provides — or even creating additional folders for further organization, as I did in Figure 25-1.

✔ All applications automatically choose the User Account folder or one of its subfolders when you use the Save As dialog box to save a file.

✔ Many folders in the User Profile folder had counterparts from previous versions of Windows. For example, Documents was once My Documents, and Music was once My Music. Generally speaking, the My part of the folder name has been dropped.

✔ Don't mess with any folders outside the My Documents folder or any folder you didn't create yourself.

✔ The User Profile folder is generally found on drive C, where Windows dwells. If your PC has other hard drives, you can also use them to store your stuff. In that case, it's okay to use the root folder on those drives.

Famous yet forbidden folders

In addition to needing folders for your stuff, your computer needs folders for the stuff Windows uses and folders for your applications. I call them *forbidden* folders; don't mess with them!

Windows. Windows itself lives in the Windows folder, which may be named WINNT on some computers. This folder contains many files and a heck of a lot of subfolders, all of which comprise the Windows operating system and its support programs. *Touch ye not the files that lurketh there!*

Program Files. The software you use on your PC also has its own home plate, the *Program Files folder.* Within that folder are numerous subfolders, one each for the various programs installed on your computer — or perhaps one general folder for all programs from a specific vendor. Look, but don't touch.

Other folders. The computer's C drive is chock-full of folders. What do they do? I don't know! I don't think anyone knows, but that's not the point. The point is to use only your User Account folder and its subfolders for your stuff. Any other folder is considered hands off.

> ✔ You may occasionally hear the Windows folder (and its subfolders) referred to by their official corporate name: *system folders.*

> ✔ Although you may someday poke around inside a forbidden folder, don't mess with anything there.

> ✔ The root folder of the hard drive is considered forbidden.

> ✔ Don't mess with any folder you didn't create yourself! You can look, but don't do anything else!

The Windows Explorer Program

One duty of an operating system is to help you organize the stuff you create. It's Windows job to put files on the hard drive, organize the files into folders, and keep track of all that stuff. Furthermore, Windows presents the file and folder information to you in a simple manner, which allows you to control your files and folders without the necessity of a second brain. The tool you use to help manipulate those files and folders is the Windows Explorer program.

Windows Explorer is one of the easiest programs to run. My favorite way to start it is to press Win+E on the keyboard. You can also open the Computer or User Account icon on the desktop or choose Computer or your user account name from the Start button menu. The Windows Explorer program is shown in Figure 25-2.

In Figure 25-2, Windows Explorer displays the files and folders found in the Documents folder. You can see Documents as the last item (on the right) on the address bar. Also visible are the Navigation pane with the Favorite Links area and Folders list, and the Details pane.

TIP

> ✔ Windows Explorer isn't the same program as Internet Explorer.

> ✔ You control what's visible in the Windows Explorer window by using the Organize toolbar button's menu. Choose a pane to view, or summon the traditional menu bar, from the Layout submenu.

> ✔ The size and appearance of the icons in the Windows Explorer window depend on settings you make from the Views toolbar button.

> ✔ Toolbar buttons come and go in Windows Explorer, depending on what you're doing and which type of icon is selected.

> ✔ To open a folder, double-click its icon. Folders all open in the same window, unless you configure Windows to open each folder in its own window (which I don't recommend because it can get terribly busy).

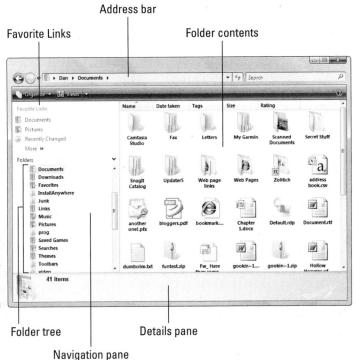

Address bar

Favorite Links

Folder contents

Figure 25-2:
Windows
Explorer.

Folder tree

Details pane

Navigation pane

Let There Be Folders

Creating a folder is easy. Remembering to use the folder is the hard part. But when the organizing mood hits you or you start a new project or you just want to keep some files separate from others, create a folder. Follow these steps:

1. Open the parent folder.

Folders must be created on media and in a folder, even if it's the root folder of the media. Therefore, the first step you need to do is to open a folder window in which you'll create your new folder.

2. Click the Organize button on the toolbar.

3. Choose New Folder from the menu.

The new folder appears as an icon in the window. Its name is New Folder, but note that the name is *selected*. It means that you can type a new folder name immediately.

4. Type a short, descriptive name for the folder.

I often have folders named Stuff or Stow or even Junk into which I put things I don't know where else to put. But don't fret over the name; you can always rename a folder later.

5. Press Enter to lock in the name.

The new folder is ready to use.

You can double-click the new folder's icon to open it. A blank window appears because it's a new folder and has no contents. See Chapter 26 for information on copying or moving files into the folder.

✔ Be clever with the name! Remember that this folder will contain files and possibly other folders, all of which should relate somehow to the folder's name.

✔ Generally speaking, folders are manipulated like files. After creating a folder, you can rename it, move it, copy it, delete it, or make a shortcut to the folder. See Chapter 26 for those details.

✔ A special type of folder is the *Compressed Folder*, also known as a Zip file. Of course, discussing compressed folders pushes this book more into the topic of Windows itself. So if you want to read more about Compressed Folders, refer to a good Windows book.

The Open Dialog Box

As you use your computer, you often find yourself digging through folders with the Open or Browse dialog box, off to fetch a file somewhere on disk. For example, you want to open that document you worked on yesterday, the one that contains your plans for winning the Junior Miss Avocado Pageant.

The Open dialog box, depicted in Figure 25-3, is summoned by using the Open command. Similarly, its sister the Browse dialog box appears when you issue a Browse command. Both ways, the purpose of the dialog box is to hunt down a specific file on disk.

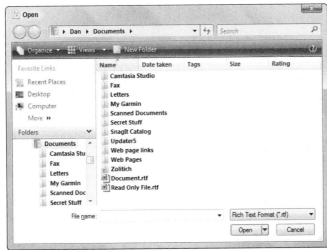

Figure 25-3:
The typical Open dialog box.

Yes, the Open dialog box looks and works a lot like a Windows Explorer window. It has the same panes, toolbar, and file list. The bonus information specific to opening files, however, is found near the bottom of the dialog box.

The File Name text box allows you to manually enter a filename — which is a typically silly and nerdy thing to do, so I don't recommend it.

The menu button, the one that says Rich Text Format (*rtf) in Figure 25-3, is used to help narrow the type of file listed in the Open dialog box. By narrowing the list, you can more easily scope out the file you want.

Finally, you click the Open button to open the selected file. Note that the Open button often has a menu button next to it. Clicking that button displays options for opening a file.

- ✔ Note that not every program can open every type of file. Programs work best on the files they create themselves.

- ✔ When you're really stuck finding a file, use the Windows Search command. See Chapter 26.

Chapter 26

File Control

In This Chapter

▶ Selecting groups of files

▶ Moving or copying files and folders

▶ Duplicating files

▶ Copying files to removable media

▶ Making a file shortcut

▶ Deleting and undeleting files

▶ Renaming files and folders

▶ Finding lost files

*Y*our files represent the stuff you create on your computer. As such, they're very important to you. The operating system understands this, and it gives you a smattering of tools to control, manipulate, and maintain your files. Control is the issue here! Like nuclear fuel or a room full of kindergarteners, your files must be contained. This chapter describes the tools you need to use to control your files.

Working with Groups of Files

Before you can mess with any file, you must select it. As with singing, you can select files individually or in groups.

To select a single file, click its icon once with the mouse. Click. A selected file appears highlighted on-screen, similar to the one shown in Figure 26-1. The file is now ready for action.

    ✔ Clicking a file with the mouse *selects* that file.

    ✔ Selected files appear highlighted in the folder window.

> ✔ You can select files in only one window at a time. You cannot select files across multiple folders.
>
> ✔ File manipulation commands — Copy, Move, Rename, and Delete, for example — affect only selected files.

Figure 26-1:
The icon
(file) on the
right is
selected.

Selecting all files in a folder

To select all files inside a folder, click the Organize button on the toolbar and choose the Select All command. This command highlights all files in the window — including any folders (and all the folders' contents) and marks them as ready for action.

You can also use the Ctrl+A keyboard shortcut to select all files in a folder.

Selecting a random smattering of files

Suppose that you need to select four icons in a folder all at once, similar to what's shown in Figure 26-2. Here's how to do that:

Figure 26-2:
A random
smattering
of files is
selected.

1. **Click to select the first file.**

   Point the mouse at the file's icon and click once.

2. **Press and hold the Ctrl key on the keyboard.**

   Either Ctrl (control) key works; press and hold it down.

3. **Click to select the next file.**

   By holding the Ctrl key, you can select as many files as your clicking finger desires. (If you don't hold it down, clicking one file unselects anything that's already selected.)

4. **Repeat Step 3 until you have selected all the files you want.**

   Or, until your clicking finger gets sore.

5. **Release the Ctrl key when you're done selecting files.**

Now you're ready to manipulate the selected files as a group.

To deselect a file from a group, just Ctrl+click it again.

Selecting a swath of files in a row

To select a queue of files, such as those shown in Figure 26-3, pursue these steps:

Name ▲	Size	Type	Artist
Bach's Brandenburg Concerto...	142 KB	MIDI Sequence	
Back to the Future.mid	39 KB	MIDI Sequence	
Beethoven's 5th Symphony.rmi	91 KB	MIDI Sequence	
Beethoven's Fur Elise.rmi	21 KB	MIDI Sequence	
bewitched.mid	9 KB	MIDI Sequence	
bigtop.mid	30 KB	MIDI Sequence	
bjs-ming.mid	6 KB	MIDI Sequence	
bohemian rhapsody.mid	51 KB	MIDI Sequence	
brunes.mid	47 KB	MIDI Sequence	
Bumble Bee.mid	14 KB	MIDI Sequence	
bumble.mid	21 KB	MIDI Sequence	
bwv538f.mid	25 KB	MIDI Sequence	
bwv538t.mid	36 KB	MIDI Sequence	
bwv948.mid	14 KB	MIDI Sequence	
Can't do that sum.mid	11 KB	MIDI Sequence	
CANYON.MID	21 KB	MIDI Sequence	
cartoons.mid	5 KB	MIDI Sequence	
Classical Gas.mid	8 KB	MIDI Sequence	
Dance of the Sugar-Plum Fair...	21 KB	MIDI Sequence	
Debussy's Claire de Lune.rmi	28 KB	MIDI Sequence	
doom1.mid	18 KB	MIDI Sequence	
elvis.mid	16 KB	MIDI Sequence	
EURYDICE.MID	90 KB	MIDI Sequence	
figaro.mid	38 KB	MIDI Sequence	

Figure 26-3: A group of files in a row is selected.

1. **Click the Views menu button on the toolbar and choose List from the menu.**

2. **Click to select the first file in your group.**

3. **Press and hold the Shift key.**

   Either Shift key on the keyboard works.

4. Click to select the last file in your group.

By holding down the Shift key, you select all the files between the first click and the second click, as shown in Figure 26-3.

5. Release the Shift key.

The files are now ready for action.

This file selection technique works best in List view. It works in other file views as well, though not as predictably.

You can take advantage of various file sorting commands to arrange the files in the list. Right-click in the folder window and use the Sort By submenu, or the Group By or Stack By submenus, to help organize how the icons line up.

Lassoing a group of files

Another way to select files as a group is to lasso them. Figure 26-4 illustrates how to do it by dragging over the files with the mouse.

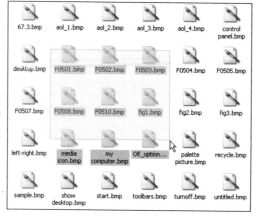

Figure 26-4:
Lasso a group of files with the mouse.

To lasso the files, start by pointing the mouse above and to the left of the icon horde you want to rope. Holding down the mouse button, drag down and to the right to create a rectangle surrounding ("lassoing") the file icons, as shown in Figure 26-4. Release the mouse button, and all the files you have lassoed are selected as a group. A vocal "Yee-ha!" is considered appropriate in this circumstance.

Unselecting stuff

To unselect a file, simply click anywhere in the folder (but not on an icon). Or, you can close the folder window, in which case Windows immediately forgets about any selected files.

Files Hither, Thither, and Yon

Files don't stand still. You find yourself moving them, copying them, and killing them off. If you don't do those things, your hard drive gets all junky and, out of embarrassment, you're forced to turn off the computer when friends come over.

Moving or copying files to another folder

Files are moved and copied all the time. *Moving* a file happens when you transplant it from one folder to another folder. *Copying* happens when you duplicate a file, by keeping the original in its place and making an exact copy elsewhere.

Windows has about a jillion different ways to copy and move files. Rather than bore you with every possible alternative, here's the way I prefer to move or copy a file or group of selected files:

1. **Select the files or folders you want to move or copy.**

2a. **For moving, click the Organize button on the toolbar and choose the Cut command from the menu.**

2b. **For copying, click the Organize button on the toolbar and choose the Copy command from the menu.**

    Yes, you can cut and copy files just like you can cut and copy text and graphics. Of course, neither action means squat until you actually paste.

3. **Open the destination folder.**

    Using the Windows Explorer window to browse to the folder, on whatever media, into which you want to move or copy the file (or files).

4. **Click the Organize button and choose the Paste command.**

    The files are moved or copied from their current location to the folder you selected.

The Copy command makes file duplicates, and the Move command moves the files.

- Moving folders moves all the files and subfolders inside that folder. Be careful when you do this: Windows may lose track of the documents previously opened in those folders.

- You can also use the handy keyboard shortcuts: Ctrl+C for Copy, Ctrl+X for Cut, and Ctrl+V for Paste.

- To cancel the operation, simply press the Esc (escape) key before you paste the files. This action restores the cut files to a nondimmed state.

- Don't eat the paste.

Moving or copying files can be such a drag

Perhaps the easiest way to move or copy a file is to have both the file's source window and the destination window open on the desktop at the same time. To move, simply drag an icon from one window to the other. To move a group, select the icons and then drag them from one window to the other.

Note that Windows displays a bubble beneath the icon for the files you're dragging. The bubble displays the total number of files being manipulated, and whether you're moving or copying the files.

When you drag files between two folders on the hard drive, Windows *moves* the files. But when you drag files between two different media (say, the hard drive and a memory card), Windows *copies* the files.

You can override Windows tendency to move or copy files by using the keyboard when you drag files:

- To copy the files, press and hold the Ctrl key as you drag the mouse.
- To move the files, press and hold the Shift key as you drag the mouse.

Duplicating a file

To make a duplicate, simply copy a file to its same folder. Use any of the techniques for copying files that I cover earlier in this chapter.

The duplicate is created with the suffix – Copy added to the original name. That's your clue that the file is a duplicate of the original stored in the same folder.

Copying a file to removable media

For some reason, people have a hang-up with copying files to a memory card or to any removable disk. It's quite simple to do. Here's how:

1. **Ensure that a media is properly attached, or *mounted,* to your computer.**

   For example, stick the digital memory card in the card reader.

2. **Select the files to copy.**

3. **Right-click the selected files and choose File⇨Send To, and then choose the removable media from the submenu.**

   The Send To submenu lists all available removable disk drives to which you can send the file — even a recordable CD or DVD, if your PC is blessed with such hardware.

   The files are copied to the drive as soon as you choose the command.

Always make certain that a disk is in the drive and that the disk is ready to accept files before you copy.

✔ To copy files to another hard drive, use the Move or Copy commands, covered earlier in this chapter.

✔ Be sure that you properly unmount a digital media card before you remove it from the drive. Refer to Chapter 9.

✔ See Chapter 28 for more information on writing to a recordable CD or DVD.

Creating shortcuts

A file *shortcut* is a 99 percent fatfree copy of a file. It enables you to access the original file from anywhere on a computer's disk system, without the extra baggage required to copy the file all over creation. For example, you can create a shortcut to the Microsoft Word program and put it on the desktop for easy access. Such is the essence of the file shortcut.

Making a shortcut is done the same way as copying and pasting a file, as discussed in the section "Moving or copying files to another folder," earlier in this chapter. The difference comes when you paste: Right-click in the destination folder and choose the Paste Shortcut command from the pop-up menu.

✔ To quickly create a shortcut on the desktop, right-click an icon and choose Send To⇨Desktop (Create Shortcut) from the pop-up menu.

Shortcut to the old graveyard

- A shortcut icon has a little arrow in a white box nestled into its lower left corner (see the margin). This icon tells you that the file is a shortcut and not the real McCoy.

REMEMBER

- Shortcuts are often named with the suffix Shortcut. You can edit out the Shortcut to part, if you like. Refer to the section "Renaming files," later in this chapter.

- Have no fear when you're deleting shortcuts: Removing a shortcut icon doesn't remove the original file.

Deleting files

Part of maintaining the disk drive closet is the occasional cleaning binge or spring-cleaning bustle. This task involves not only organizing files and folders by moving and copying them but also cleaning out the deadwood — removing files you no longer want or need.

To kill a file, select it and press the Delete key on your keyboard. You can also use the Delete command on the Organize toolbar button's menu. Or, if you can see the Recycle Bin icon on the desktop, drag the files with the mouse and drop them right on the Recycle Bin icon. Phew! The file is gone.

- Windows may warn you about deleting a file. Are you *really* sure? You probably are, so click Yes to delete the file. (Windows is just being utterly cautious.)

WARNING!

- You can delete folders just like files, but keep in mind that you delete the folder's contents — which can be dozens of icons, files, folders, jewelry, small children, widows, and refugees. Better be careful with that one.

- Never delete any file or folder unless you created it yourself.

- Programs aren't deleted in Windows; they're uninstalled. See Chapter 27.

Undeleting files (Files of the Undead!)

TIP

If you just deleted a file — and I mean *just deleted* it — you can choose the Undo command (Ctrl+Z) from the Organize toolbar button's menu. That gets it back.

If Edit➪Undo doesn't do it, or undo it (or whatever), take these steps:

1. **Open the Recycle Bin on the desktop.**

   If the Recycle Bin icon isn't visible on the desktop, click the far left triangle on the Windows Explorer address bar and choose Recycle Bin from the menu that appears.

2. **Select the file you want recovered.**

3. **Click the Restore This Item button on the toolbar.**

   The file is magically removed from Recycle Bin limbo and restored afresh to the folder and disk from which it was so brutally seized.

4. **Close the Recycle Bin window.**

Windows has no definite time limit on how long you can restore files; they can be available in the Recycle Bin for months or even years. Even so, don't let the convenience of the Recycle Bin lull you into a false sense of security. Never delete a file unless you're certain that you want it gone, gone, gone.

Files can be permanently deleted by pressing Shift+Delete on the keyboard. They aren't stored in the Recycle Bin and cannot be recovered. That's why you should use only the Shift+Delete command to seriously remove files you no longer want.

Renaming files

Windows lets you rename any file or folder at any time. You may want to do this to give the folder a better, more descriptive name, or you may have any number of reasons to give an icon a new name. Here's how it's done:

1. **Click the icon once to select it.**

2. **Choose the Rename command from the Organize toolbar button's menu.**

   The file's current name is highlighted or selected — just like selected text in a word processor.

3. **Type a new name or edit the current name.**

4. **Press the Enter key to lock in the new name.**

Note that all files *must* have a name. If you don't give the file a name (you try to leave it blank), Windows complains. Other than that, here are some file renaming points to ponder:

- ✔ Before pressing the Enter key (refer to Step 4), you can press the Esc key to undo the damage and return to the file's original name.

- ✔ Windows doesn't let you rename a file with the name of an existing file; no two items in the same folder can share the same name.

- ✔ If you have hidden the filename extensions, it may appear that two files share the same name. Note, however, that such files can be of two different types and have two different icons.

✔ You can undo the name change by pressing the Ctrl+Z key combination or choosing Edit⇨Undo from the menu. You must do it *immediately* after the booboo occurs in order for it to work.

✔ The keyboard shortcut for renaming files is F2. I prefer using this key to choosing the menu item because my hands need to be on the keyboard to type the new filename anyway.

Windows lets you rename a group of icons all at once. It works the same as renaming a single icon, except that when the operation is completed, all selected icons have the same new name plus a number suffix. For example, you select a group of icons and press the F2 key. When you type **Picture** as the group filename, each file in the group is given the name Picture (2), Picture (3), and so on, up to the last file in the group — Picture (24), for example.

Finding Wayward Files

Losing track of your files in Windows is no big deal. Unlike losing your glasses or car keys, Windows sports a powerful Search command. Lost files are found almost instantly. Even the Amazing Kreskin couldn't find things faster!

To find a file in Windows, use any Search window. You may see one in the upper right corner of Windows Explorer. Or, find one at the bottom of the Start button menu. Wherever the file is, simply type the name of the file you're looking for. Press the Enter key and soon you're inundated with matching files — even with matching text within files. And no waiting!

Here are some searching tips:

✔ It helps to start in a high-up folder, such as your User Account folder or the Computer folder window. The search progresses "downward" through the folders.

✔ Clicking the Advanced Search link at the bottom of the Search Results window allows you to narrow the search's focus a tad. You can enter a date range, for example.

✔ If your keyboard has a Windows key, you can press Win+F, where the F means *find*. This action summons the Search Results window.

✔ The toolbar in the Search Results window helps you narrow the search's focus.

✔ This book's wee li'l companion, *PCs For Dummies Quick Reference* (Wiley Publishing, Inc.) contains many more Search window options and variations for finding just about any file based on its type, size, or date.

Chapter 27

Software, Programs, Applications

In This Chapter

▶ Installing new programs

▶ Starting programs

▶ Quickly running recent programs

▶ Accessing popular programs

▶ Creating desktop shortcuts

▶ Removing software

▶ Updating and upgrading software

*T*he PC hardware may be dumb, and the operating system may be in charge, but in order to get any work done on your computer, you need software. Specifically, you need those workhorse applications that transform your whimsical musings into something substantial, by using the power of the computer's hefty I/O muscle to convert your keystrokes and mouse movements into something wonderful and new — or stagnant and rotten, depending on whether you love your work.

I find the main problem with software to be the terminology. Just how many words are there for a computer program? *Software* is the big term. *Computer program* is technical, though more technical is *executable*. Then there are the applications and the software suites. No matter the jargon, this chapter covers the job of setting up and using those programs on your PC.

How do I quit all other programs?

Many installation programs ask you to "quit all other programs" before you proceed with installing the new software. The reason is that installation is monitored to make uninstalling easier. Having other programs run "in the background" can disturb this process. Also, because some programs require the computer to be reset after installation, if you haven't yet saved your data, you're out of luck.

To make sure that no other programs are running, press the Alt+Tab key combination. If Windows switches you to another program or window, close it. Keep pressing Alt+Tab until the only program you see is the installation program. That way, you ensure that all other running programs have closed. (And there's no need to close any background applications or other processes.)

Software Installation

Software is what makes your computer do the work. But the program itself doesn't magically jump from the mostly empty software box and into your computer. It requires effort on your behalf. This isn't anything technical. In fact, it's so easy that few software boxes even bother to contain instructions. When that's the case, you can start reading here:

1. **Open the software box.**

   You need a knife or scissors to remove the shrink wrap and potential impenetrable transparent plastic seal over the box flap.

   Try not to rip up the box. You want to keep it intact, either for long-term storage or in case the store lets you return the software. Most stores don't. When they don't, you can try reselling the software on eBay.

2. **Savor the industrial epoxy odor of the box's insides.**

3. **Locate the installation disc or discs.**

   If you have more than one, note in which order they're used; the discs should be numbered, and you want to start with the first disc, which should also be labeled INSTALL.

   Sometimes, a DVD is included, which means that you can use that single DVD, rather than multiple CDs, to install the program.

   In addition to the installation disc, you may have other discs, bonus programs, supplements, and libraries of clip art. You don't need to install everything, but you should find the Install disc.

4. **Scour the box for printed information.**

   Specifically, you want to find a Read Me sheet or *Getting Started* booklet.

You may have a manual in the box. It's a joke. Gone are the days when computer software came with manuals. The manual is now "on the disc," in the form of a help file, which isn't very helpful.

If installation instructions are in the box, follow them.

5. Insert the installation disc into the drive.

6. Start the installation program.

If you're lucky, the installation program runs automatically when you insert the disc into the PC's DVD drive.

7. Obey the instructions on the screen.

Read the information carefully; sometimes, they slip something important in there. My friend Jerry (his real name) just kept clicking the Next button rather than read the screen. He missed an important notice saying that an older version of the program would be erased. Uh-oh! Poor Jerry never got his old program back.

You may also be hit with a User Account Control (UAC) warning here. If so, enter the administrator password or click the Continue button to proceed.

8. Choose various options.

The software asks for your name and company name, and maybe for a serial number. Type all that stuff in.

Don't freak if the program already knows who you are. Windows is kinda clairvoyant in that respect.

When you're asked to make a decision, the option that's already selected (the *default*) is typically the best option. Only if you know what's going on and *truly care* about it should you change anything.

You can find the serial number inside the manual, on the CD-ROM case, on the first disc, or on a separate card that you probably threw away even though I told you to keep everything in its original box. Don't lose that number! I usually write down the serial number inside the manual or on the software box itself.

9. Files are copied.

Eventually, the installation program copies the files from the installation disc to your hard drive for full-time residence.

If asked, replace one CD with another. This process may go on for some time.

10. It's done.

The installation program ends. The computer may reset at this point. That's required sometimes when you're installing special programs that Windows needs to know about. (Windows is pretty dumb after it starts.)

Start using the program!

How do I disable my antivirus software?

The better antivirus programs constantly monitor your computer to check for new viruses. So, whenever you install new software, the antivirus software may stand up and say "Wait a minute!" and prevent the installation. The only way around this problem is to temporarily disable the antivirus software.

The easiest way to disable antivirus software is locate the antivirus program's tiny icon in the Notification Area. Right-click that icon and choose the Disable command from the pop-up menu. After doing so, you may proceed with installation. Remember, however, to reenable the antivirus software after installing the new program. One way to do that is to restart Windows, which most new programs require after installation anyway.

Granted, the preceding steps are vague and general. Hopefully, your new software comes with more specific instructions. Refer to the sidebars nearby for important information on some commonly asked installation questions.

✔ You must have administrator privileges to install new software on your computer. This is fine; most users set themselves up as administrators anyway. Also, if more than one person uses your computer, be sure that you install the software for everyone to use.

✔ Many applications require some form of validation or registration, which means that you need to connect to the Internet to complete the installation process. For folks without an Internet connection, a phone number might be provided to help activate the product the old-fashioned, human way.

Running a Program

After the software gets into your PC, the next thing you want to do is Run That Program. As with other things in Windows, there are many different, strange, and potentially useful ways to run your programs. The following sections describe some of the more popular methods.

Finding a program on the Start button menu

All new software you install should set itself up on the Start button menu, on the All Programs submenu. In fact, if the software did things properly,

Windows displays a pop-up bubble on the Start button that says "New software installed" (or something similar) and highlights the new program's location.

To run your program, obey these steps:

1. **Click the Start button.**

2. **Choose All Programs to pop up the All Programs menu.**

3. **Click your program's icon on the menu.**

    Clicking the program's icon on the menu runs the program; the Start menu thing goes away, and your program's window appears on the screen.

4. **If the program cannot be found, locate the program's submenu and then go back to Step 3.**

    Some programs may be buried on submenus and even more submenus. It all depends on how the All Programs menu is organized.

Yeah, the All Programs menu can be a mess! You can organize that menu, but that's really the topic of another book.

The program itself isn't installed on the All Programs menu. What you see there is merely a *shortcut* icon, or tiny copy of the program. The program itself is most likely located in its own subfolder in the Program Files folder on drive C. (Refer to Chapter 26 for more information on shortcuts.)

Accessing recent programs

Every time you run a program in Windows, it appears on the Start button menu, on the left side, in an area I cleverly refer to as the Recently Used Programs list. Figure 27-1 shows you where the list is.

Choose any program on the list to immediately run it again — no wading through the All Programs menu required! Note that programs fall off that list as you run new programs.

Putting your program in the pin-on area

If you prefer to have your program appear right on the Start menu, where it's most handy, consider adding the program to the pin-on area, as shown in Figure 27-1. Programs "pinned" to the Start button menu stay there come hell or high water or so-called computer expert nephews visiting from Indiana.

Recently used programs list

Pin-on area

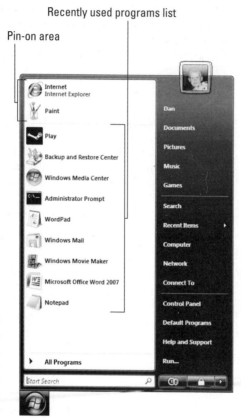

Internet Internet Explorer	Dan
Paint	Documents
Play	Pictures
Backup and Restore Center	Music
Windows Media Center	Games
Administrator Prompt	Search
WordPad	Recent Items ▶
Windows Mail	Computer
Windows Movie Maker	Network
Microsoft Office Word 2007	Connect To
Notepad	Control Panel
	Default Programs
	Help and Support
▶ All Programs	Run...

Figure 27-1:
Programs
found on the
Start button
menu.

Start Search

To add any program to the pin-on area, right-click the program's icon and
choose the Pin to Start Menu command from the pop-up menu.

You can click any program icon, even a program on the Recently Used
Programs list or a program icon found on the All Programs menu.
Remember: Right-click.

Creating a desktop shortcut icon

When a program installs itself on your computer, it sets up a command or
even a submenu full of commands on the Start button menu's All Programs
menu. The program may also create a shortcut icon on the desktop, which
allows you even faster access to the program. Well, it allows access any time
you see the desktop.

If you enjoy having shortcut icons on the desktop, you can add any program (or folder or file) to the desktop as a shortcut. Simply locate the program's icon or shortcut icon, right-click that icon, and choose Send To⇨Desktop (Create Shortcut) from the pop-up menu. The shortcut file is created, and its icon appears on the desktop.

Putting an icon on the Quick Launch bar

Another handy place to put frequently used programs is on the Quick Launch bar, which is where the Quick Launch bar gets its name. If it were the Quick Lunch bar, you would put sandwiches down there, not program icons.

The easiest way to put a program icon on the Quick Launch bar is to drag the program's shortcut icon from the desktop and onto the Quick Launch bar. Refer to the preceding subsection for information on creating a desktop shortcut icon.

Uninstalling Software

To remove any newly installed program, you use an uninstall program. You *do not* merely delete the program or its folder.

Nearly all programs you install come with an uninstall program or feature. The program to remove the software is commonly named Uninstall, and it might be found on the Start button menu's All Programs menu, right by the icon used to start the program. Figure 27-2 illustrates such a configuration: An Uninstall program appears on my PC's All Programs menu and removes the program DOSBox.

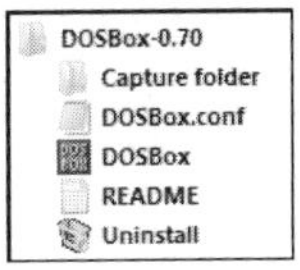

Figure 27-2:
An uninstall
program on
an All
Programs
submenu.

- DOSBox-0.70
- Capture folder
- DOSBox.conf
- DOSBox
- README
- Uninstall

When you cannot find an obvious uninstall program, you can turn to
Windows and follow these steps:

1. **Open the Control Panel.**

2. **From the Control Panel Home, choose the link Uninstall a Program,
   found beneath the Programs heading; from the Control Panel Classic
   view, double-click to open the Programs and Features icon.**

   No matter how you get there, the Programs and Features window
   appears, as shown in Figure 27-3. That window lists all software installed
   on your PC.

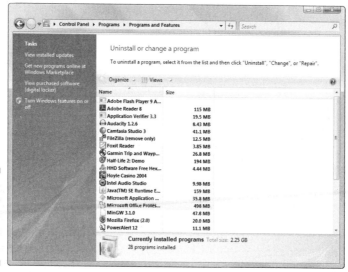

Figure 27-3:
The Add or
Remove
Programs
dialog box.

3. **Select the program you want to uninstall.**

4. **Click the Uninstall/Change button on the toolbar.**

5. **If prompted by a User Account Control, type the administrator password or click the Continue button.**

6. **Continue reading instructions on the screen to uninstall the program.**

The uninstall directions vary from program to program. Windows itself doesn't
remove the program; it's really the software developer's job to create the uninstall program. So the procedure varies.

Some stubborn programs don't fully remove themselves. They may leave behind a smattering of files, shortcut icons, empty folders. You can remove an empty folder yourself, if you like. (Folders are deleted just like files; see Chapter 26.) Avoid deleting any program or file installed in the Windows folder or any of its subfolders.

Updating and Upgrading Your Software

After a novel is written, it's finished. Subsequent reprints correct a few misspellings and typos, but that's about it. Software, on the other hand, is *never* finished. It's too easy to change. Most software packages are updated once every year or two, and sometimes more often. Software upgrades happen less frequently.

What's the difference between an update and an upgrade? *Updates* are gradual and tiny. They repair, or *patch,* software you've already purchased. For example, an update may fix a bug or problem. An upgrade can fine-tune some features. And, generally speaking, updates are free.

What about upgrading Windows?

I recommend keeping Windows up-to-date with frequent updates, as discussed in Chapter 23. But what about upgrades to Windows? After all, Windows is your PC's operating system, the main program in charge. So, unlike upgrading other software on your PC, upgrading Windows is a Big Deal. You should weigh your upgrade decision carefully.

Microsoft produces a new version of Windows about once every three years (though Windows Vista took five years to appear after Windows XP). As with previous Windows upgrades, the newer version offers better features and a different way of doing things than the previous version. You have to ask yourself a key question: "Do I need those features?" If not, don't bother with the update.

Perhaps the most important question is "Will my software be compatible with the new version of Windows?" In many cases, existing software has trouble with the new version of Windows, especially games and graphics software. Will software developers offer updates to their programs to make them compatible with the new version of Windows? Or will you have to pay more to upgrade those programs? And finally, will your current PC hardware be able to handle the new version of Windows?

In my world, it has been too expensive and too much of a bother ever to upgrade Windows. Instead, I simply buy a new computer, one that comes with the new version of Windows pre-installed. That always works best for me, and it should for you as well.

Upgrades, however, are complete revisions of the entire program. An upgrade presents a new version of the software, along with a version number. For example, the latest version of Microsoft Office is an upgrade, not an update. Also, upgrades cost money.

My advice: Update frequently. If the manufacturer offers a patch or a fix, install it as recommended. But updates are necessary only when the new features or modifications are things that you desperately need or when the upgrade addresses security issues. Otherwise, when the current version is doing the job, don't bother.

✔ Update: a minor fix to some software you own. A patch. No charge.

✔ Upgrade: a new version of the program. You pay for it.

✔ Refer to Chapter 23 for my advice on updating Windows.

✔ Consider each upgrade offer on its individual merits: Will you ever use the new features? Do you need a word processor that can print upside-down headlines and bar charts that show your word count? Can you really get any mileage out of the intranet version when you're a sole user sitting at home?

✔ Here's something else to keep in mind: If you're still using DoodleWriter 4.2 and everybody else is using DoodleWriter 6.1, you may have difficulty exchanging documents. After a while, newer versions of programs become incompatible with their older models. If so, you need to upgrade.

✔ In an office setting, everybody should be using the same software version. (Everybody doesn't have to be using the *latest* version, just the *same* version.)

Chapter 28

Making Your Own Discs

In This Chapter

▶ Confirming that you have a proper DVD/CD drive

▶ Buying discs

▶ Understanding disc formats

▶ Inserting a disc

▶ Working with the disc in Windows

▶ Using an RW disc

▶ Labeling CD-R discs

▶ Throwing a disc out

*I*n a world where your typical teenager creates more music CDs in a day than your average music store sells in a week, it's difficult to believe that computers haven't always been disc factories. Yet ever since PCs first came with CD-ROMs, users have wanted to burn their own discs.

Computers are a natural for creating things, even disks. Back in the vacuum tube era, floppy disks were created hand over fist. But floppy disks were never (if at all) used for storing music — or even a heck of a lot of information. The CD, and later the DVD, provided a useful method of storing not only music and movies but also lots of computer data. In fact, it's really no big deal now to make your own discs — CD or DVD. This chapter shows you the ropes.

Your Personal Disc Factory

The PC is adept at spitting out discs. The key is having the right combination of hardware and software to get the job done. The hardware probably came standard with your PC, especially if you purchased your computer in the past couple of years. The software is supplied with Windows Vista, which is the first version of Windows to directly support writing to both types of discs — CD and DVD.

Checking the hardware

Your computer most likely came with a DVD drive, which is also capable of reading CDs. To create a disc, however, you need a recordable DVD drive, one that creates DVDs in addition to reading them. If the drive is the SuperDrive, it can also create CDs.

For more information on the DVD drive, refer to the section "The DVD Drive" in Chapter 9.

Obtaining the proper disc

To create your own discs, you have to buy discs, specifically the proper disc for your PC's type of recordable drive. That would seem easy, but it's not. The reason it isn't easy is that recordable disc formats evolved, and several standards are available.

Fortunately, most DVD drives that can create discs support all the common disc formats. This doesn't do away with the confusion, so here's my handy disc guide to help you choose which disc format to use:

CD-R: This disc, in the standard recordable CD format, can be written to only once and never erased or used again.

CD-RW: In this standard rewriteable (RW) CD format, the disc works just like a CD-R, though it can be completely erased and used again.

DVD-R: This is the most popular DVD recordable format, compatible with both computers and home-movie DVD players.

DVD+R: This is the second most popular DVD recordable format, much faster than DVD-R but not as compatible.

DVD-RW: This is the erasable version of the DVD-R format. As with a CD-RW, these recordable DVDs can be completely erased and recorded to again.

DVD+RW: The fully erasable version of the DVD+R format.

Other formats may be available as well, such as the older DVD-RAM format. These rare formats, happily, are quickly fading from the scene.

- ✔ Refer to Chapter 9 for information on disc capacity; the capacity for recordable discs is the same as that of the RO (read-only) discs.

- ✔ Discs are cheap! I recommend buying them on spools in 25-, 50-, or 100- disc packs. (You may not think that the discs are cheap, but when CD-Rs first came out they were about $5 a pop. Recordable DVDs were originally $15 each.)

✔ Some CD-R discs are better than others. Although a pal of mine says that any old CD-R will do, I stick with the brands I know and use the special high-speed discs. My data is important to me, so I don't mind paying extra.

✔ Some CD-Rs are labeled specifically for music. These music CD-Rs are of a lower quality than data CD-Rs because music doesn't have the same accuracy demands as data storage.

✔ The RW format discs are more expensive than the other, write-once disc formats.

Disc-writing software

Windows has had the ability to create CDs for quite some time, for storing data or storing music, by using the Windows Media Player. Windows Vista is the first version of Windows to fully support creating DVDs as well as CDs. The procedure works the same for both types of disc, as well as with the individual format variations (the R and RW differences).

✔ For more information on creating a music CD, refer to Chapter 18.

✔ Windows also comes with programs for making movie DVDs. The Windows Movie Maker is a good choice for when you're starting out with digital video. See Chapter 17.

✔ Third-party disc creation programs exist, such as the popular Nero program. This book covers only the Windows method for creating discs.

Choosing the right format

When Windows creates, or *initializes,* a recordable disc, it provides you with an opportunity to select the disc format. In this context, *format* refers to the way information is recorded on the disc. It's a technical thing, and the details are as boring as an in-flight magazine article, but it helps to know a bit about the formats when you choose to create a disc.

The two disc formats are Live File System and Mastered. They both control how information is written to the disc:

Live File System: In this format, information is written to the disc immediately. You can eject the disc, use it in another computer, and then reinsert the disc and keep adding files to it. You can use the disc until it's full.

Mastered: This format collects files to be written to the disc, storing them on the PC's hard drive. All waiting files are written to the disc at one time. Then the disc is *closed*, and further writing to the disc is prevented.

Of the two formats, the Mastered format is more compatible with other CD and DVD drives, and it makes the most efficient use of disc space. The Live File System, however, works more like traditional removable media in a PC.

You can create any disc — CD or DVD, R or RW, plus or minus — using either format.

Your Very Own Data Disc

As long as you have the proper DVD or CD drive, plenty of discs, and Windows Vista, you can create your own data discs. The following sections describe the procedure.

Inserting the disc

As with all removable media, you begin your CD or DVD creation journey by sticking the disc into the drive. Here's the 411:

1. **Put a recordable disc into the drive.**

   Windows is smart enough to recognize the disc and asks you what to do with it by using the AutoPlay dialog box, as shown in Figure 28-1. Though the figure illustrates what happens for a CD-R, similar options are shown when you insert a DVD-R or DVD+R.

Figure 28-1:
A blank
CD-R is
detected.

2. **Select the option Burn Files to Disc.**

   The Burn a Disc dialog box shows up.

3. **Type a name for the disc.**

   Name the disc based on its contents. Or, you can just accept the current date, which is already shown in the dialog box.

4. **Click the Show Formatting Options button to reveal format choices.**

   You can skip this option when you want to use the Live File System; skip to Step 6.

5. **Choose Live File System or Mastered.**

   Review the section "Choosing the right format," earlier in this chapter, for more information.

6. **Click the Next button.**

   For the Live File System, Windows formats the disc, preparing it for use. This goes rather quickly.

7. **Start using the disc.**

The disc is *mounted* into your PC's permanent storage system. Windows automatically opens the root folder window for the disc, and you can also see the disc's icon in the Computer window. You can now use the disc just like any other media in your computer; see the next section.

- ✔ Your computer may automatically recognize the disc and mount it without interrupting you. Groovy.

- ✔ If the drive doesn't recognize the disc, the disc might be defective. Fetch another.

What to put on the disc?

The burning burning-question is "What kind of data should you put on a CD-R?" Obviously, you don't want to use a CD-R like a removable hard drive. That's because the disc can be used only once. When it's full, it's done! It cannot be erased. Therefore, I recommend using CD-R data discs for *archiving* and data transfer.

Archiving is just a fancy word for storage. For example, when I'm done writing a book, I archive all the text documents, figures, pictures, — even my contract — on a disc. Even if the files don't fill up the disc, that's okay; archiving is not about

maximizing storage potential. With the files safely saved on the CD-R, I can delete them from my hard drive and make that space available for something else. And, if I ever need the files again, they're handy on the archive CD.

Discs are also excellent for moving information between computers, which is why new software comes on a CD or DVD. I use discs to send files in the mail that are too big to send by e-mail. (How big? Anything larger than 10MB is too big for e-mail.)

Working with the disc in Windows

After mounting the recordable disc, you can work with it just like you work with the hard drive: Copy files to the disc window. Use the Send To command from a right-click (pop-up) menu. Create folders, even subfolders. Rename and manage files as you normally do.

For a Live File Format disc, information is written to the disc as soon as you copy it over. That's why it's called the *Live* File System; your interaction with the disc is pretty much real-time.

For a Mastered-format disc, you send what are essentially shortcut icons to the disc's window. Those icons dwell in the window until the disc is ejected and they're finally written. So, until the disc is ejected and written to, you're free to manipulate files and folders on the disc image without affecting anything written to the disc.

For either format, you can use the Burn button on the toolbar to copy selected files to the disc for either immediate burning (Live File System) or eventual burning (Mastered).

✔ Icons may appear ghostly until you initially eject a disc created with the Live File System. That's perfectly okay.

✔ On a Mastered disc, files appear with the download flag over their icons. This means that the file is ready to be written to the disc but has not yet been written.

✔ Erasing, renaming, or moving a file after it has been burned to a Live File System–formatted disc wastes disc space. If possible, try to do your file manipulations *before* you burn the files to the disc.

Ejecting a recordable disc

What happens when you eject a recordable disc depends on which format you chose:

Live File Format: You can eject a Live File Format disc at any time. Windows alerts you that the disc is being prepared so that other PCs can access the information. Then the disc is ejected.

Mastered. You can eject a Mastered disc at any time; the disc just pops out of the drive. To write information to the mastered disc, see the next section.

Of course, the advantage of a Life File Format disc is that you can reinsert it into your PC and continue writing files. (See the preceding section.) You can do this — insert the disc, write files, eject the disc — repeatedly until the disc is full and cannot be written to any more.

Finishing a Mastered format disc

When you choose the Mastered format for your disc, files must be burned to the disc. This doesn't happen by ejecting the disc. Nope, you have to follow these steps:

1. **Open the Computer window or the DVD drive's window.**

2. **Click the Burn to Disc toolbar button.**

   The Burn to Disc dialog box appears. (The Burn to Disc button appears only when you're using a recordable disc created using the Mastered format.)

3. **(Optional) Enter a name for the disc.**

   The recording speed is, doubtless, okay — though one school of thought says that choosing the *slowest* recording speed ensures the best performance.

4. **Click the Next button.**

   Wait as the files are burned to the disc.

The disc is ejected automatically when it's done.

With a Mastered disc, you cannot write any additional information to the disc after it's written. The disc can, however, be read by a wider variety of computers than a similar disc created using the Live File System.

Erasing an RW disc

RW discs work just like their R disc sisters. All the information in the previous sections applies to RW discs. The main difference is the addition of a toolbar button that lets you reformat the RW disc and start over.

 To reformat the RW disc, open its window or the Computer window and click the Erase This Disc toolbar button. Follow the directions on the screen to completely erase the disc and start over. Note that this operation may take some time, especially for DVD-RW discs.

- RW discs are different from other recordable discs. It says *RW* on the label, and the disc is more expensive, which is most obvious when you try to taste this disc.

- RW discs may not be readable in all CD or DVD drives. If you want to create a CD with the widest possible use, burn a CD-R rather than a CD-RW disc. For a DVD, use the DVD-R format.

- It's often said that RW discs are best used for backing up data because they can be reused over and over. However, on a disc-per-disc basis, it's cheaper to use non-RW discs instead.

Labeling the disc

I highly recommend labeling all removable media, from recordable discs to memory cards. Even if you name things only A or B, that's fine because it helps you keep track of things.

- Label your disc *after* it's been written to. That way, you don't waste time labeling what could potentially be a bad disc (one that you would throw away).

- I use a Sharpie to write on the disc. Write on the label side; the other side is the one containing your important data. You don't want to write on that.

- Do not use a sticky label on your CD-R. Only if the label specifically says that it's chemically safe for a CD-R should you use it. Otherwise, the chemicals in the standard type of sticky label may damage the disc and render the information that's written to it unreadable after only a few months.

Disposing a Disc

Sure, you can just toss a disc into the trash. That's okay — in most places. Some communities classify a DVD or CD as hazardous, and it must be properly disposed of or sent off for recycling.

If you don't want anyone else to read the disc, you probably don't want to throw it away intact. The best solution is to destroy the disc by getting a paper shredder that can also handle CDs and DVDs.

Some folks say that you can effectively erase a disc by putting it in a microwave oven for a few seconds. I don't know whether I trust or recommend that method. And, don't burn a disc; its fumes are toxic.

Part VI
The Part of Tens

The 5th Wave   By Rich Tennant

"I got this through one of those mail order PC companies that let you design your own system."

In this part . . .

I enjoy lists, which is probably due to the same mental defect that lets me cram my brain with trivia. Part of my feasting on knowledge involves reading lots of trivia, and I feel the best trivia is organized into lists, such as Ten Fatal North American Insect Bites or Ten Things Surgeons Have Left in Patients' Bodies or Ten Places Hikers Go and Never Return. Why is it always ten? I give up! But in that fine decimal tradition, I present the final part of this book, trivial or not, which lists helpful chapters organized into topics of ten useful computer tips, suggestions, and information.

Chapter 29

Ten Common Beginner Mistakes

In This Chapter

▶ Not properly quitting Windows

▶ Buying too much software

▶ Buying incompatible hardware

▶ Not buying enough supplies

▶ Not saving your work

▶ Not backing up files

▶ Opening or deleting unknown things

▶ Trying to save the world

▶ Replying to spam

▶ Opening a program attached to e-mail

Sure, you can make a gazillion mistakes with a computer, whether it's deleting the wrong file or dropping the color laser printer on your toe. But I have narrowed the list to ten. These are the day-to-day operating mistakes that people tend to repeat until they're told not to or until they read about it here.

Not Properly Shutting Down Windows

When you're done with Windows, shut it down. Choose the Shut Down command from the Start button menu. The PC automatically turns itself off.

Refer to Chapter 4 for detailed PC shutdown instructions.

Buying Too Much Software

Your PC probably came out of the box with dozens of programs preinstalled. (No, you're not required to use them; refer to Chapter 27, the section about uninstalling software.) Even with all that software preinstalled, don't overwhelm yourself by getting *more* software right away.

Buying too much software isn't really the sin here. The sin is buying too much software and trying to learn it all at once. The buy-it-all-at-once habit probably comes from buying music, where it's okay to lug home a whole stack of CDs from the store. You can listen to several CDs over the course of a few days. They're enjoyable the first time, and they age well. Software, on the other hand, is gruesome the first day and can take months to come to grips with.

Have mercy on yourself at the checkout counter and buy software at a moderate rate. Buy one package and figure out how to use it. Then move on and buy something else. You learn faster that way.

Buying Incompatible Hardware

This doesn't happen as often as it once did, back in the days before the PC consumed nearly every other type of computer. But you may still find yourself, for example, buying the wrong memory card. I did that once, and it was an expensive mistake!

Know your PC! Review Chapters 1 and 2. That way, you don't buy that FireWire-only external hard drive when your PC lacks a FireWire port or try to add an AGP expansion card when your computer's motherboard has only PCIe slots. (See Chapter 6.)

Always check your hardware before you buy it! Especially if you're shopping online — if you're not sure that the hardware is compatible, phone the dealer and ask those folks specifically.

Not Buying Enough Supplies

Buy printer paper in those big boxes. You *will* run out. Buy extra paper and a variety of papers for different types of printing (drafts, color, high-quality, and photo, for example). Buy a spool of 100 discs. Get a few extra memory cards. Keep extra printer ink cartridges on hand. You get the idea.

Not Saving Your Work

Whenever you're creating something blazingly original, choose the Save command and save your document to the hard disk. When you write something dumb that you're going to patch up later, choose the Save command too. The idea is to choose Save whenever you think about it — hopefully, every few minutes or sooner.

Save! Save! Save!

You never know when your computer will meander off to watch a cooking show on the Food Channel while you're hoping to finish the last few paragraphs of that report. Save your work as often as possible. And, always save it whenever you get up from your computer — even if it's just to turn to a dictionary to ensure that Emeril didn't make up the word *ganosh*.

Not Backing Up Files

Saving work on a computer is a many-tiered process. First, save the work to your hard drive as you create it. Then, at the end of the day, back up your work to external media, such as a CD-R or memory card. Always keep a duplicate, safety copy of your work somewhere because you never know.

At the end of the week (or month), run the Windows backup program. I know that this process is a pain, but it's much more automated and easier to do than in years past. (Note that Backup doesn't come with all flavors of Windows Vista.)

Opening or Deleting Unknown Things

Computers have both hardware and software rules about opening or deleting unknown items. On the software side, I have a rule:

Delete only those files or folders you created yourself.

Windows is brimming with unusual and unknown files. Don't mess with 'em. Don't delete them. Don't move them. Don't rename them. And, especially, don't open them to see what they are. Sometimes opening an unknown icon can lead to trouble.

On the hardware side, don't open anything attached to your PC unless you absolutely know what you're doing. Some hardware is meant to open. New console cases have pop-off and fliptop lids for easy access. They make upgrading things a snap. If you open a console, remember to unplug it! It's okay to open your printer to undo a jam or install new ink or a toner cartridge. Even so, don't open the ink or toner cartridges.

Other hardware items have Do Not Open written all over them: the monitor, keyboard, and modem.

Trying to Save the World

Avoid that hero instinct! People new to PCs and fresh on e-mail somehow feel emboldened that they're personally responsible for the health, safety, and entertainment of everyone else they know on the Internet. Let me be honest: If you're just starting out, be aware that those of us already on the Internet have seen that joke. We have seen the funny pictures. We know the stories. And, everyone has already sent us that e-mail saying that if you send it to seven people you know, somehow Bill Gates will write you a check for $4,000.

Please don't be part of the problem. Telling others about viruses and *real* threats is one thing, but spreading Internet hoaxes is something else. Before you send out a blanket e-mail to everyone you know, confirm that you're sending the truth. Visit a few Web sites, such as www.truthorfiction.com or www.vmyths.com. If the message you're spreading is true, please include a few Web page links to verify it.

Thanks for being part of the solution and not part of the problem!

Replying to Spam E-Mail

Don't reply to any spam e-mail unless you want more spam. A popular trick is for spammers to put some text that says "Reply to this message if you do not want to receive any further messages." Don't! Replying to spam signals the spammers that they have a "live one," and you then get even more spam. Never, ever, reply to spam!

Opening a Program Attached to an E-Mail Message

You can receive photos via e-mail. You can receive sound files. You can receive any types of documents. You can even receive Zip file archives or compressed folders. These files are all okay to receive. But, if you receive a program (EXE or COM) file or a Visual Basic Script (VBS) file, do not open it!

The only way to get a virus on a PC is to *run* an infected program file. You can receive the file okay. But, if you open it, you're dead. My rule is "Don't open any EXE file you receive by e-mail."

- ✔ If you have to send a program file by e-mail, write or phone the recipient in advance to let the person know that it's coming.

- ✔ When in doubt, run antivirus software and scan the file before you open it.

- ✔ Some types of viruses can come in Microsoft Word documents. Antivirus software may catch these viruses, but in any case, confirm that the sender meant to send you the file before you open it.

Chapter 30

Ten Things Worth Buying for Your PC

In This Chapter

▶ Mouse pad and wrist pad

▶ Antiglare screen

▶ Keyboard cover

▶ More memory

▶ Larger, faster hard drive

▶ Ergonomic keyboard

▶ Uninterruptible power supply

▶ Headset

▶ Scanner or digital camera

▶ Portable digital music player

I'm not trying to sell you anything, and I'm pretty sure that you're not ready to burst out and spend, spend, spend on something — like another computer (unless it's someone else's money). Still, some toys — or, shall I say, *companions* — are worthy of your PC's company. Here's the list of items I recommend. Some are not that expensive, and I don't sell any of them on my own Web site!

Mouse Pad and Wrist Pad

If you have a mechanical (not optical) mouse, you need a mouse pad on which to roll it. Get one; the varieties are endless — plus, the mouse pad ensures that you have at least one tiny place on your desktop that's free of clutter for rolling the mouse around.

A *wrist pad* fits right below your keyboard and enables you to comfortably rest your wrists while you type. This product may help alleviate some repetitive-motion injuries that are common to keyboard users. Wrist pads come in many exciting colors, some of which may match your drapery.

Antiglare Screen

Tawdry as it may sound, an *antiglare screen* is nothing more than a nylon stocking stretched over the front of your monitor. Okay, they're *professional* nylons in fancy holders that adhere themselves to your screen. The result is no garish glare from the lights in the room or outside. An antiglare screen is such a good idea that some monitors come with them built-in.

Glare is the number-one cause of eyestrain while you're using a computer. Lights usually reflect in the glass, either from above or from a window. An antiglare screen cuts down on the reflections and makes the stuff on your monitor easier to see.

Some antiglare screens also incorporate antiradiation shielding. I'm serious: They provide protection from the harmful electromagnetic rays spewing out of your monitor even as you read this page! Is this necessary? No.

Keyboard Cover

If you're klutzy with a coffee cup or have small children or spouses with peanut-butter-smudged fingers using your keyboard, a keyboard cover is a great idea. You may have even seen one used in a department store: It covers the keyboard snugly, but still enables you to type. It's a great idea because, without a keyboard cover, all that disgusting gunk falls between the keys. Yech!

In the same vein, you can also buy a generic dust cover for your computer. This item preserves your computer's appearance but has no other true value. Use a computer cover only when your computer is turned off (and I don't recommend turning it off). If you put the cover on your PC while the PC is turned on, you create a minigreenhouse, and the computer gets way too hot and could melt. Nasty. This type of heat buildup doesn't happen to the keyboard, so keeping the keyboard cover on all the time is okay — cool, in fact.

More Memory

Any PC works better with more memory installed. The upper limit on some computers is something like 16GB of RAM, which seems ridiculous now, but who knows about two years from now? Still, upgrading your system to 1GB or 2GB of RAM is a good idea. Almost immediately, you notice the improvement in Windows and various graphics applications and games. Make someone else do the upgrading for you; you just buy the memory.

Larger, Faster Hard Drive

Hard drives fill up quickly. The first time, it's because you keep lots of junk on your hard drive: games, things people give you, old files, and old programs you don't use any more. You can delete those or archive them to a disc for long-term storage. Then, after a time, your hard drive fills up again. The second time, it has stuff you really use. Argh! What can you delete?

The answer is to buy a larger hard drive. You can add an external hard drive quickly and easily or have one installed inside the console. Buying a faster model is a great way to improve the performance of any older PC without throwing it out entirely.

Ergonomic Keyboard

The traditional computer keyboard is based on the old typewriter keyboard (the IBM Selectric, by the way). Why? It doesn't have to be. No mechanics inside the keyboard require the keys to be laid out in a staggered or cascading style. Repetitive typing on this type of keyboard can lead to various ugly motion disorders (VUMDs).

To help you type more comfortably, you can get an ergonomic keyboard, such as the Microsoft Natural Keyboard. This type of keyboard arranges the keys in a manner that's comfortable for your hands, to keep everything lined up and not tweaked out, like on a regular computer keyboard.

A UPS

The *uninterruptible power supply (UPS)* is a boon to computing anywhere in the world where the power is less than reliable. Plug your console into the UPS. Plug your monitor into the UPS. If the UPS has extra battery-backed-up sockets, plug your modem into it too.

✔ Chapter 4 has information on using a UPS as well as using a power strip.

✔ Using a UPS doesn't affect the performance of your PC. The computer couldn't care less whether it's plugged into the wall or a UPS.

Headset

A headset is like a pair of headphones but with the addition of a microphone. This item may seem useless, until you consider how many ways such a gizmo can be used on a modern PC. First of all, headsets are great for playing online games and for communicating on the Internet (as opposed to using a telephone), and they're an ideal choice when you decide to tackle computer dictation (Chapter 18.)

✔ I use a USB headset, which doesn't interfere with my PC's external speakers.

✔ Try to get a headset with a volume adjuster and mute button built in.

Scanner or Digital Camera

Scanners and digital cameras are really the same thing, just in different boxes. A *scanner* is a flatbed-like device used for scanning flat things. A *digital camera* is a portable scanner with a focused lens, which lets it "scan" things out in the nonflat real world. Both gizmos do the same thing: Transfer an image from the cold harshness of reality into the fun digital world of the computer.

If you already have a manual camera, getting a scanner is a great way to start your computer graphics journey. You can easily scan in existing photos and, after they're digitized, store them in the computer or e-mail them to friends.

Digital cameras are also great investments, although they're more expensive than scanners. The future of photography is digital, so buying one now or later is probably on your list of things to do before you die.

Also see Chapter 16.

Portable Digital Music Player

In case you haven't heard or read it somewhere, the CD player is dead. In fact, music pundits are saying that music CDs will soon be a thing of the past. The next and final resting place for all your music will be your computer. The portable extension of that music will be a digital music player, also known as an *MP3 player*.

The most popular digital music player is the Apple iPod. Although the iPod is an Apple product, it's fully compatible with your PC, including the popular iTunes music program. Other digital music players exist as well. Ensure that the one you get has enough storage for all your music, is compatible with your PC, and has a handy way of talking with the computer as well as recharging its battery.

Refer to Chapter 18 for more information on digital music and using a portable music player.

Chapter 31

Ten Tips from a PC Guru

In This Chapter

▸ Remember that you're in charge

▸ Realize that computer nerds love to help

▸ Use antivirus software

▸ Don't fret over upgrading software

▸ Don't reinstall Windows to fix things

▸ Perfectly adjust your monitor

▸ Unplug your PC when you open its case

▸ Subscribe to a computer magazine

▸ Avoid the hype

▸ Don't take this computer stuff too seriously

I don't consider myself a computer expert or genius or guru, though many have called me those nasty names. I'm just a guy who understands how computers work. Or, better than that, I understand how computer people think. They may not be able to express an idea, but I can see what they mean and translate it into English for you. Given that, here are some tips and suggestions so that you and your PC can go off on your merry way.

Remember That You Control the Computer

You bought the computer. You clean up after its messes. You feed it CDs when it asks for them. You control the computer — simple as that. Don't let that computer try to boss you around with its bizarre conversations and funny idiosyncrasies. It's really pretty dopey; the computer is an idiot.

If somebody shoved a flattened can of motor oil in your mouth, would you try to taste it? Of course not. But stick a flattened can of motor oil into a CD drive, and the computer tries to read information from it, thinking that it's a CD. See? It's dumb.

You control that mindless computer just like you control an infant. You must treat it the same way, with respect and caring attention. Don't feel that the computer is bossing you around any more than you feel that a baby is bossing you around during 3 a.m. feedings. They're both helpless creatures, subject to your every whim. Be gentle. But be in charge.

Realize That Most Computer Nerds Love to Help Beginners

It's sad, but almost all computer nerds spend most of their waking hours in front of a computer. They know that it's kind of an oddball thing to do, but they can't help it.

Their guilty consciences are what usually make them happy to help beginners. By passing on knowledge, they can legitimize the hours they while away on their computer stools. Plus, it gives them a chance to brush up on a social skill that's slowly slipping away: the art of *talking* to a person.

✔ Always be grateful when you're given help.

✔ Avoid relatives who claim to be nerds and desire to "fix" your PC for you. Don't try to be nice to them; treat your PC like your wallet. You wouldn't hand it over to anyone, right? Remember, it's easier to sue someone you don't know.

Use Antivirus Software

It's a sad statement, but to really enjoy your computer, you have to invest in some antivirus software. You really need the protection that such a program offers — even if you're careful. Every PC that's running Windows and connected to the Internet is at risk. There are no exceptions.

✔ See Chapter 23 for more computer security advice.

✔ Yes, pay the money and buy the annual subscription to keep your antivirus software up to date.

- Some antivirus programs come with other Internet security software as well, including spyware protection and perhaps a firewall. Yes, those things are worth the cost.

- There's no need to run two antivirus (or spyware or firewall) programs at once. One program is enough to do the job.

Understand That Upgrading Software Isn't an Absolute Necessity

Just as the models on the cover of *Vogue* change their clothes each season (or maybe I should say "change their *fashions*" each season), software companies issue perpetual upgrades. Should you automatically buy the upgrade?

Of course not! If you're comfortable with your old software, you have no reason to buy the new version. None!

The software upgrade probably has a few new features in it (although you still haven't had a chance to check out all the features in the current version). And, the upgrade probably has some new bugs in it too, making it crash in new and different ways. Feel free to look at the box, just as you stare at the ladies on the cover of *Vogue*. But don't feel obliged to buy something you don't need.

Don't Reinstall Windows

A myth floating around tech-support sites says that the solution to all your ills is to reinstall Windows. Some suspect that tech-support people even claim that it's common for most Windows users to reinstall at least once a year. That's rubbish.

You *never* need to reinstall Windows. All problems are fixable. It's just that the so-called tech-support people are lazy and resort to a drastic solution as opposed to trying to discover what the true problem is. If you press them, they *will* tell you what's wrong and how to fix it.

In all my years of using a computer, I have never reinstalled Windows or had to reformat my hard drive. It's not even a good idea just to refresh the bits on the hard drive or whatever other nonsense they dish up. There just isn't a need to reinstall Windows ever. Period.

Refer to my book *Troubleshooting Your PC For Dummies* (Wiley) for all the various solutions you can try instead of reformatting your hard dive or reinstalling Windows.

Perfectly Adjust Your Monitor

I don't have much explaining to do here. Keeping the monitor turned up too brightly is bad for your eyes, and it wears out your monitor more quickly.

 To adjust a CRT monitor to pink perfection, turn the brightness (the button with the little sun) all the way up and adjust the contrast (the button with the half moon) until the display looks pleasing. Then, turn the brightness down until you like what you see. That's it!

Unplug Your PC When You Upgrade Hardware

Newer PCs don't have a flippable on-off switch, like the older models do. When you open the case to upgrade or add an expansion card, your belly (if it's like my belly) may punch the power-on button, and, lo, you're working in a hazardous electrical environment. To prevent that, unplug the console before you open it for upgrading.

You don't need to unplug the console or even turn off the PC when you add a USB or FireWire device. (You need to unplug it if you add a USB expansion card, however.)

Subscribe to a Computer Magazine

Oh, why not? Browse the stacks at your local coffeehouse-slash-music-store-slash-bookstore. Try to find a computer magazine that matches your tastes.

- ✔ One magazine that seems to be worthy for computer beginners is *SmartComputing*. Look for it in a magazine stand near you.
- ✔ What sells me on a magazine are the columns and the *newsy* stuff they put up front.
- ✔ Some magazines are all ads. That can be great if you like ads, or it can be boring.
- ✔ Avoid the nerdier magazines, but I probably didn't need to tell you that.

Shun the Hype

The computer industry is rife with hype. Even if you subscribe to a family-oriented computer magazine, you still read about the latest this or the next-biggest-trend that. Ignore it!

My gauge for hype is whether the thing that's hyped is shipping as a standard part of a PC. I check the ads. If they're shipping the item, I write about it. Otherwise, it's a myth and may not happen. Avoid being lured by the hype.

 ✔ When hype becomes reality, you read about it in this book.

 ✔ Former hype I have successfully ignored: Pen Windows, push technology, Web channels, Shockwave, Microsoft Bob, Windows CE, and tablet PCs.

 ✔ Hype that eventually became reality: USB, CD-R, shopping on the Web (or *e-commerce*), DVD drives, digital cameras, and home networking.

Don't Take It So Seriously

Hey, simmer down. Computers aren't part of life. They're nothing more than mineral deposits and petroleum products. Close your eyes and take a few deep breaths. Listen to the ocean spray against the deck on the patio; listen to the gurgle of the marble Jacuzzi tub in the master bedroom.

Pretend that you're driving a convertible through a grove of sequoias on a sunny day with the wind whipping through your hair and curling over your ears. Pretend that you're lying on the deck under the sun as the Pacific Princess chugs south toward the islands where friendly, wide-eyed monkeys eat coconut chunks from the palm of your hand.

You're up in a hot air balloon, swirling the first sip of champagne and feeling the bubbles explode atop your tongue. Ahead, to the far left, the castle's spire rises through the clouds, and you can smell Chef Claude's awaiting banquet.

Then slowly open your eyes. It's just a dumb computer. Really. Don't take it too seriously.

Index

• *Symbols & Numerics* •

\ (backslash) key, 138
. (period) in filenames, 290
3-D graphics, supporting, 123
16 bits, PC sound sampled at, 164
404 error, 258
802.11 wireless networking standard,
      232, 234

• *A* •

A-B switch for a printer, 91
Accelerated Graphics Port. *See* AGP
account folder. *See* User Profile folder
acoustic coupler modem, 176
ACPI (Advanced Configuration and Power
      Interface), 186
ad hoc network, 238
Add a Printer toolbar button, 158
Add or Remove Programs dialog box, 324
Add Printer Wizard, 158
Address bar in Windows Explorer, 303
address for memory, 97
addresses, e-mail, 260
Adjust Date/Time command, 81
administrator privileges required to install
      new software, 320
administrator's UAC, 281–282
Adobe Photoshop Elements, 198
Advanced Configuration and Power
      Interface (ACPI), 186
Advanced Power Management (APM)
      specification, 186
Advanced Search link in the Search Results
      window, 316

AGP (Accelerated Graphics Port)
      expansion slot, 79
      port, 123
AIFF (Audio Interchange File Format), 224
air flow
      in the console, 23
      for the microprocessor, 76
      in PCs, 185
air vents, 21–22, 24
ALL CAPS, e-mail messages in, 260
All Programs menu on the Start button
      menu, 62, 63
all-in-one printers, 150, 152
Alt key, 136
Alt+Tab key combination, 318
AMD microprocessors, 76
animation, displaying pop-up windows, 274
annual subscription for antivirus software,
      350
antenna, wireless adapter with, 234
antiglare screen, 344
antiradiation shielding, 344
antivirus software
      described, 279
      disabling, 320
      investing in, 350–351
Any key, 138
APM (Advanced Power Management)
      specification, 186
Appearance Settings dialog box, 127
applications (programs)
      accessing recent, 321
      adding and removing, 158, 324
      antivirus software, 279, 320, 350–351
      attached to e-mail messages, 341
      described, 14–15, 294

applications (programs) *(continued)*
  finding on the Start button menu, 320–321
  putting in the pin-on area, 321–322
  quitting all other, 318
  running, 320–323
archiving, data discs for, 331
arrow keys on the keyboard, 134
ATA (Advanced Technology Attachment), 107
ATAPI. *See* ATA
ATI adapters, 126
ATI Radeon, 123
Attach File to Message button, 269
attachments
  grabbing with Windows Mail, 268–269
  opening, 269
  saving in Windows Mail, 268
  sending and receiving with e-mail, 268
  sending in Windows Mail, 269–270
attributes of files, 287
Au file format, 224
Audacity sound recording program, 173
audio. *See also* music
  abilities of PCs, 163–167
  connections, 31–33
  control in Windows, 167–169
  file types, 224
Audio Interchange File Format (AIFF), 224
audio microphone
  configuring, 168
  described, 32
  jack, 24–25, 27
  options for, 167
  setting up for speech recognition, 227
audio speakers
  configuring in Windows, 168
  described, 19, 164–166
  in a monitor, 124
  positioning, 165–166
  switching to headphones, 169
Audio Video Interleave (AVI) file, 216
author, e-mail address of, 5

automatic updates, accepting from Windows, 278
AutoPlay dialog box
  displaying for a disc, 111
  for a CD-R, 330
  for a memory card, 114
AVI (Audio Video Interleave) file, 216

• B •

back posture, 141
background, changing, 128–129
backing up files, 339
backslash (\) key, 138
Balanced power-management plan, 187
bank of memory, 95
base station
  configuring, 242
  in a network, 233
batteries in cordless mice, 144
battery, internal to a PC, 82–83
battery-powered PCs, power-saving options, 188–189
Bcc field in Windows Mail, 261
beginners
  common mistakes, 337–341
  helped by computer nerds, 350
bidirectional cable for a printer, 36
bidirectional connection with DSL, 179
binary counting system, 97
binary information in files, 286
BIOS (Basic Input/Output System). *See* chipset
BIOS Setup utility, 45
bits
  described, 97
  handled by a microprocessor, 77
black and white, printing in, 259
black ink, instead of color, 154
blackout, 39
blind-carbon-copying of an e-mail message, 261

blue UACs, 282
Bluetooth standard, 236
BMP (Windows Bitmap) file format, 199
boot disk, finding, 109
boxes
  keeping, 30
  unpacking, 29–30
Break key, 138
brightness, adjusting for an image, 202–203
broadband modems
  connecting, 35
  described, 177–178
  types of, 178
brownout, 39
Browse dialog box, 305
browser home page, 257–258
browsing. *See also* Internet Explorer (IE)
  a network, 245
  the Web, 257–258
Burn a Disc dialog box, 330–331
Burn button on the toolbar, 332
Burn to Disc toolbar button, 333
burning songs to a CD, 225
buttons on a monitor, 124
bytes
  measuring memory in, 96–97
  measuring the size of a file, 288

• *C* •

C drive, 108
cable modem, 178
cables. *See also* USB cables
  connected to expansion cards, 78
  described, 19, 32
  length of, 32
  networking, 234–235
  for printers, 36, 156
camera, digital, 193–195, 346–347
Camera Raw (CRW) format, 199
Cancel button for printing, 162
capacity of a hard drive, 108

capitalization in filenames, 289
capturing a video signal, 208
case
  closing, 74
  opening, 73–74
case sensitivity of filenames, 289
Cat 5 networking cable, 234
cathode ray tube. *See* CRT monitors
CD drives
  booting from, 109
  described, 20–21
  speed rating of, 110–111
CD-R discs
  about, 328
  compared to CD-RW, 224
  for music, 329
  quality of, 329
CD-RW discs, 328
CDs
  about, 347
  burning, 225
  capacity of, 110
  disc-writing software, 329
  disposing of, 334
  ejecting, 111–112, 332–333
  inserting into drives, 111
  labeling, 334
  making your own, 224–225, 327–334
  moving information between computers, 331
  naming, 331
  obtaining proper, 328–329
  playing musical, 170
  ripping music from, 221
center/subwoofer jack, 24–26
central processing unit (CPU), 20. *See also* microprocessor
chair, adjusting, 141
Change Plan Settings options, 55
channels, changing in live TV, 210–211
child folder, 299
chipset, 83

classic Start menu, 62

clicking with a mouse, 145, 147

client-server network, 232

clock

  displayed by Windows, 80

  in a PC, 80–82

  setting, 81

  updating date-and-time stamps, 288

closing the console or case, 74

codecs, 217

color laser printers, 150

color printers, inks or toners in, 153

color tone, fixing in older photographs, 203

colors, adjusting, 131–132

COM port, 36. *See also* serial port

commercials, skipping, 213

communications software, 181

compact discs. *See* CDs

CompactFlash memory cards, 114

components, 19

Compressed Folder, 304

compressed folders, downloading, 267–269

compressor-decompressor, 217

computer cables. *See* cables

Computer icon, 66

computer magazines, subscribing to, 352

computer memory. *See* memory

Computer Name/Domain Changes dialog

  box, opening, 239–240

computer nerds, helping beginners, 350

computer networking. *See* networking

computer packaging, 29–30

computer printers. *See* printer(s)

computer software. *See* software

Computer window

  displaying, 66, 292

  viewing permanent storage devices, 117

computers. *See* PCs (personal computers)

COM/serial connector, 24–26

condenser mics, 167

configuration program for a router, 241

configuring

  file sharing, 247–248

  for Internet use, 256

  microphone, 168

  modems, 180–181

  network, 233

  routers, 240–242

  speakers, 168

  Windows Media Center, 209

connecting to the Internet, 256–257

connection for a modem, 181–182

connection information for a network, 238

connectors, 85

console

  backside of, 22–24

  closing, 74

  described, 18–20, 30

  front of, 20–22

  inside the, 71–74

  opening, 73–74

  plugging things into, 31–37

  setting up, 30

  turning on, 44

console buttons, 21–22

Contacts folder, 300

containers, files as, 286

Context key, 139

contrast, adjusting for an image, 202–203

Control Panel

  changing the date/time format, 80

  Classic view, 64–65

  displaying the Sound dialog box, 167

  Home window, 64–65

  Programs and Features window, 324

control panels on printers, 152–153

conventions in this book, 3–4

Copy command, 311

Copy suffix, 312

copying files, 311–312

copyrighted images on the Web, 264

cordless mice, 143–144

CPU (central processing unit), 20. *See also* microprocessor
Critical Stop event, sound associated with, 171
cropping images, 201
CRT monitors
    about, 121–122
    adjusting, 352
    compared to LCD, 122
Crucial Web site, 102–103
CRW (Camera Raw) format, 199
Ctrl key
    holding down to select files, 308–309
    holding to copy files, 312
    location option in the Mouse Properties dialog box, 147
    uses of, 136
Ctrl+A, 308
Ctrl+C, 264, 312
Ctrl+D, 258
Ctrl+Esc, 62
Ctrl+J, 221
Ctrl+P, 159–160, 259
Ctrl+S, 294
Ctrl+V, 264, 312
Ctrl+X, 312
Ctrl+Z (Undo command), 314, 316
cursor, 135
cursor keypad on the keyboard, 134
Cut command, 311
CYMK (cyan, yellow, magenta, black), 154

• D •

data CD-Rs, 329
data discs
    creating, 330–331
    recording, 330–334
    working with in Windows, 332
Data DVD option in Media Center, 214
data files, 287

data storage, external
    adding, 115–116
    described, 115–116
    removing, 116
date, setting in a PC, 81
Date and Time Properties dialog box, 82
Date and Time Settings dialog box, 81
date-and-time format in Windows, 80
date-and-time stamp on a file, 287
daughterboards. *See* expansion cards
DCIM folder on a memory card, 195
default printer
    setting, 158–159
    in Windows, 157
deleting
    files, 314
    folders, 314
    RW disc contents, 333–334
demodulation, 175
desktop
    creating a shortcut on, 313, 322–323
    described, 60–61
Desktop Background window, 128
Desktop folder, 300
desktop PC, 18
desktop shortcut icon, creating, 322–323
destination folder for a file, 311
Details pane in Windows Explorer, 303
DHCP, 242
dialup access, network connection for, 256
dialup connection, canceling, 257
dialup modem
    adding an external, 180
    configuring an internal, 180–181
    connecting, 34–35
    described, 175–177
    hanging up, 183
    setting up, 179–181
    using, 181–183
dictating to PCs, 226–228
digital cameras, 193–195, 346–347
digital jacks, 35

digital monitor connector, 25
digital music players, 347
Digital Subscriber Line (DSL), 178
digital video, 215
digital video connector, illustrated, 26
digital video recorders (DVR), 208
digital-to-VGA adapter, 35
DIMMs (Dual Inline Modular Memory), 95
dip, 39
directional antenna, 234
directories. *See* folders
disc drive letter, mapping a network folder
    as, 250
disc formats, 328–329
disconnecting from a dialup connection,
    256
discs. *See also* CDs
  about, 347
  burning, 225
  capacity of, 110
  disposing of, 334
  ejecting, 111–112, 332–333
  inserting into drives, 111
  labeling, 334
  making your own, 224–225, 327–334
  moving information between computers
    with, 331
  naming, 331
  obtaining proper, 328–329
  playing musical, 170
  ripping music from, 221
disc-writing software, 329
disk drive cage, inside the console, 72–73
disk drives. *See also* hard drives
  alternative forms of, 112
  described, 107
  lights, 21–22
  sharing entire, 249
  types of, 106
disk media in a disk drive, 107
disk memory, 12
disk storage, sharing, 231

display
  adjusting to see small things, 130
  defined, 120
Display Pointer Trails option in the Mouse
    Properties dialog box, 147
Display Settings dialog box, 131
display size, adjusting, 131–132
disposing of discs, 334
.doc filename extension, 291
document scanners
  compared to digital cameras, 194
  described, 195–198, 346–347
  operation of, 196–197
documents and files
  about, 286
  attributes of, 287
  canceling the printing of, 162
  contents of, 286–287
  copying to removable media, 313
  creating, 294–296
  creating shortcuts for, 313–314
  date and time of, 287
  deleting, 314
  described, 15, 198, 286
  describing, 287–288
  downloading, 263
  dragging between two folders, 312
  duplicating, 312
  finding, 316
  in folders, 288
  lassoing a group of, 310
  moving or copying, 311–312
  naming, 287–290, 295
  not backing up, 339
  opening, 94
  opening or deleting unknown, 339
  renaming, 315–316
  saving, 94
  saving as a different type, 296
  saving to disk, 294–296
  selecting, 307–311
  selecting a few, 308–309

selecting a row of, 309–310
selecting all in a folder, 308
sending between two computers, 263
size of, 287
types of, 286, 288
undeleting, 314–315
of unknown format, 269
unselecting, 311
uploading, 263
working with groups of, 307–311
Documents folder
  described, 300
  displaying files and folders found in,
    302–303
Documents subfolder in the User Profiles
    folder, 66
dots per inch (dpi), 197
double quotes in Google searches, 259
double-clicking with a mouse, 145
downloading
  files, 263
  software from the Internet, 265–267
Downloads folder
  deleting files from, 267
  described, 300
dpi (dots per inch), 197
Drafts folder in Windows Mail, 260
dragging
  files between two folders, 312
  with a mouse, 145
Dragon Naturally Speaking, 228
DRAM chips, 95
DRD-R format, erasable version of, 328
drive A, 112, 117
drive B, 117
drive C, 117
drive for DVDs
  creating CDs and DVDs, 109
  described, 20, 21, 109–110, 220
  inserting a boot disc into, 110
  making discs with, 328
  speed rating of, 110–111

drive letters
  assigning to shared folders, 245
  identifying storage media, 117
  rules for assigning, 118
drive mechanism of a disk drive, 107
drivers
  described, 15
  finding on the Internet, 265
dropping an object with a mouse, 145
DSL (Digital Subscriber Line), 178
DSL modem, 178
Dual Inline Modular Memory (DIMM), 95
duplicating files, 312
dust cover for a PC, 344
DVD drives
  creating CDs and DVDs, 109
  described, 20–21, 109–110, 220
  inserting a boot disc into, 110
  making discs with, 328
  speed rating of, 110–111
DVD logo, 110
DVD recordable formats, 328
DVD+R discs, 328
DVD-R discs, 328
DVD-RAM format, 328
DVD+RW discs, 328
DVD-RW discs, 328
DVDs
  burning from recorded TV, 213–214
  capacity of, 110
DVR (digital video recorder), 208
dynamic microphones, 167
dynamic random access memory (DRAM)
    chips, 95

• E •

editing images, 201–204
802.11 wireless networking standard, 232
ejecting
  discs, 111–112
  memory cards, 114–115

ejecting *(continued)*
  a music CD, 221
  recordable discs, 332–333
electrical storm, turning off PCs during, 57
electrical surge, 39
e-mail addresses, entering, 260
e-mail attachments
  grabbing with Windows Mail, 268–269
  opening, 269
  saving in Windows Mail, 268
  sending and receiving with e-mail, 268
  sending in Windows Mail, 269–270
e-mail messages
  blind-carbon-copying of, 261
  opening programs attached to, 341
e-mail program in Windows, 259–261
e-mail server, your ISP's, 255
Enable Transparency check box, 127
energy, saving, 185
Energy Star program, 185
Enter key, 138–139
Erase This Disc toolbar button, 333
ergonomic keyboard, 345. *See also*
  keyboard(s)
Escape (Esc) key
  about, 138
  canceling an operation, 312
  making the Start button menu go away, 62
Ethernet. *See also* NICs (network adapter
  cards)
  networking standard, 232
events, assigning sounds to, 170–172
EXE extension, 292
executable files, 292
expansion, future, 20–21
expansion cards, 23, 78–79
expansion slots, 23, 78–79
extensions. *See* filename extensions
external devices, assigning drive letters to,
  118
external dialup modems
  adding, 180
  described, 177

external storage
  adding, 115–116
  described, 115–116
  removing, 116
Extract button in the Extract Compressed
  (Zipped) Folders window, 267

• F •

F1 key, 67, 138
F2 key, 316
F5 key, 244
face down, top side down symbol, 154
face down, top side up symbol, 154
face up, top side down symbol, 155
face up, top side up symbol, 155
fan
  in the console, 23
  for the microprocessor, 76
Favorite Links area in Windows
  Explorer, 303
Favorites, adding Web pages to, 258
Favorites folder, 301
fax machine, as a printing device, 157
fax modems, dialup modems as, 177
file(s)
  about, 286
  attributes of, 287
  canceling the printing of, 162
  contents of, 286–287
  copying to removable media, 313
  creating, 294–296
  creating shortcuts for, 313–314
  date and time of, 287
  deleting, 314
  described, 15, 198, 286–288
  downloading, 263
  dragging between two folders, 312
  duplicating, 312
  finding, 316
  in folders, 288
  graphics, 198–205
  lassoing a group of, 310

moving or copying, 311–312
naming, 287–290, 295
not backing up, 339
opening, 94
opening or deleting unknown, 339
renaming, 315–316
saving, 94
saving as a different type, 296
saving to disk, 294–296
selecting, 307–311
selecting a few, 308–309
selecting a row of, 309–310
selecting all in a folder, 308
sending between two computers, 263
size of, 287
types of, 286, 288
undeleting, 314–315
of unknown format, 269
unselecting, 311
uploading, 263
working with groups of, 307–311
File Download dialog box, 265–266
File menu, Save commands on, 294–295
File Name text box in the Open dialog box,
    305
file sharing, turning on, 248
File Transfer Protocol (FTP), 270
filename extensions
  described, 291
  details about, 291–292
  for graphics files, 199
  renaming, 293
  seeing or hiding, 292
filenames
  case sensitivity of, 289
  described, 287
  forbidden characters, 290
  length of, 290
file-naming rules, 290
FileZilla, 270
film DVDs, programs for making, 329

film negatives, scanning, 198
finding. *See* searching
firewall. *See also* Windows Firewall
  defined, 276–277
  enabling a router's, 241
  operations of, 277
  testing, 277
firewall protection in a router, 235
FireWire port. *See also* IEEE 1394 connector
  networking computers using, 235
FireWire symbol, 90
flash animation, displaying pop-up
    windows, 274
flash memory, 96
flat screen monitors, 122
flipping images, 203–204
floppy disk drives, 21, 112
floppy disks, 107
folder icon in Windows, 298
folders
  creating, 304
  deleting, 314
  described, 288, 297–298
  files in, 288
  forbidden, 301–302
  as key to organizing files, 298
  naming, 289, 304
  opening, 298, 303
  opening or deleting unknown, 339
  renaming, 315–316
  selecting all files in, 308
  sharing, 248–249
  unsharing, 251
Folders list in Windows Explorer, 303
footprint of a PC, 18
forbidden characters in filenames, 290
forbidden folders, 301–302
Form Feed button on a printer, 152
format for a recordable disc, 329–330
forward slash (/) key, 138
404 error, 258

FreeCell, playing to learn a computer
mouse, 145
FTP (File Transfer Protocol), 270
function keys on the keyboard, 134

• G •

gadgets in the Sidebar, 61
game controller. *See* gamepad connector
gamepad connector, 34
GB (gigabyte) of memory, 97
Getting Started booklet, 318
GHz (gigahertz), 77
gibi (Gi), 101
GIF (Graphics Interchange Format), 199
gigabyte (GB) of memory, 97
gigahertz (GHz), 77
Google, searching with, 259
GPU (graphics processing unit), 123
graphical images. *See also* icons
  adjusting contrast or brightness, 202–203
  copyrighted on the Web, 264
  cropping, 201
  editing, 201–204
  flipping, 203–204
  getting into PCs, 193–198
  resizing, 201–202
  rotating, 203–204
  saving from Web pages, 264
  scaling, 201–202
  selecting a program to manage, 194–195
  viewing in Windows, 204–205
graphical links in Web pages, 258
graphics adapters
  described, 120, 122–123
  disabling on the motherboard, 123
graphics file formats, 198–200
graphics file types, changing, 200–201
graphics files, working with, 198–205
Graphics Interchange Format (GIF), 199
graphics port. *See* AGP (Accelerated
  Graphics Port)
graphics processing unit (GPU), 123

graphics systems of a PC, 120–123
grayscale, printing in, 259
guide
  recording TV shows found in, 212
  viewing in Windows Media Center, 211

• H •

hanging up a modem, 183
hard copy
  described, 19
  printing, 150
hard disk drives, capacity and speed of,
  108
hard drives. *See also* disk drives
  adding to a PC, 108
  purchasing larger, faster, 345
  storing images on, 195
hardware
  basic PC, 18–20
  buying incompatible, 338
  described, 13
  keyboards. *See* keyboards(s)
  for making discs, 328
  memory cards. *See* memory cards
  for networking, 232–236
  opening, 340
  printers. *See* printer(s)
  screen. *See* monitors; screen
  upgrading safely, 352
hardware firewall, 241
HDTV capable tuners, 208
headphones
  switching to speakers, 169
  using, 166
headphones/speakers connector, 24–25
headsets
  described, 166
  purchasing, 346
heat dissipation in computers, 185
heating ducts, running networking cable
  through, 235

Help (F1) key, 67, 138
Help and Support Center, 67
Help and Support command, 67
Help engine, quitting, 67
Hibernate option
  described, 49
  for the power button, 54
Hibernation, 51–52
Hide Extensions for Known File Types
    option, 292
hiding filename extensions, 292
High Performance power-management
    plan, 187
High Performance Serial Bus. *See* IEEE port
high-speed modems. *See* broadband
    modems
hoaxes, 340
home page, setting, 257–258
horizontal orientation
  choosing for printing Web pages, 259
  printing in, 161
.HTML filename extension, 291
hub
  described, 235
  for a network, 233
  of a network, 235–236
human engineering, 272, 279
humidity, avoiding, 31
hype, shunning, 353

• *1* •

IBM PC, 15
icons
  described, 61
  on the desktop, 60
  for desktop, 322–323
  displaying Control Panel items as, 64
  enlarging, 130
  renaming a group of, 316
  representing files in Windows, 293
  shortcut compared to regular, 314

for storage devices, 117
  on a typical PC monitor, 125
  in Windows Explorer, 303
IDE, 107
IEEE 1294 port, 235
IEEE 1394 (FireWire) connector, 24–27. *See*
    also FireWire port
IEEE cables, 90
IEEE connectors, 33
IEEE port, 33, 89–90
I.Link. *See* IEEE port
images. *See also* icons; pictures
  adjusting contrast or brightness, 202–203
  copyrighted on the Web, 264
  cropping, 201
  editing, 201–204
  flipping, 203–204
  getting into PCs, 193–198
  resizing, 201–202
  rotating, 203–204
  saving from Web pages, 264
  scaling, 201–202
  selecting a program to manage, 194–195
  viewing in Windows, 204–205
impact printers, 150
Import Pictures and Videos to My
    Computer option, 195
Import Pictures using Windows option, 195
incompatible hardware, buying, 338
Industry Standard Architecture (ISA), 79
infrared (IR) cordless mice, 143–144
infrared connector, illustrated, 27
initializing a recordable disc, 329
ink cartridges
  changing, 154
  in inkjet printers, 153
ink for printers, 153–154
inkjet paper, 155
inkjet printers, 150–151
ink/toner replacement for printers, 152
Input and Output. *See* I/O (Input/Output)

input devices
  described, 11
  mice as, 142
inserting
  discs into disc drives, 111
  memory cards, 114
insertion pointer, 135
Install Updated Automatically option in
    Windows Update, 278
installation of software, 318–320
installation program, starting, 319
instructions for a processor, 12
Intel, microprocessors from, 76
interface
  of a disk drive, 107
  of a graphics adapter, 123
  of Windows, 59–63
internal clock
  displayed by Windows, 80
  in a PC, 80–82
  setting, 81
  updating date-and-time stamps, 288
internal dialup modem, 176–177, 180–181
Internet
  accessing, 254–257
  configuring Windows for, 256
  connecting to, 256–257
  described, 254
  downloading software from, 265–267
  obtaining software from, 265–268
Internet Explorer (IE)
  browsing the Web using, 257–258
  running to test the Internet, 256
  security features of, 272
  security tools in, 273–275
  starting, 273
Internet hoaxes, spreading, 340
Internet programs, running more than one,
    256
Internet service provider. *See* ISP
Internet time, synchronizing with, 82
invisible SSID, 241

I/O (Input/Output), 10–11
I/O connectors on the motherboard, 75
I/O panel on the console, 23–26
I/O port, 86
IP addresses, providing dynamically, 242
iPod
  described, 347
  designed for iTunes software, 224
  making MP3 players popular, 223
ISA expansion slot, 79
ISP (Internet service provider)
  choosing, 254–255
  information needed from, 255
  malware assistance from, 272
iTunes, 221, 224

• J •

jacks, 86
joystick connector, 34
joystick port, 26–27
JPG (Joint Photographic Experts Group)
    file format, 199
JPG images, converting TIFF images to, 200
jukeboxes, available for Windows, 221

• K •

Kaspersky Anti-Virus, 279
KB (kilobytes) of memory, 96–97
Kensington SmartSockets power strips, 39
keyboard(s)
  connecting, 34
  controlling in Windows, 140–141
  described, 19
  ergonomic, 345
  keys on special, 139
  layout of, 134–135
keyboard connector, 24, 27
keyboard cover, 344
keyboard port, 34, 91
Keyboard Properties dialog box, 140–141

keys
  abbreviations on, 136
  repeating, 140
kilobits per second, measuring modem
    speed, 178
kilobytes (KB) of memory, 96–97·
KVM switch, 90

• *L* •

labeling discs, 334
LAN (local area network), 232
landscape orientation
  printing in, 161
  for printing Web pages, 259
laptop PCs
  described, 18
  update options for, 278
laser in a CD or DVD drive, 107
laser paper as inkjet paper, 155
laser printers
  described, 150
  not plugging into power strips, 39
  plugging in directly into wall sockets, 39
lassoing files, 310
LCD monitors, 121–122, 132
LED sensor in an optical mouse, 143
left (main) button on a mouse, 142–143
left handers, mouse adjustments for, 148
legacy ports
  described, 90–91
  on a PC, 86
lightning storm, turning off PCs during, 57
lights on the console, 21–22
Line In connector, 32
Line in jack, 24–25, 27
line noise, 39
Links folder, 301
liquid crystal display. *See* LCD monitors
Live File Format disc
  ejecting, 332–333
  interaction with, 332

Live File System format
  described, 329–330
  selecting, 331
live TV
  pausing, 210–211
  watching, 210–211
Live TV subcategory in the Windows Media
    Center, 210–211
local area network (LAN), 232
local sharing, 249
lock keys on the keyboard, 137
locking PCs, 48, 50–51
Log Off command on the Shutdown
    menu, 50
logging in to Windows, 46–47
logging off PCs, 48, 50
long-term storage, 12, 94
lossy compression, 199
LPT port, 91
LPT1, 158

• *M* •

MAC address, getting, 241–242
Macintosh computer, 16
Macintosh iPod
  described, 347
  designed for iTunes software, 224
  making MP3 players popular, 223
magazines, subscribing to computer, 352
magnetic oxide in disk media, 107
Magnifier tool in Windows, 226
mail addresses, entering, 260
mail attachments
  grabbing with Windows Mail, 268–269
  opening, 269
  saving in Windows Mail, 268
  sending and receiving with e-mail, 268
  sending in Windows Mail, 269–270
mail messages
  blind-carbon-copying of, 261
  opening programs attached to, 341

mail program in Windows, 259–261

mail server, your ISP's, 255

malware, 272–273

manual. *See also* online manual

  for a printer, 153

manual/envelope feeder in a printer, 151

Map Network Drive dialog box, 250

mapped network drive, disconnecting, 251

mapping a folder to a disk drive letter, 250

margins, setting for printing, 160–161

Mastered disc, ejecting, 332

Mastered format

  described, 330

  selecting, 331

Mastered format disc

  finishing, 333

  interaction with, 332

Mavis Beacon Teaches Typing software,
  135

MB (megabyte) of memory, 97

Mbps (megabits per second), 234

McAfee VirusScan, 279

mebi (Mi), 101

mechanical mouse, 143

media, mounting, 313

Media Access Control address. *See* MAC

  address, getting

Media Center

  configuring, 209

  interface of, 209–210

  recording TV programs, 211–212

  using, 208

  using across a network, 248

media PC, 207

Media Player

  compared to Windows Media Center, 208

  controlling audio files, 170

  interface of, 220

  running, 220–221

  working with portable music devices, 223

media playlist, 220, 222

media sharing, turning on, 248

Media sharing setting in the Network and
  Sharing Center window, 248

megabits per second (Mbps), 234

megabyte (MB) of memory, 97

megapixel, 197

memory. *See also* RAM (random access
  memory)

  adding to a PC, 101–103

  described, 12, 93–94

  determining the amount of, 98–99

  in a graphics adapters, 122

  measuring, 96–97

  saving contents to a file, 106

  sizes of, 98

  upgrading, 345

memory addresses, 97

memory card reader in a printer, 151–152

memory card slots, 21

memory cards

  copying files to, 313

  described, 106, 113

  ejecting, 114–115

  inserting, 114

  plugging into PCs, 194

  types of, 113–114

  usage limitation of, 115

memory chips, 95

Memory Sticks, types of, 114

menu bar in Internet Explorer, 257

messages, e-mail. *See* e-mail messages

Mi (mebi), 101

mice. *See* mouse

microcomputers, 15

microphone

  configuring, 168

  described, 32

  options for, 167

  setting up for speech recognition, 227

microphone jack, 24–25, 27

Microphone Setup Wizard, 168

microprocessor

  described, 75–76

  determining the type of, 77–78

in a graphics system, 123
muscle and speed of, 76–77
naming, 76
Microsoft, security patches from, 279
Microsoft Natural Keyboard, 345
Microsoft Windows. *See* Windows
MIDI file format, 171
MIDI files, converting to audio file
    formats, 225
Mini 1394 DV connector, 24–25
mini-DIN connector for audio input, 32–33
mini-tower PC, 18
mirrors for downloading, 267
Mixer, choosing from the volume control
    pop-up, 169
modem connector, 24–25, 27
modems
  broadband, 35, 177–178
  connecting, 34–35
  defined, 175–176
  sharing, 231
  speed of, 178–179
  types of, 176–179
modifier keys on the keyboard, 135–136
modular components, 73
modulation, 175
monitor buttons, 124–125
monitor connector, 27
monitor/adapter relationship in a graphics
    system, 120–121
monitors. *See also* screen
  adjusting, 141, 352
  adjusting the display of, 124–126
  connecting, 35
  defined, 120
  described, 18–19
  entering a low-power state, 187
  physical description of, 124
  resolution of, 197
  turning off, 57
  types of, 121–122

moon button, setting, 55
motherboard
  described, 72–75
  sound-generation hardware on, 164
Motion Pictures Experts Group format, 216
mounting
  discs into a PC's permanent storage
    system, 331
  media, 313
mouse
  connecting, 34
  described, 19, 142–143
  double-clicking, 145, 147
  operations, 144–145
  variations of, 144
  wireless, 91
mouse body, 142–143
mouse connector, 24, 27
mouse pads
  with built-in wrist elevators, 141
  purchasing, 343
mouse pointer
  controlling on the screen, 144
  locating a lost, 146–147
mouse port, 34, 91
Mouse Properties dialog box, 146
MOV file, 216
movie DVDs, programs for making, 329
moving
  files, 311–312
  with a mouse, 145
MP3 (MPEG-1 Audio Layer 3) format, 224
MP3 audio files, 171
MP3 players
  attaching to PCs, 223
  described, 223, 347
MPEG (Motion Pictures Experts Group)
    format, 216
MPEG-1 Audio Layer 3 format, 224
multiboot system, 52
MultiMediaCard (MMC), 114

music. *See also* audio
  organizing into playlists, 220, 222
  ripping from CDs, 221
music CD-Rs, 329
music CDs, making your own, 224–225
Music folder
  described, 301
  saving files in, 173
  in the User Profile folder, 171
music players, digital, 347
Music subfolder in the User Profiles folder, 66
Musical Instrument Digital Interface, 171
Musicmatch Jukebox, 221
My Documents folder. *See* Documents folder
My Music folder. *See* Music folder
My Network Places. *See* Network window

• *N* •

name, assigning to a computer, 239
naming
  discs, 331
  files, 287–290, 295
  folders, 289, 304
Narrator program in Windows, 226
narrowband modem. *See* dialup modem
Natural Keyboard, 345
Navigation pane in Windows Explorer, 303
negatives (film), scanning, 198
Nero program, 329
network(s)
  ad hoc, described, 238
  browsing, 245
  choosing public or private, 238
  configuring, 233
  connecting to using Windows, 237–238
  graphical map of, 246–247
  hub in, 235–236
  plugging in, 35

network adapter cards, 234
Network and Sharing Center, 65–66
Network and Sharing Center window
  displaying, 236–237
  opening, 182
  sharing settings in, 247–248
Network area of the Network and Sharing
    Center window, 237
Network Connections Details box, 241
network connector, 24–26
network discovery, turning on, 246
Network discovery setting in the Network
    and Sharing Center window, 247
network drives, adding to a computer
    system, 118
network folder
  accessing, 249–250
  mapping as a disk drive letter, 250
network layouts, typical, 233
network map, viewing, 246–247
network name, setting your
    computer's, 239
Network Neighborhood. *See* Network
    window
network printers
  accessing, 252
  described, 157
  using, 252
Network window
  browsing folders from, 249–250
  browsing the network from, 245
  described, 66
  refreshing, 244
  in Windows, 244–246
networking
  control of, 65–66
  hardware for, 232–236
  software used for, 236–242
  standards, 232
networking cable, wiring with, 235
networking jack, 35

NICs (network adapter cards), 234
No Signal message on a monitor, 124
Norton AntiVirus, 279
notebook/laptop PC. *See* laptop PCs
Notification Area
  described, 60–61, 63
  "networking buddies" icon in, 238
  updates pop-up bubble in, 279
  Volume icon, 169
null modem, 179
Num Lock key, 134, 137
number 0, compared to uppercase letter O,
  137
number 1, compared to lowercase letter *l*,
  137
numbers, at the beginning of filenames,
  290
numeric keypad
  on the keyboard, 134
  keys for working with numbers, 140
NVIDIA adapters, 126
NVIDIA GeForce, 123

• *O* •

OCR (optical character recognition), 198
Ogg file format, 224
online manual, 67
On-Line or Select on a printer, 152
on-off button on a monitor, 124
on-off switch, true, 55
on-screen display for a monitor, 125
Open button in the Open dialog box, 306
Open dialog box, 305–306
Open Folder to View Files option, 195
open stand, 224
opening
  the console or case, 73–74
  files, 15, 94
  folders, 298
  hardware, 340
  information in Windows, 106

opening folders
  about, 298
  unknown, 339
  in Windows Explorer, 303
operating system, 13–14, 59
optical character recognition (OCR), 198
optical mouse, 143
orange UACs, 282
Organize button on the toolbar, 304
orientation, changing for an image, 203–204
OS. *See* operating system
Outlook Express. *See* Windows Mail
output, 11
output devices, 11

• *P* •

packaging (packing material)
  keeping, 30
  unpacking, 29–30
padlock button in the Start button menu, 51
Page Setup command
  selecting landscape orientation, 259
  selecting paper size, 155
Page Setup dialog box, 160–161
Paint program, opening a graphics image
  in, 200
paper
  buying, 338
  for printers, 154–155
  types of, 155
paper feed in a printer, 151
paper output tray in a printer, 151–152
paper sizes, selecting, 161
paperclip icon in Windows Mail, 268
parent folders, 299
Parental Controls in Windows Vista, 272
partitioning a drive, 108
password
  entering into Windows, 47
  entering manually, 256
  for a user account, 46
  for a wireless network, 242

Password Hint link, 47
password protected sharing, 248
Paste command, selecting, 311
Paste Shortcut command, selecting, 313
patches, installing to Windows, 278
patching software, 325
pathnames, backslash (\) key in, 138
Pause key, 138
pausing live TV, 210–211
PC Setup program, 45
PCI Express, 79
PCI Express slot, 123
PCI slots, 79
PCs (personal computers)
  adding memory to, 101–103
  assigning names to, 239
  clock, 80–82
  controlling, 349–350
  described, 15–16
  dictating to, 226–228
  getting images into, 193–198
  graphics systems of, 120–123
  inner guts of, 72–73
  introduction to, 9–16
  leaving turned on, 56–57
  locking, 50–51
  memory requirements of, 99
  not taking so seriously, 353
  power-saving options for battery-
    powered, 188–189
  resetting for automatic updates, 279
  setting up, 29–42
  television on, 209–215
  transferring files between two, 179
  turning into TVs, 207–209
  turning off, 48–54
  turning on, 37–42, 44–46
  types of, 17–18
  unplugging when upgrading hardware,
    352

peer-to-peer network
  compared to an ad hoc, 238
  described, 232
Pentium microprocessor, 76
periods in filenames, 290
Peripheral Component Interconnect. *See*
    PCI Express
peripherals
  described, 85
  monitors as, 124
  turning on, 44
permanent storage
  described, 105
  types of devices for, 106
  uses of, 106
personal computers. *See* PCs
Personalization window
  Desktop Background, 128
  Display Settings, 131
  Screen Saver, 129
  viewing, 126
  Windows Color and Appearance, 127
phishing
  described, 273
  fighting with Internet Explorer, 274–275
Phishing Filter in Internet Explorer, 275
Phone and Modem Options icon, viewing,
    180
phone headsets
  described, 166
  purchasing, 346
phosphor burn-in, 130
photo printers, 150
photocopier paper, as general-purpose
    paper, 155
photo-editing programs, 198
photographic papers, 155
picture size of a monitor, 124
pictures. *See also* images
  selecting as background, 128
  sending as e-mail attachments, 270

Pictures folder
  described, 301
  storing images in, 195
Pictures subfolder in the User Profiles
    folder, 66
ping, 199
pin-on area, putting programs in, 321–322
pixels
  described, 132
  number displayed, 131
platters in hard drives, 107
Play button in the Windows Media Player
    window, 220
Playback tab in the Sound dialog box, 168
playlist
  creating, 220, 222
  editing, 222
plenum cable, 235
PNG (Portable Network Graphics) format,
    199
pointer. *See* cursor; mouse pointer
Pointer Options tab in the Mouse
    Properties dialog box, 146–147
pointing with a mouse, 145
Pop-up Blocker submenu in Internet
    Explorer, 274
pop-ups, 273
portable music players, 223, 347
Portable Network Graphics (PNG) format,
    199
portrait orientation, printing in, 161
ports, 86, 277
posture for typing, 141
power
  turning on, 37–42
  for USB devices, 87–88
power button
  described, 21–22, 43
  disabling, 54
  functions of, 53–54
  panic shut down, 54

programming, 52
  on the Start menu, 55–56
power connector, 23, 27
power lines, spikes through, 39
power management
  described, 185–186
  standards, 186
power of two, 98
Power Options in System Settings, 53–54
Power Options window
  controlling Sleep mode, 51
  displaying, 186
  opening, 55
  preset plans in, 187
power outage, 39
Power Save power-management plan, 187
power strip
  described, 37–39
  turning on, 44
power supply, 72–73, 83–84
power surge, 39
powered USB hub, 88
power-management plan
  choosing, 187
  creating, 188
Preview button on the toolbar, 204
Print dialog box
  described, 159–160
  displaying, 259
  Properties button, 259
Print Preview command, 160, 258
Print Screen key, 132
Print toolbar icon, 160
printer(s)
  adding manually, 158
  all-in-one printers, 150, 152
  connecting, 35–36
  control panels on, 152–153
  controlling in Windows, 156–159
  described, 19
  ink for, 153–154
  operation of, 159–162

printer(s) *(continued)*
  paper for, 154–155
  parts of, 151–152
  resolution of, 197
  setting default, 158–159
  setting up, 156
  sharing, 231, 251–252
  turning on, 44
  types of, 150–151
  unsharing, 252
printer cable
  described, 36
  purchasing, 156
printer connector, 24–25, 27
printer paper, buying, 338
printer port, 91
printer sharing, turning on, 248
Printer sharing setting in the Network and
    Sharing Center window, 247
printer's window, displaying, 162
Printers window, opening, 251
printing
  in reverse order, 161
  stopping, 161–162
  Web pages, 258–259
private network, 238
PRN port, 91
processing, described, 11–12
processor
  described, 12, 75–76
  determining the type of, 77–78
  in a graphics system, 123
  muscle and speed of, 76–77
  naming, 76
program files, 287
Program Files folder, 267, 302
programmable power button, 53
programs (applications)
  accessing recent, 321
  adding and removing, 158, 324

antivirus software, 279, 320, 350–351
attached to e-mail messages, 341
described, 14–15, 294
finding on the Start button menu, 320–321
putting in the pin-on area, 321–322
quitting all other, 318
running, 320–323
Programs and Features window in the
    Control Panel, 324
Properties button in the Print dialog
    box, 259
protecting against viruses. *See* antivirus
    software
public folder sharing, 248
Public folder sharing setting in the
    Network and Sharing Center
    window, 247
public network, 238
public-level folders, accessing, 248
purging recorded TV, 214–215

Quick Launch bar
  described, 60–61
  putting an icon on, 323
QuickTime, obtaining a free copy of, 216
"quit all other programs" message, 318
quotes in Google searches, 259

• R •

radio frequency mice, 143–144
rain storm, turning off PCs during, 57
RAM (random access memory), 12, 94, 96.
    See also memory
Read Me sheet with software, 318
README file in downloaded software, 266
read-only drive, DVD drive as, 109
read-only memory (ROM), 96
read-write head on a hard drive, 107

recharging cradle for a cordless mouse, 144

recordable disc formats, standards for, 328

recordable discs
  ejecting, 332–333
  putting into a drive, 330

recordable DVD drive, 328

recorded shows, removing, 215

recorded TV
  burning DVDs from, 213–214
  purging, 214–215
  watching, 213

recording
  scheduling for TV programs, 212–213
  sounds, 172–173
  TV programs, 211–212

Recording tab in the Sound dialog box, 168

recovery drive, drive D as, 108

Recycle Bin, opening on the desktop, 314–315

Recycle Bin icon
  described, 66
  dragging files into, 314

recycling ink cartridges, 153

red UACs, 282

Refresh button in Internet Explorer, 258

registration of software, 320

reinstalling Windows, 351

removable media
  copying files to, 313
  labeling, 334

removing
  discs, 111–112
  memory cards, 114–115
  a music CD, 221
  programs, 324
  recordable discs, 332–333
  RW disc contents, 333–334

Rename command
  for files, 293
  from the Organize toolbar button's
    menu, 315

renaming
  filename extensions, 293
  files, 315–316
  folders, 315–316

repeat delay, 140

repeat rate, 140

repetitive stress injury (RSI), avoiding, 141

repository, 265

reset button, 22

resizing images, 201–202

resolution
  adjusting, 131–132
  of the desktop, 61
  of a PC monitor, 197
  of printers, 197
  setting for a scanner, 197

Resolution slider in the Display Settings
    dialog box, 131

resources, sharing, 231–232

Restart command from the Shutdown
    menu, 49, 52

restarting
  a PC, 49
  Windows, 52

Restore This Item button in the Recycle
    Bin, 315

"restricted content" TV channels, 210

Return key. *See* Enter key

reusability of memory, 94

reverse order, printing in, 161

right button, on a mouse, 142–143

right-clicking with a mouse, 145

right-dragging with a mouse, 145

ripping music from CDs, 221

RJ-45 jack, 35

ROM (read-only memory), 96

ROM drive, 109

root directory. *See* root folder

root folder
  described, 298–299
  of the hard drive, 302

root hub, 88

rotating images, 203–204

routers

with built-in firewall protection in a router, 235

configuring, 240–242

described, 235

in networks, 233

RS-232 serial port, 36. *See also* serial port

RSI (repetitive stress injury), avoiding, 141

running programs, 320–323

RW discs

compared to other recordable discs, 334

erasing, 333–334

as more expensive, 329

readability of, 334

• *S* •

SATA. *See* Serial ATA interface for a disk drive

satellite modem, 178

Save As command, 294–295

Save As dialog box

described, 264, 295–296

naming files, 289

Save As Type drop-down list, 296

Save As Type menu button, saving graphics files, 200

Save Attachments dialog box in Windows Mail, 268

Save command, 339

Save commands in Windows, 294–295

Save Games folder, 301

saving

files, 94, 294–296

songs to a CD, 225

your work, 339

scaling images, 201–202

scanners

compared to digital cameras, 194

described, 195–198, 346–347

operation of, 196–197

Scanners and Cameras option in Control Panel, 216

scheduling the recording of TV programs, 212

screen. *See also* monitors

defined, 120

taking a picture of, 132

Screen Resolution slider, setting display resolution, 131

screen saver

disabling, 130

displaying, 129–130

Screen Saver Settings dialog box, 129–130

Scroll Lock key, 137

Search Results window, opening, 316

Searches folder, 301

searching

for files, 316

the Web, 259

secret panel door, 21–22. *See also* I/O panel on the console

Secure Digital (SD) cards, types of, 114

security

firewalls. *See* firewall

passwords. *See* password

spyware, 273, 279–280

against viruses. *See* antivirus software

Security Center window, 275–276

security patches, accessing the latest from Microsoft, 279

Select All command, 308

selecting files

all in a folder, 308

a few, 308–309

a row of, 309–310

Serial ATA interface for a disk drive, 107

serial connector, 24–25

serial number, finding for software, 319

serial port, 36, 91

series

recording all programs in a TV, 212

removing, 215

servers
  in a client-server network, 232
  for downloading, 267
Service Set Identifier. *See* SSID
Setup program, accessing, 45
Share button on the toolbar, 249
share name, changing, 249
shared folders in a network, 245
shared network resources, displaying, 245
shared printers, 157
shared video memory, 100
sharing
  configuring Windows to enable, 247–248
  folders, 248–249
  printers, 251–252
  resources, 231–232
Shield icon
  labeling required administrator
    approval, 281
  on the Start menu power button, 279
ShieldsUP (Gibson Research), 277
Shift key
  holding to move files, 312
  holding to select files, 309–310
  uses of, 136
Shift+Delete command, permanently
    deleting files, 315
shortcut icons
  compared to regular, 314
  creating on the desktop, 322–323
Shortcut suffix, 314
shortcuts, creating for files, 313–314
Show Color Mixer button, 127
Show More arrow, 276
Show More button, 248
Shut Down command
  described, 49, 52–53
  from the Start button menu, 337
Shut Down option
  described, 49
  for the power button, 54
shutdown, options for, 48–50
Shutdown menu, accessing, 49–50

shutting down Windows properly, 337
Sidebar, 60, 61
sitting at a computer, 141
16 bits, PC sound sampled at, 164
size of files, 287
skin for Windows Media Player, 221
sleep button, 22. *See also* moon button,
    setting
Sleep command from the Shutdown menu,
    49, 51
Sleep mode
  described, 48, 51
  enabling with the power button, 54
Slide Show button on the toolbar, 205
slide-in type of disk drive, 111
slide-out tray for a disc drive, 111
Slideshow program, running, 205
SmartComputing magazine, 352
SmartMedia cards, 114
SmartSockets power strips, 39
Snap To option in the Mouse Properties
    dialog box, 147
Snipping Tool, 132
software
  antivirus software, 279, 320, 350–351
  applications, 14
  buying too much, 338
  defined, 12
  described, 13
  downloading from the Internet, 265–267
  drivers, 15
  installing, 266, 318–320
  memory requirements of, 99
  operating system in a computer, 13–14
  other, 14–15
  programs, 15
  with scanners, 198
  uninstalling, 323–325
  updating and upgrading, 325–326
  utilities, 15
  for writing discs, 329
software boxes, keeping intact, 318

Solitaire, playing to learn a computer mouse, 145
Sony/Phillips Digital Interconnect Format. *See* SPDIF connectors
sound(s)
  assigning to events, 170–172
  playing in Windows, 170
  recording, 172–173
Sound dialog box
  opening, 170–171
  Playback tab, 168
  Recording tab, 168
  Sounds tab, 171–172
  in Windows, 167
sound files, copying to audio CDs, 225
sound hardware
  adding to a PC, 164
  controlling, 167
Sound Recorder program in Windows, 172–173
sound samples on the Internet, 172
Sounds list, preselected sounds on, 171
Sounds tab in the Sound dialog box, 171–172
SourceForge.net Web page, 265
spaces in filenames, 290
spam e-mail, replying to, 340
SPDIF connectors, 24–25, 27–28, 33
Speaker Setup Wizard, 168
speakers
  configuring in Windows, 168
  described, 19, 164–166
  in a monitor, 124
  positioning, 165–166
  switching to headphones, 169
speakers connector, 24–25
speakers jack, 28
speaking, PC capable of, 226
speaking to PCs, 226–228
special buttons on a mouse, 142–143
special characters in filenames, 290
speech recognition in Windows, 227

Speech Recognition microphone window, 227–228
Speech Recognition Options window, 227
speech tutorial, taking, 227
speed
  double-click rate, 145
  of memory, 94
  of a microprocessor, 77
speed rating of DVD and CD drives, 110–111
Spelling button in Windows Mail, 260
spikes, 39
spyware
  described, 273
  protecting against, 279–280
SSID (Service Set Identifier)
  making invisible, 241
  for a wireless network, 241–242
Stand By mode. *See* Sleep mode
Standard account, UAC when using, 281
standard recordable CD format, 328
standard rewriteable (RW) CD format, 328
Start button
  described, 60, 62
  on the taskbar, 61
Start button menu
  customizing, 62
  described, 62–63
  finding programs on, 320–321
  Help and Support command, 67
  padlock button, 51
  programs pinned to, 321–322
  Shut Down command, 337
Start menu, power button, 55–56
Start Sync button, 223
starting
  PCs, 44–46
  Windows, 46–48
startup error messages, 46
sticky labels, not using on CD-Rs, 334
Stop button in Internet Explorer, 258
stopping printing, 161–162

storage, 12
storage media, capacity of, 106
storage of data, external
  adding, 115–116
  described, 115–116
  removing, 116
storms (electrical), turning off PCs
    during, 57
stylus mouse, 144
subfolders, 299
subject, entering for an e-mail address, 260
subwoofer, 164–165
subwoofer jack, 24–25
supplies, not buying enough, 338
surge, 39
surge protection, power strip with, 39
surround left/right jack, 24–25, 28
surround sound, setting up, 164–166
Suspend mode. *See* Sleep mode
S-Video connector, 28, 36
S-Video output, 26
Switch User command on the Shutdown
    menu, 48–49, 51
switches, 235
system folders, 302
system password in the Setup program, 45
System Request key, 138
System Settings window, Power Options,
    53–54
system tray. *See* Notification Area
system unit. *See* console
System window
  displaying memory, 98–99
  microprocessor and RAM summary,
    77–78
  opening, 239

● *T* ●

Tab key, 139
Tagged Image File Format (TIFF) graphics
    standard, 199

taskbar, 60, 61
tasks, switching between, 61
TB (terabyte) of memory, 97
technical support from an ISP, 255
telephone, connecting to a computer, 34
television, watching on PCs, 209–215
television signal, required by a
    TV tuner, 208
temperatures, best for PCs, 31
temporary storage, 12. *See also* memory
terabyte (TB) of memory, 97
terminal or communications software, 181
text, saving from a Web page to disk, 264
text documents, 286
three-dimensional graphics,
    supporting, 123
thumbnails of images stored in a PC, 204
TIFF (Tagged Image File Format) graphics
    standard, 199
TIFF images, converting to JPG, 200
time. *See also* clock
  required to download files, 267
  setting in a PC, 81
time server, 82
timeout value for sleeping a computer, 188
title bar, file name appearing on, 295
Toner [is] low warning, 154
toner in laser printers, 153
tools, 15
tower system PC, 18
trackball, 144
transparencies (slides), scanning, 198
tray types for disc drives, 111
Trojan programs, 273
turning off PCs, 48–53, 54
turning on PCs, 37–42, 44–46
TV
  turning a PC into, 207–209
  watching live, 210–211
TV channels, changing, 210–211

TV programs
  recording, 211–212
  scheduling the recording of, 212–213
  watching recorded, 213
TV tuners
  connecting, 208–209
  described, 208
twisted pair, 179
two, powers of, 98
typewriter keys on the keyboard, 134
typing
  learning, 135
  posture for, 141

• *U* •

UAC dialogs, 280–282
undeleting files, 314–315
Undo command (Ctrl+Z), 314, 316
uninstalling software, 323–325
uninterruptible power supply. *See* UPSs
Universal Serial Bus ports. *See* USB ports
Unnamed Network in the Connect to a
    Network window, 238
unpacking boxes, 29–30
unplugging PCs while upgrading hardware,
    352
unpowered USB hubs, 88
unsecured wireless networks, 238
unselecting files, 311
unsharing
  folders, 251
  printers, 252
updates
  listing of Windows, 278
  repairing or patching software, 325
updating
  software, 325–326
  Windows, 277–279
upgrades, 326

upgrading
  memory, 345
  software, 325–326, 351
  Windows, 325
uploading files, 263
uppercase
  Caps Lock key, 137
  in filenames, 289
  typing e-mail in ALL CAPS, 260
UPSs (uninterruptible power supplies)
  described, 40–42, 346
  setting sleep values when running on, 189
URLs, typing, 258
USB (Universal Serial Bus) port, 86
USB cables. *See also* cables
  connecting cameras to PCs, 194
  described, 36–37, 87
  for printers, 156
USB connectors, 24, 28
USB devices
  acting as hubs, 88
  connecting, 36–37, 87
  plugging in, 36–37
  removing, 88
USB hub, 88–89
USB interface for a disk drive, 107
USB ports
  compared to IEEE, 90
  using to add external storage, 115
USB symbol, 86
USB-powered devices, 87
user, switching, 48–49
user account, creating in Windows, 46
User Account Control (UAC) warning
    dialog boxes, 280–282
User Account Folder window, displaying,
    300
user account name, 300
User Profile folder
  described, 66, 299–301
  subfolders in, 300–301
utilities, 15

• *V* •

validation of software, 320
vents, 21–22, 24
vertical orientation, printing in, 161
VGA (Video Gate Array), 123
VGA connectors, described, 23–25, 35
video(s)
  creating or viewing your own, 215
  editing, 217–218
video adapter card, memory chips on, 100
video capture card, 208
video cards. *See* graphics adapters
video chat, 216
video conference, 216
video driver, 15, 126
Video DVD option in Media Center, 214
video editing program, 217–218
video files, types of, 216–217
video memory, 100
video RAM, 122
Video subfolder in the User Profiles
    folder, 66
Videos folder, 301
video/VGA connector, 23–25
viewing images in Windows, 204
virtual memory, 100
virus, 273
virus protection software
  described, 279
  disabling, 320
  investing in, 350–351
Vista. *See* Windows Vista
visual interface. *See* skin for Windows
    Media Player
visually impaired, tools for, 226
voice recognition, 227–228
voltage switch, 23
volume, adjusting in Windows, 169
volume control, speakers with, 166
volume control slider, 169

Volume icon in the Notification Area, 169
VPU (visual processing unit), 123
VRAM, 122

• *W* •

wall socket, power coming from, 39
wallpaper
  changing, 128–129
  creating, 129
  setting images as, 264
warning banner on blocked pop-ups, 274
warranty card, filling out, 30
watts, rating power supplies in, 84
WAV (Waveform) audio format, 224
WAV files, 171
Web
  browsing, 257–258. *See also* Internet
      Explorer (IE)
  described, 257
  searching, 259
Web browser, connecting to the router, 240
web camera, 215–216
Web domain of an ISP, 255
Web page addresses
  removing all previously typed, 257
  of routers, 240
Web pages
  displaying for routers, 241
  keeping stuff from, 263–264
  printing, 258–259
  saving images from, 264
  saving text from, 264
  saving to disk, 258–259
Web site(s)
  checking with the phishing filter, 275
  for this book, 5
webcam, 215–216
WEP (Wired Equivalent Privacy),
    setting, 241

wheel button on a mouse, 142–143
Win key
  popping up the Start button menu, 62
  uses of, 136
Win+Break, 77
Win+E, 302
Win+F, 316
Win+L, 50
Window Color and Appearance in the
    Personalization window, 127
Windows. *See also* Windows Vista
  adjusting monitor display, 126–132
  audio control in, 167–169
  changing the appearance of windows, 127
  configuring for the Internet, 256
  configuring to enable sharing, 247–248
  connecting to a network, 237–238
  controlling printers, 156–159
  controlling the keyboard in, 140–141
  defending, 279–280
  folders used by, 301–302
  interface of, 59–63
  manually configuring modems, 180
  mouse in, 146–148
  Narrator program, 226
  Network window, 244–246
  not properly shutting down, 337
  as the operating system, 14
  playing sounds in, 170
  power management in, 186–189
  reinstalling, 351
  restarting, 52
  starting, 46–48
  supporting creation of DVDs and CDs, 329
  updating, 277–279
  upgrading, 325
  viewing images in, 204–205
  working with data discs, 332
windows, pop-up
  blocking in Internet Explorer, 274
  described, 273
Windows backup program, running, 339

Windows Bitmap file format, 199
Windows Defender
  described, 272, 279–280
  starting, 280
Windows Explorer program, 302–303
Windows Explorer window, compared to
    the Open dialog box, 305
Windows Firewall. *See also* firewall
  described, 272, 276–277
  starting, 277
Windows folder, 302
Windows Help system, 67
Windows Mail
  described, 260
  grabbing an attachment with, 268–269
  saving attachments, 268
  sending attachments, 269–270
Windows Media Audio (WMA) file format,
    171, 224
Windows Media Center
  configuring, 209
  interface of, 209, 210
  recording TV programs, 211–212
  using, 208
  using across a network, 248
Windows Media Player
  compared to Windows Media Center, 208
  controlling audio files, 170
  interface of, 220
  running, 220–221
  working with portable music devices, 223
Windows Media Video (WMV) format, 216
Windows Movie Maker, 217–218, 329
Windows Security Center
  described, 275–276
  starting, 276
Windows Sidebar, 60–61
Windows Update service, 278
Windows Vista. *See also* Windows
  activating network discovery, 246
  flavors of, 4
  password required for, 47

recommendation for, 1
software setup of a network, 236–242
Windows Vista Aero interface in the Start button menu, 62–63
WINNT folder, 302
wire for wired networks, 233
Wired Equivalent Privacy (WEP), setting, 241
wireless devices, 37
wireless hub, placement of, 236
wireless keyboards
  described, 135
  using traditional keyboard and mouse ports, 91
  working directly with Media Center, 209
wireless networking standards, 232, 234
wireless networks, unsecured, 238
wireless NIC, 234
wireless routers, supporting wired networks, 235
wires in a wired network, 234
WMA (Windows Media Audio) file format, 171, 224
WMV (Windows Media Video) format, 216
word order in Google searches, 259
work, not saving, 339
workgroup
  described, 239–240
  joining, 239–240
  shown in the Network window, 244

World Wide Web. *See* Web
worm, 273
wrist pad
  described, 141
  purchasing, 344
writing songs to a CD, 225

• X •

X number, rating DVD and CD drives, 110–111
xD cards, 114

• Y •

yellow UACs, 282

• Z •

zero, typing, 137
zero bytes, file of, 288
Zip file
  described, 304
  installing from, 267–268
Zoom menu in the IE window, 257
Zoom tool, 202

Notes

BUSINESS, CAREERS & PERSONAL FINANCE

0-7645-9847-3

0-7645-2431-3

Also available:

- Business Plans Kit For Dummies
  0-7645-9794-9
- Economics For Dummies
  0-7645-5726-2
- Grant Writing For Dummies
  0-7645-8416-2
- Home Buying For Dummies
  0-7645-5331-3
- Managing For Dummies
  0-7645-1771-6
- Marketing For Dummies
  0-7645-5600-2

- Personal Finance For Dummies
  0-7645-2590-5*
- Resumes For Dummies
  0-7645-5471-9
- Selling For Dummies
  0-7645-5363-1
- Six Sigma For Dummies
  0-7645-6798-5
- Small Business Kit For Dummies
  0-7645-5984-2
- Starting an eBay Business For Dummies
  0-7645-6924-4
- Your Dream Career For Dummies
  0-7645-9795-7

HOME & BUSINESS COMPUTER BASICS

0-470-05432-8

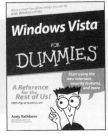

0-471-75421-8

Also available:

- Cleaning Windows Vista For Dummies
  0-471-78293-9
- Excel 2007 For Dummies
  0-470-03737-7
- Mac OS X Tiger For Dummies
  0-7645-7675-5
- MacBook For Dummies
  0-470-04859-X
- Macs For Dummies
  0-470-04849-2
- Office 2007 For Dummies
  0-470-00923-3

- Outlook 2007 For Dummies
  0-470-03830-6
- PCs For Dummies
  0-7645-8958-X
- Salesforce.com For Dummies
  0-470-04893-X
- Upgrading & Fixing Laptops For Dummies
  0-7645-8959-8
- Word 2007 For Dummies
  0-470-03658-3
- Quicken 2007 For Dummies
  0-470-04600-7

FOOD, HOME, GARDEN, HOBBIES, MUSIC & PETS

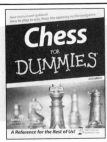

0-7645-8404-9

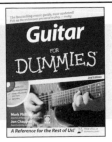

0-7645-9904-6

Also available:

- Candy Making For Dummies
  0-7645-9734-5
- Card Games For Dummies
  0-7645-9910-0
- Crocheting For Dummies
  0-7645-4151-X
- Dog Training For Dummies
  0-7645-8418-9
- Healthy Carb Cookbook For Dummies
  0-7645-8476-6
- Home Maintenance For Dummies
  0-7645-5215-5

- Horses For Dummies
  0-7645-9797-3
- Jewelry Making & Beading For Dummies
  0-7645-2571-9
- Orchids For Dummies
  0-7645-6759-4
- Puppies For Dummies
  0-7645-5255-4
- Rock Guitar For Dummies
  0-7645-5356-9
- Sewing For Dummies
  0-7645-6847-7
- Singing For Dummies
  0-7645-2475-5

INTERNET & DIGITAL MEDIA

0-470-04529-9

0-470-04894-8

Also available:

- Blogging For Dummies
  0-471-77084-1
- Digital Photography For Dummies
  0-7645-9802-3
- Digital Photography All-in-One Desk Reference For Dummies
  0-470-03743-1
- Digital SLR Cameras and Photography For Dummies
  0-7645-9803-1
- eBay Business All-in-One Desk Reference For Dummies
  0-7645-8438-3
- HDTV For Dummies
  0-470-09673-X

- Home Entertainment PCs For Dummies
  0-470-05523-5
- MySpace For Dummies
  0-470-09529-6
- Search Engine Optimization For Dummies
  0-471-97998-8
- Skype For Dummies
  0-470-04891-3
- The Internet For Dummies
  0-7645-8996-2
- Wiring Your Digital Home For Dummies
  0-471-91830-X

* Separate Canadian edition also available
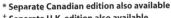
† Separate U.K. edition also available

Available wherever books are sold. For more information or to order direct: U.S. customers visit www.dummies.com or call 1-877-762-2974.
U.K. customers visit www.wileyeurope.com or call 0800 243407. Canadian customers visit www.wiley.ca or call 1-800-567-4797.

SPORTS, FITNESS, PARENTING, RELIGION & SPIRITUALITY

0-471-76871-5   0-7645-7841-3

Also available:
- Catholicism For Dummies
  0-7645-5391-7
- Exercise Balls For Dummies
  0-7645-5623-1
- Fitness For Dummies
  0-7645-7851-0
- Football For Dummies
  0-7645-3936-1
- Judaism For Dummies
  0-7645-5299-6
- Potty Training For Dummies
  0-7645-5417-4
- Buddhism For Dummies
  0-7645-5359-3

- Pregnancy For Dummies
  0-7645-4483-7 †
- Ten Minute Tone-Ups For Dummies
  0-7645-7207-5
- NASCAR For Dummies
  0-7645-7681-X
- Religion For Dummies
  0-7645-5264-3
- Soccer For Dummies
  0-7645-5229-5
- Women in the Bible For Dummies
  0-7645-8475-8

TRAVEL

0-7645-7749-2   0-7645-6945-7

Also available:
- Alaska For Dummies
  0-7645-7746-8
- Cruise Vacations For Dummies
  0-7645-6941-4
- England For Dummies
  0-7645-4276-1
- Europe For Dummies
  0-7645-7529-5
- Germany For Dummies
  0-7645-7823-5
- Hawaii For Dummies
  0-7645-7402-7

- Italy For Dummies
  0-7645-7386-1
- Las Vegas For Dummies
  0-7645-7382-9
- London For Dummies
  0-7645-4277-X
- Paris For Dummies
  0-7645-7630-5
- RV Vacations For Dummies
  0-7645-4442-X
- Walt Disney World & Orlando
  For Dummies
  0-7645-9660-8

GRAPHICS, DESIGN & WEB DEVELOPMENT

0-7645-8815-X   0-7645-9571-7

Also available:
- 3D Game Animation For Dummies
  0-7645-8789-7
- AutoCAD 2006 For Dummies
  0-7645-8925-3
- Building a Web Site For Dummies
  0-7645-7144-3
- Creating Web Pages For Dummies
  0-470-08030-2
- Creating Web Pages All-in-One Desk
  Reference For Dummies
  0-7645-4345-8
- Dreamweaver 8 For Dummies
  0-7645-9649-7

- InDesign CS2 For Dummies
  0-7645-9572-5
- Macromedia Flash 8 For Dummies
  0-7645-9691-8
- Photoshop CS2 and Digital
  Photography For Dummies
  0-7645-9580-6
- Photoshop Elements 4 For Dummies
  0-471-77483-9
- Syndicating Web Sites with RSS Feeds
  For Dummies
  0-7645-8848-6
- Yahoo! SiteBuilder For Dummies
  0-7645-9800-7

NETWORKING, SECURITY, PROGRAMMING & DATABASES

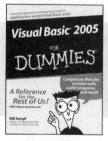

0-7645-7728-X   0-471-74940-0

Also available:
- Access 2007 For Dummies
  0-470-04612-0
- ASP.NET 2 For Dummies
  0-7645-7907-X
- C# 2005 For Dummies
  0-7645-9704-3
- Hacking For Dummies
  0-470-05235-X
- Hacking Wireless Networks
  For Dummies
  0-7645-9730-2
- Java For Dummies
  0-470-08716-1

- Microsoft SQL Server 2005 For Dummies
  0-7645-7755-7
- Networking All-in-One Desk Reference
  For Dummies
  0-7645-9939-9
- Preventing Identity Theft For Dummies
  0-7645-7336-5
- Telecom For Dummies
  0-471-77085-X
- Visual Studio 2005 All-in-One Desk
  Reference For Dummies
  0-7645-9775-2
- XML For Dummies
  0-7645-8845-1

HEALTH & SELF-HELP

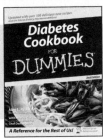

0-7645-8450-2

0-7645-4149-8

Also available:

Bipolar Disorder For Dummies
0-7645-8451-0

Chemotherapy and Radiation
For Dummies
0-7645-7832-4

Controlling Cholesterol For Dummies
0-7645-5440-9

Diabetes For Dummies
0-7645-6820-5* †

Divorce For Dummies
0-7645-8417-0 †

Fibromyalgia For Dummies
0-7645-5441-7

Low-Calorie Dieting For Dummies
0-7645-9905-4

Meditation For Dummies
0-471-77774-9

Osteoporosis For Dummies
0-7645-7621-6

Overcoming Anxiety For Dummies
0-7645-5447-6

Reiki For Dummies
0-7645-9907-0

Stress Management For Dummies
0-7645-5144-2

EDUCATION, HISTORY, REFERENCE & TEST PREPARATION

0-7645-8381-6

0-7645-9554-7

Also available:

The ACT For Dummies
0-7645-9652-7

Algebra For Dummies
0-7645-5325-9

Algebra Workbook For Dummies
0-7645-8467-7

Astronomy For Dummies
0-7645-8465-0

Calculus For Dummies
0-7645-2498-4

Chemistry For Dummies
0-7645-5430-1

Forensics For Dummies
0-7645-5580-4

Freemasons For Dummies
0-7645-9796-5

French For Dummies
0-7645-5193-0

Geometry For Dummies
0-7645-5324-0

Organic Chemistry I For Dummies
0-7645-6902-3

The SAT I For Dummies
0-7645-7193-1

Spanish For Dummies
0-7645-5194-9

Statistics For Dummies
0-7645-5423-9

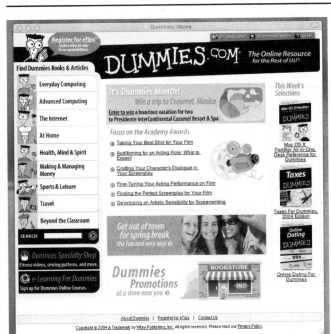

Get smart @ dummies.com®

- **Find a full list of Dummies titles**
- **Look into loads of FREE on-site articles**
- **Sign up for FREE eTips e-mailed to you weekly**
- **See what other products carry the Dummies name**
- **Shop directly from the Dummies bookstore**
- **Enter to win new prizes every month!**

* Separate Canadian edition also available
† Separate U.K. edition also available

Available wherever books are sold. For more information or to order direct: U.S. customers visit www.dummies.com or call 1-877-762-2974.
U.K. customers visit www.wileyeurope.com or call 0800 243407. Canadian customers visit www.wiley.ca or call 1-800-567-4797.

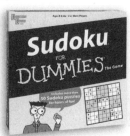

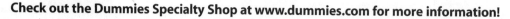